Air Battle for Arnhem

ONE WAY TICKET

Those lazy coils of tow-ropes laid
Along the runways all displayed,
To herald an amazing feat,
The take-off, of an Airborne fleet;
Dakotas, Stirlings, in position
Airborne troops of the First Division,
All waiting for the last command
To lift this army from the land.
The word at last, the engines roared,
The tow-ropes leapt with one accord,
Between the planes and Horsa gliders,
Linking tugs and glider riders,
Lifting the first the gliders rose,
The tow-ropes whipped from tail to nose.
September Forty Four it was, at noon as I recall,
A sunny day, a pleasant day, a day to suit us all,
And as we climbed into the sky,
A sight so marvellous met the eye,
Three hundred Horsa gliders flew,
Above the slipstream, straight and true.
Then out into the Netherlands,
This giant fleet prepared to land,
The canopies of parachutes
Just filled the air like summer fruits.
As idle domes they floated down,
To land so softly on the ground;
Then suddenly our hearts stood still,
The tow-ropes gone, and what a thrill
To watch the ground come up to meet
The gliders of this airborne fleet.
We hit the ground and skidded on,
The landings safe, the first job done,
Machine-guns chattered, rifles cracked,
But through all this the troops unpacked,
Then moved off at a hasty pace,
Eight miles to go, to reach that place,
Called ARNHEM.

By Colin Fowler
Credit Stuart Eastwood and
his book *When Dragons Flew*

Air Battle for Arnhem

Alan W. Cooper

Pen & Sword
AVIATION

First published in Great Britain in 2012 by
Pen & Sword Aviation
an imprint of
Pen & Sword Books Ltd
47 Church Street
Barnsley
South Yorkshire
S70 2AS

ISBN: 978-1-78159-108-6

A CIP catalogue record for this book is available from the British Library.

Typeset in 11pt Ehrhardt by
Mac Style, Beverley, E. Yorkshire

Printed and bound in the UK by the MPG Books Group Ltd

Pen & Sword Books Ltd incorporates the Imprints of Pen & Sword Aviation,
Pen & Sword Family History, Pen & Sword Maritime, Pen & Sword Military,
Pen & Sword Discovery, Wharncliffe Local History, Wharncliffe True Crime,
Wharncliffe Transport, Pen & Sword Select, Pen & Sword Military Classics,
Leo Cooper, The Praetorian Press, Remember When, Seaforth Publishing
and Frontline Publishing.

For a complete list of Pen & Sword titles please contact
PEN & SWORD BOOKS LIMITED
47 Church Street, Barnsley, South Yorkshire, S70 2AS, England
E-mail: enquiries@pen-and-sword.co.uk
Website: www.pen-and-sword.co.uk

Contents

Introduction 1

Chapter 1   Pre-Arnhem 3

Chapter 2   Operation Comet 9

Chapter 3   46/38 Groups and Squadrons 11

Chapter 4   Arnhem 17

Chapter 5   Operation Market Garden 20

Chapter 6   Sunday 17 September 1944 26

Chapter 7   Monday 18 September 1944 42

Chapter 8   Tuesday 19 September 1944 53

Chapter 9   Wednesday 20 September 1944 80

Chapter 10   Thursday 21 September 1944 92

Chapter 11   Saturday 22 September 1944 114

Chapter 12   Saturday 23 September 1944 117

Chapter 13   Sunday 24 September 1944 124

Chapter 14   Sunday 25 September 1944 126

Chapter 15   Post-Mortem 129

Chapter 16   The Outcome 141

Chapter 17   Post-War 149

Awards to The Royal Air Force for the Battle of Arnhem 155
RAF Losses at Arnhem 158
RAF Losses at the Battle of Arnhem: September 1944 160
Index 193

Contents

Introduction

Sixty years ago a battle took place that, if it had succeeded could have shortened the war by six months. The operation to take the bridges at Arnhem was given the code name Operation 'Market Garden', Market was the air side of the operation and Garden the subsequent ground operations.

It was the end product of many such planned operations that had been cancelled in the run up to Arnhem in September 1944.

But to put on an operation of such magnitude in such a short time was asking a great deal, and for it to be successful was asking even more.

The main problem was communication between the ground forces and the re-supply aircraft manned by men of the Royal Air Force.

It is their efforts and courage at Arnhem that the book *Air Battle for Arnhem* is about.

Over a period of seven days, troops of the 6th Airborne were taken to their positions by the RAF in towed gliders and in subsequent days the aircrews showed courage of the highest order in ensuring that the troops were kept supplied with ammunition and food to sustain them in their efforts to take the bridges at Arnhem.

Their courageous efforts were costly, 309 aircrew and seventy-nine air despatchers were killed, and a loss of 107 aircraft included in these losses the men of the RAF who supported the main re-supply armada.

One of the pilots on operations at Arnhem was Jimmy Edwards later a well known face and voice on television and radio. He many years later at an aircrew dinner said 'I never fired a bullet or dropped a bomb,' which sums up the role played by one of the main players, the Dakota, which flew at 500 feet into an area still in enemy hands but unfortunately not known to the RAF to drop supplies to the men on the ground. This was undertaken time after time.

Another of those and in the same squadron as Jimmy was David Lord, who for his valour at Arnhem was awarded the Victoria Cross, the only one awarded to the RAF for the Battle of Arnhem although more could have been awarded.

The role of the air despatchers, or AD's as they were known, has not been forgotten in this book and are on all occasions considered to be part of the aircrew on operations to Arnhem. Their efforts to make sure the supplies were released from the aircraft to the besieged men on the ground, was a vital factor in getting what supplies could be got to the troops.

The RAF's role at Arnhem has not been written until now.

This is their story *Air Battle for Arnhem* .

Chapter 1

Pre-Arnhem

In August 1944 the Germans were retreating back to Germany, and a plan to take advantage of this by using the 1st Airborne Division, who had been formed in August and were now up to strength but kicking their heels in the UK, was being considered.

The raw material for this planning was provided by three American and two British airborne divisions, plus the 1st Polish Parachute Brigade and the 52nd (Lowland) Division, the air transport from the US had the IX Troop Carrier Command, and from the RAF No 38 and 46 Groups being the means of transport for the troops.

In overall command was Lieutenant General, Lewis Hyde Brereton of the US Army Air Force, who had commanded the US 9th Air Force in the Mediterranean, arrived in England on 10 September 1943 and took over the 9th Air Force. In August 1944, he also took over the VII Air Support Command of the US 8th Air Force. He had began as a sailor and transferred to the army, serving in the First World War where he was heavily decorated with the US Distinguished Flying Cross, French *Croix de Guerre* and *Lègion d'honneur*, at the time he said 'I was flying like hell and a lot of Germans got in my way.' He had flown B-17 bombers in the Pacific before coming to Europe.

Between 6 June and 17 September 1944, no less than eighteen airborne operations were planned but cancelled for one reason or another.

A number of these operations were cancelled because the advancing army on the ground in Europe were reaching areas planned for airborne operations, making such assaults unnecessary.

To undertake such an operation meant having the closest co-operation with the Royal Air Force, the only means of getting troops and supplies to the target area.

Field Marshal Montgomery had two options open to him, he could stay where he was on the threshold of Germany, or he could cross the three-river barrier in one foul swoop.

With three airborne divisions ready Brereton chose the latter, the 82nd and 101st US forces and the British 1st Airborne Division, which were given the task of forming a corridor; the axis would be Eindhoven-Veghad-Grave-Nijmegen Arnhem Road and the bridges at Grave, Waal at Nijmegen, as well as the lower bridge over the Lower Rhine at Arnhem.

On 26 August 1944 it was decided that the selection of Lille as the place to land a large airborne force was unsound with German resistance still organised even in retreat: –

(i)   The flight to this area would be through flak defences, which were too strong.
(ii)   Maintenance by air to this area on a large scale could not be guaranteed.
(iii)   The landing fields and weather in this area are comparatively poor.
(iv)   An airborne operation on the other hand to capture intact the Port of Boulogne, Calais, or Dunkirk seemed both the more desirable and practicable. A port in the north of France which was fully intact would be of vital importance.

On 1 September it was thought to land a force in the Liege area instead, as the Lille area was unsatisfactory.

It seemed to show a lack of knowledge of the limitations and capabilities of airborne troops by Brereton, a report suggested that mainly the Royal Air Force not the army was laid down by the War Office and Air Ministry, after the disasters at Sicily in 1943 should control the necessity of airborne operations.

The above idea was cancelled on 4 September.

On 2 September 1944 a plan was hatched for consideration with the 1st Airborne Division to be landed in the area of Tournai and seize a bridgehead over the Escaut River for the purpose of assisting the Central and Northern Allied Army Groups, destroying the German Army by blocking withdrawal routes to the east.

This would consist of 1,533 aircraft and 598 gliders of which 1,055 were to be used for dropping parachute troops, 120 tug aircraft towing two gliders each and 358 tug aircraft towing one glider each, followed by a further 1,311 aircraft plus 2,067 gliders. This operation would have the code name 'Linnet'.

It would be carried out by the 1st Airborne Division, who would land in the area of Maastricht, with the US 82nd Airborne Division landing in the area of Tongress, and the US 101st Airborne Division landing to the west of Liege.

The route was Beachy Head, Le Treport, Arras and Tournai, with re-supply missions flown as required on D-Day, 3 September.

Because of weather conditions on 4 September 'Linnet II' (The Maastricht Gap) was cancelled but the troops however were kept on full alert, with a thirty-six-hour warning of a new operation. On 5 September the port of Antwerp was captured.

Montgomery wanted to make a full blooded thrust to Berlin, and on 5 September proposed a plan to General Brereton to seize the Rhine bridges from Arnhem to Wesel and prepare the way for his ground forces to advance to the north of the Ruhr.

On 6 September it was stated that Montgomery's plan to land troops in the Arnhem area was similar to the two previous ones, but preferable in that the force was to be of a more reasonable size and the need for troops in this advance area was likely to be great, but the plan would prove a difficult one to justify unless a practical route could be found for the troop carriers to maintain an airhead in the areas of Arnhem in the event of the airborne troops not being relieved.

The new plan was to seize the Rhine bridges from Arnhem to Wesel in order to prepare for a ground advance to the north of the Ruhr; it was given the code name 'Comet' and focused on the Nijmegen–Arnhem area.

D-Day for 'Comet' was planned for 8 September but postponed for twenty-four hours. The air despatchers of 63rd Airborne Composite Company RASC, 6th Airborne Division, received orders to stand by to load a further 100X3 tons of equipment from 63 Company dumps to be despatched in Stirling aircraft flying from Keevil, Harwell, and Fairford airfields. On 9/10 September it was again postponed for twenty-four hours and finally on the 11th cancelled.

The troops of the 1st Airborne Division scheduled for 'Linnet' were still in place in Swindon and other Wiltshire areas, and the US and Polish airborne troops were still in bases elsewhere around the UK.

On the 10th a request had come from 21 Army Group to investigate an airborne operation on Walcheven Island, which at the time seemed the best aerial method of assault yet put forward. It was to be carried out in conjunction with Bomber Command. The plan:

(a) Enable the port of Antwerp to be used.
(b) Cut off the escape of five German Divisions hemmed in on the Belgium Coast.

However, this was rejected by General Brereton.

Operation 'Comet' did not go down well with some, to them it seemed impossible, particularly as it was a large operation and could mean time wasted, therefore the Germans would have time to bring strong defences into the area.

On 14 September came orders from the War Office that 63 Company were to be mobilised by the 30th and ammunition was conveyed to airfields. On 16 September this was reversed and the 'Monty' plan with the code name 'Market

Garden', 'Market' for the air operation and 'Garden' for the ground operation was completed with the experts in 38 Group saying the losses would be forty per cent killed, twenty per cent missing and twenty per cent damaged, it would either be an exercise or a slaughter. The plan was rather leisurely with only one sortie or drop a day, which it was felt was unsound. If it was to be a success then there seemed little justification for dropping and flying in masses of supplies for such a long period, while getting everything in as quickly as possible was vitally important. For weather and air support reasons it was highly desirable to get the whole force down as quickly as possible.

The plan:-

(i)   Night before D-Day, 38 and 46 Groups and some of the Groups of IX Troop Carrier Command, to drop paratroops, whose main tasks would be to protect the glider landing zones and neutralise dangerous flak. It was felt that German night fighters could be prevented but only for one night from interfering with this operation.

(ii)   Dawn D-Day. The remaining troop carrier aircraft to land mainly gliders.

(iii) Mid-day, D-Day, 38 Group aircraft and the other first lift aircraft to bring in further gliders and paratroops.

(iv)   Evening D-Day. The second lift aircraft to bring in the balance of gliders and paratroops.

This would mean three complete divisions on the ground in eighteen hours, but there were reservations about the fact that they seemed to be in place with no alternative plan in the event of running into difficulties.

The 'Linnett' force would be enlarged to three, possibly four, divisions, plus the Polish Parachute Brigade who were based in Lincolnshire, Leicestershire and Rutland. The only major units not to have been moved were the six parachute battalions. The glider ropes had been moved to the vicinity of airfields where aircraft glider towing squadrons were based.

On 17 September came a Warning Order: Resupply Operation 'Market'.

At the outbreak of war with the formation of parachutists, it became necessary for a suitable design for a container to drop supplies, the outcome a metal skinned container 6 feet long by 15 inches in diameter and capable of carrying up to 600lbs, which would fit in the bomb bay of a Whitley bomber.

No story of the RAF's contribution to the Battle of Arnhem would be complete without the dedication and contribution of the air despatchers of the Royal Army Service Corps. In 1940 with the conception of airborne troops it soon became evident that some form of air despatcher organisation was required, and it was within the framework of the airborne forces that the R.A.S.C Air Despatch was to come to fruition. In 1941, the unit was logistic support until it was brought into the airborne fold, when 31 Brigade converted and became known as the 1st Air Landing Brigade, and 31 Brigade Transport Company was renamed on 9 December 1941 as the 1st Air Landing Brigade Transport Company R.A.S.C. This then became 250 Airborne Light Composite Company R.A.S.C. In 1942 their activities were limited to packing and loading containers into the Whitley aircraft. The containers had an opening at both ends, but had its limitations with only a small weight capacity. Experiments were made on an idea by Lieutenant Colonel Packe, dropping all manner of equipment and supplies in a wicker basket from 600 feet. This went on until October 1942 when trials were carried out on a C47 Dakota aircraft using roller conveyer equipment.

In 1943, 93 and 253 Companies joined the division and dropping went on in the Middle East and North Africa. In 1943 the 6th Airborne Division was being formed, and the first Logistic Unit was 716 formed in June 1943, later joined by 398 and 63 as follows:

63 Airborne Composite Company R.A.S.C
398 Airborne Composite Company R.A.S.C
716 Airborne Light Composite Company R.A.S.C

In 1944, with the invasion of Europe expected that year, the pressure was on to train sufficient personnel in air supply duties as aircrew. A great number of USAAF Squadrons had arrived in the theatre equipped with Dakotas, and in the spring of 1944, 46 Group was formed.

Initially the projection was 800 men (200X four man air crews), this was soon realised to be unrealistic with the 1st Airborne Division, and 253 Company was designated to operate also, each would have 200 personnel (50X4 crews) trained.

In March 1944 an order was given for all air despatchers to wear gym shoes not boots when operating in aircraft due to the slippery metal floors.

The supply bases were in the area between Oxford and Salisbury.

233 Troop Carrying Company R.A.S.C became the first soon to be formed air despatch unit and would come under the command of HQ 48 Air Despatch. On 14 March 1944, fifty-five per cent of the company volunteered for air despatch duties. On completion of their training, they were to report to OC Airborne Supplies Training Wing at Amesbury, Wiltshire. In May 1944, the 799 and 800 Companies were formed under the command of HQ 48 Air Despatch.

In June 1944, HQ 49 Air Despatch were to be formed having the two Airborne Companies 253 and 63 under command plus a separate company 720, with many of the men who were to man 49 Air Despatch were found from within the airborne formations. This had the effect of collaborating a wealth of experience which was to be put to good use as HQ 49 Air Despatch were given the task of planning for Arnhem.

On 18 August 1944, HQ Air Despatch Group was formed.

On 1 September a warning order was given to HQ 49 Air Despatch for 253 Company to provide 32X4 men crews and 32X2 men crews, along with 50X4 men crews, from 63 Company. On 7 September operation 'Comet' 253 Company with 50X3 ton vehicles, plus 50X4 men, reported to Saltby Airfield for a re-supply mission. 63 Company were also asked for the same numbers and to report to Folkingham Airfield. On 8 September a further 100X3 ton vehicles from 63 Company were loaded for despatch to Stirling's, operating from Fairford, Harwell and Keevil.

The aircraft being used for supply missions at Arnhem were the Dakota, Halifax and Stirling Bombers. The Dakota was loaded with six containers and ten panniers; the Halifax carried four containers and ten panniers. The Stirling carried twenty-four containers and four panniers. To discharge panniers from a Dakota the pilot would fly a course at the lowest possible speed and height, the four despatchers normally commanded by a corporal and dropping sixteen panniers in eight to twelve seconds, working on the orders of the pilot. In the Stirling there were only two despatchers who like the aircrew used the intercom system and the containers dropped from the bomb bay, and controlled by the aircrew, panniers were dropped from a hole in the deck when the bomb doors were open. The Dakota loads were dropped with the help of a gravity roller system through the side door, whereas in the Stirling the air despatchers had to manhandle their load to the hole in the deck to make a drop. Prior to the take off the supplies were delivered by lorry and manhandled aboard into the belly of the Stirling or up the rollers on the Dakota.

The despatchers were provided with an observer's parachute which was worn on the front of their bodies and operated by a ripcord with a D-Ring. They were kept in a corner of the aircraft to avoid deploying them while undertaking their despatch duties. As with aircrew little training in the use of a parachute was given, with the hope you would never have to use it.

The main airfields used were Broadwell, Blake Hill Farm, Down Ampney, and occasionally Lyneham and Fairford. Eight air despatchers had three companies, 223, 799 and 800, which were located at Burford, St Margaret and Down Ampney. On 18 September, 63 Company were to provide crews for thirty-three Stirlings and twenty-one Dakotas. The balance to be provided by 49 Company RASC Air Despatch: 253 Company of 33X two man crews operating from Harwell, on Stirlings.

In March 1944, 223 Troop Carrying Company RASC based in Northern Ireland were the first to become an Air Despatch Company initially under HQ 48 Air Despatch, then the 36 Lines of Communication Column RASC, and later HQ 48 Air Despatch which had been formed on 18 August 1944.

On 7 September, 253 and 63 Company, were posted to Saltby Airfield for operation 'Comet', but it was cancelled on 11 September then put forward to 17 September as a warning order for 'Market'.

Chapter 2

Operation Comet

At the time of the decision to go ahead with Comet/Market there were four alternatives:

1. To seize the airfields at Berlin;
2. To seize the German Naval base at Kiel but only if the Germans were at the point of surrender or collapse;
3. To secure Walcheron Island at the mouth of the Schelde Estuary; for the purpose of assisting the opening of the port of Antwerp. Cancelled because the Germans could easily flood the island. Code Name (Infatuate)
4. Get the 1st and 3rd Armies through the west wall or across the Rhine; all to take place in U.S General Bradley's section and this required his approval.

There were other considerations, Chartres-Rambouillet code name 'Transfigure', Boulogne code name 'Boxer; Tournai, code name 'Linnet; The Maastricht Gap, code name 'Linnet II', Aachen, code name 'Naples; Cologne, code name 'Naples II', Trier, code name 'Milan; The ground between Neuwied and Koblenz, code name 'Milan II', Saarbrucken, code name 'Choker' and the cities of Mainz and Mannheim, code name 'Choker II'. History shows that none of these plans were chosen.

Another plan was similar to 'Market' at Arnhem, but upstream at Wesel. Many thought this would have been better and avoid the gap and increasing German strength along the Dutch-Belgium border.

Operation 'Comet' which was Field Marshal Montgomery's idea was a plan to drop the 1st Airborne Division by parachute and glider into enemy territory, to capture five bridges in the area of Eindhoven-Nijmegen and Arnhem. Once secured the British tanks of the 21st Army Group would then link up with the American troops and secure the crossings.

This was planned for 9 September, but only hours before it was cancelled on the basis it was too much for a single division to take all the bridges.

Bomber Command assisted by attacking six airfields in southern Holland, Deelen, Eindhoven, Gilze-Rijen, Sosterburg, Venlow and Volkel, with 675 bombers being despatched in daylight on 3 September with only one loss.

At dawn on 8 September, 822 US B17 aircraft of the US 8th Air Force attacked anti-aircraft positions and airfields along the 'Market Garden' route. One hundred and seventeen different points were assigned.

On 6 September, 38 Group Operations Order 524 was despatched to group stations. Operation 'Comet' landings would be before and just after dawn, with six gliders landing in a 'Coupe de Man' similar to Pegasus Bridge in June 1944, close to each bridge. Then 700 gliders and a large number of paratroops would follow... The RAF were trained on night operations and it was assumed the Americans would be ready as well. This was proven not to be so.

The urgency for an operation in Holland was highlighted with attack on Chiswick and Epping on 8 September by V-2 rockets fired from launching sites in Holland. Within a week twenty rockets had been fired and exploded in Greater London.

All units had been made ready for the 8th. The postponement had been made on the direct order of Montgomery because the resistance along the Albert and Meuse Escaut canals west of Antwerp was getting stronger. It was postponed from the 8th to the 9th and cancelled on the 10th.

Operation 'Comet' then became 'Market' which was the airborne plan and later to be 'Market Garden' with 'Garden' the ground plan.

The date anticipated a week later on 17/18 September 1944.

During the period 1 to 6 September the Air Officer Commander of 46 Group saw the Air Officer Commander-in-Chief, Transport Command and put forward the difficulties with the creation of the 1st Allied Airborne Army which had been imposed on his group.

In addition to being earmarked for airborne operations at home, the whole group was standing by to proceed at short notice for operations in another theatre of war. At the same time large scale and urgent demands were being made for air transport work which could only be met, in part, owing to the group having to stand by during most of this period at readiness for abortive airborne operations.

The Air Officer Commanding Transport Command, Air Chief Marshal, Sir Frederick Bowhill, GBE, KCB, DSO and Bar, in a letter of the 5th to Air Marshal, Sir Douglas Evill, KCB, DSC, AFC, Vice-Chief of the Air Staff endorsed this.

Transport aircraft were flying an average of 600 tons of supplies, mainly fuel, up to the forward units every day during the time that airborne operations were being planned and then rejected. In the four days prior to 'Market' being accepted, and its inception, the US 9th Troop Carrier Command flew 1,901 operations delivering over 5,000 tons of supplies and bringing out nearly 2,000 wounded to the rear stations.

Chapter 3

46/38 Groups and Squadrons

Number 38 Group started as 38 Wing. In August 1942 it had been recommended to become a group but this was turned down. Again, recommended in February 1943, but as before turned down on the grounds of expense for extra personnel.

In November 1943 it was finally agreed that it become a group consisting of nine squadrons and the following aircraft: two Albemarle's, one Halifax, and four Stirling's. The Halifax Squadron 298 was formed in November 1943, with ten crews from 295 Squadron and twelve from 297 Squadron. In March 1944, 'C' Flight of 298 Squadron became 644 Squadron.

Before D-Day, No 38 Group although enlarged, was still insufficient and a new group was formed as close support, flying supplies and evacuating wounded.

And so 46 Group was officially formed in January 1944, consisting of DC47 Dakota Squadrons or 'Goolie Birds' as the Americans called them. One pilot said of them "It protested, leaked oil, ran rough, rattled, ran hot and cold and rough, but she flew and flew and was always honest and a faithful maiden." This aircraft did as much to win the war as any aircraft in the Second World War as many people would endorse.

Two new squadrons were allocated to 46 Group; 512, recently formed from 24 Squadron, 271 and a nucleus of 575 were formed from 512. With three unfinished airfields available, 271 went to Down Ampney, 512 and 575 went to Broadwell and two Coastal Command Hudson Squadrons; 233 and 48 were flown to the UK from Gibraltar, 48 going to join 271 at Down Ampney and 233, when available, to go to Blakehill Farm. Another squadron was formed for Arnhem 437(RCAF) at Blakehill Farm.

In 38 Group there were ten Squadrons; They were:

190 Squadron   In 1919, and with the end of the First World War, the squadron that had been disbanded and reformed in March 1943 as an airborne forces squadron flying Stirling's. During the first two days of the landings at Arnhem,

190 flew forty-six sorties of which all but six were towing gliders, and in subsequent days they flew fifty-three sorties, lost twelve aircraft and had thirty-eight aircrew killed including their commanding officer.

At the time of Arnhem they were based at Fairford.

196 Squadron   Having been formed in 1942 as a night bomber squadron it took part in many raids on enemy ports and industrial centres in Europe. At this time 196 operated with Wellington bombers and were based at Driffield, Yorkshire with 4 Group, when it moved to 3 Group at Witchford, Cambridgeshire, it converted to Stirling bombers. In December 1943, based at Leicester East, it was transferred to the Allied Expeditionary Air Force (AEAF). In 1944 came supply dropping to the resistance in France and parachute dropping and glider pulling to Normandy, and Arnhem. In the first two days of Arnhem fifty-six sorties were flown and in the subsequent days fifty-six sorties and twenty-six aircrew killed. At the time of Arnhem they were based at RAF Keevil; a village in Wiltshire and the land for the airfield requisitioned under the emergency powers in 1941. Only one living area was destroyed; Mere Farm House. The land for Keevil in the main never did go back to the owners, as it is still used today for parachute exercises on Salisbury Plain. Today it may appear to be deserted but it is a training ground for RAF Lyneham, who used it for low level airdrop techniques from Hercules aircraft or, as are known, "Fat Albert" and a familiar sight and sound to the villagers of Steeple Ashton and Keevil.

295 Squadron   Was formed in 1942 for use with airborne forces and equipped with Whitley aircraft. In 1943 Halifax's were added to the complement of Whitley's and in October 1943, 295 converted to Albemarle's, then troop dropping at Normandy in June 1944. In July 1944 the Albemarle's were replaced by Stirling's. During Arnhem, twenty-five Stirling towing gliders were sent to Arnhem on the first day and twenty-two on the second, followed by fifty-nine re-supply sorties. The three aircraft were lost and six aircrew killed.

The Armstrong Whitworth Albermarle was a monoplane with a steel tube framework fuselage, built in three sections and a retractable tricycle landing gear. The navigator was based in the nose of the aircraft, the two pilots sat side-by-side and a radio operator in the forward fuselage.

It could carry ten troops or, as at Arnhem, tow gliders. It was originally designed as a medium bomber but never operated in this role and first flew on the 20 March 1940.

At the time of Arnhem it was based at Harwell.

296 Squadron   Was formed in 1942 operating at first with Whitley bombers and then in 1943 Albemarle's. It took part in towing sorties and took part in North Africa to supporting the attack on Sicily until being withdrawn to the UK in

October 1943. In support of the D-Day landings, 296 dropped parachutists and then later during the siege to Caen and Brest, towed gliders. During 'Market Garden' Arnhem they flew twenty-seven sorties on the first day towing Waco Hadrian gliders and then Horsas from RAF Manston. This was followed by twenty sorties towing Horsa gliders on the following two days and finally thirty re-supply sorties. Based at Brize Norton but operating from Manston for operations to Arnhem.

297 Squadron They were at first based at Brize Norton but for Arnhem operating from RAF Manston.

298 Squadron Operating from Tarrant Rushton.

299 Squadron Were formed in 1943 by expanding 'C' flight of 297 Squadron. After a short while they converted from Lockheed Venturas to Stirling's.

On the 5 June 1944, they flew twenty-three parachute dropping sorties and had seven aircraft damaged and one to flak. During the first days of Arnhem seventy-one glider towing sorties were flown followed by forty-two re-supply sorties, six aircraft and four aircrew failed to return.

570 Squadron Elements of both Albermarle squadrons, 295 and 296 became 570 Squadron that was formed at Hurn in November 1943. Glider and parachute dropping followed on D-Day and glider towing to Caen.

In July 1944, 570 converted to Stirling's and took part in 'Market Garden'.

On the first three days towing gliders on forty-six sorties and fifty-eight re-supply sorties during which time nine aircraft and twenty aircrew were lost. Based at Harwell.

620 Squadron Started as a bomber squadron in 3 Group at Chedburgh, Suffolk.

In November 1943, 620 transferred to 38 Group and was based at Fairford.

During Arnhem, forty-seven sorties were flown in the first three days and fifty-six subsequent re-supply sorties were flown. Five aircraft and six aircrew failed to return.

RAF Fairford is still open and used by the RAF and US Air Force as well as being the venue for an annual International Air Show.

644 Squadron Formed in February 1944 from a nucleus of 298 Squadron.

Flying Halifax bombers it began glider-towing exercises in preparation for D-Day. Twenty aircraft towed gliders to Normandy, including three on the first attack on the enemy battery's before the main force arrived.

At Arnhem, forty-seven sorties were flown mainly in glider towing and fifty-six re-supply operations and based at Tarrant Rushton, Dorset which was opened in 1943 and closed in 1980.

In 46 Group there were now six squadrons: They were:

48 Squadron   A First World War Squadron formed in France in 1916 until 1920 when it was renumbered No 5 Squadron but reformed as 48 in 1935. At the outbreak of the Second World War they were flying Anson aircraft on anti-submarine patrols and E–Boat patrols during the evacuation of Dunkirk.

In 1942, 48 Squadron moved to Gibraltar and it was two years before it returned to the UK and converted to Dakotas's, becoming a transport unit based at Blakehill Farm.

It flew on the first three days of Arnhem fifty glider towing sorties, its losses were heavy, nine aircraft and nineteen aircrew failed to return. At the time of Arnhem they were based at Down Ampney.

233 Squadron   Formed in 1918 but was absorbed with two other units until reformed flying Anson's and in August 1939 converted to Hudson's.

It then undertook the role of Coastal Command patrols ending up in Gibraltar where it remained until February 1944, when it returned to the UK. On arrival it converted to Dakotas. After carrying out casualty evacuation from the Normandy beachhead it took part in 'Market Garden' and undertook thirty-nine sorties towing gliders. This was followed by thirty-four re-supply sorties, three aircraft and six aircrew failed to return.

271 Squadron   Another former First World War Squadron having been formed in 1918 and disbanded within months.

It was re-designated 271 on the 1 May 1940, using out of date aircraft the Harrow and Bombay bombers. In January 1944 it converted to Dakotas and became an airborne forces unit. The Harrow aircraft were retained for ambulance flights, and on D-Day supplied twenty-two glider pulling aircraft and thereafter bringing back wounded from the beachhead.

At Arnhem it undertook forty-eight glider-pulling sorties and fifty-two re-supply sorties, five aircraft and eight aircrew failed to return. At the time they were based at Down Ampney.

In this small village there were thirty-three on the electoral roll and an average church congregation each week of fifteen. In the church All Saints there is an unusual stained glass window with a Dakota in the centre and the result of the initiative of the Down Ampney Association steered by Alan Hartley. Outside, behind the stained glass window is an RAF Garden of Remembrance. The famous composer Ralph Vaughan Williams was born here; his father being the Vicar.

The airfield was opened in 1944 and closed in 1946 where it is now a large pig farm, but has a splendid memorial to the men of 48 and 271 who served there in the Second World War.

Between 1938 and 1946 over 500 airfields were built in the UK. At the outbreak of war in 1939, the UK had only 170 airfields; in the peak of this in 1942 some 120 new airfields had been built.

437 (Husky) RCAF Squadron   Were formed at Blakehill Farm on the 14 September 1944.

Three days later it took part in the Arnhem operations and four days later suffered its first casualties, in the first two days taking part in twenty-one sorties and twenty-four re-supply sorties. Its losses were high; twelve aircraft and twelve aircrew failed to return.

Blakehill Farm was opened in 1944 and closed in 1952.

512 Squadron   Formed at RAF Hendon in June 1943 from the Dakota element of 24 Squadron. It flew forty-six glider towing sorties on the first days of Arnhem, fifteen re-supply sorties, three Aircraft and two aircrew failed to return. They were based at Broadwell, Oxfordshire, which opened in 1943 and closed in 1947.

575 Squadron   Formed at Hendon on the 1 February 1944 from the nucleus of 512 Squadron. At Arnhem the squadron flew forty-nine glider-pulling sorties and sixty re-supply sorties, on the 25/26 September 1944 being based in Brussels, one aircraft failed and five aircrew failed to return. They were based at Broadwell.

The two gliders used by the British at Arnhem was the Airspeed Horsa which had a large wingspan of 88 feet and, when fully loaded, weighed 15,250 pounds. It could carry twenty-five men and a loaded weight of 15, 500lb with a maximum speed of 150mph when on tow and 100mph when gliding. It had no throttles but the controls similar to a power-driven aircraft, a small lever painted red operated the tow-rope release. It was described as looking like a section of a London tube train but in miniature. The two pilots sat side by side, with the first pilot being on the left as in a powered aircraft.

The first Horsa prototype was towed by a Whitley bomber on the 12 September 1941, in production in 1942, was made by the furniture trade and from drawing board to being in the air took only ten months. By the time the war ended 5,000 Horsas had been built.

The other glider was the General Aircraft Hamilcar a large glider of 7 tons with a wing span of 110 feet which was longer than the Lancaster bomber and had a maximum take off weight of 36,000lb. It could carry a light tank or similar heavy weapons. Its first flight was on 27 March 1942, but it was not built in the same numbers as the Horsa and at the end of its run only 344 had been built. Its design was very interesting being made of birch wood and spruce with a fabric covered plywood skin. Both gliders had large flaps which enabled them to dive at a steep angle and get down on the ground quickly. The glider pilots did not wear parachutes but instead wore Mae West vests in the event of landing in water.

For loading vehicles and cargo purposes the nose was hinged and both pilots sat in tandem in a cockpit on the top of the fuselage 15 feet from the ground. When the Tetrarch and M22 Locust light tank was carried, the crew because of room in the glider, stayed in the tank for the whole of the flight. It was also a very safe glider with only seven pilots killed in training.

The Horsa had the great advantage over the US glider; the Waco, in that the structure of the Waco was less robust and both the Waco and its contents were more liable to damage when landing on rough ground. In addition to this, the limited size and weight carrying capacity of the Waco necessitating the carriage of guns and their prime movers in separate gliders. On the other hand the Horsa had the disadvantage of requiring a more powerful tug and was difficult to send overseas.

The use of the glider came from the Germans use of this mode of transport in May 1940. Their glider, the DFS 230, was tugged by the JU 52 aircraft and in 1940 attacked the Fort Eben Emael making it possible for the Germans to outflank the French at the Maginot Line. The British glider force began in 1940 and the Americans in May 1942.

Air Vice Marshal Leslie Hollinghurst AOC 38 Group
Born 2 January 1895.
Began in the Royal Engineers as a Sapper and then the Middlesex Regiment.
Became an under- training pilot with the Royal Flying Corps and a flying officer in October, 1917. One of the squadrons he served with was 48 which in September 1944, one of the Dakota squadrons at Arnhem.
He became Air Officer Commander of 38 (Airborne Forces) Group on the 6 November 1943.
In 1950 he became an Air Chief Marshal and was knighted in 1952. He retired in December 1952 and died in June 1971.

Air Commodore Lawrence Darvall AOC 46 Group
Born 24 November 1898.
Began in the army and awarded a Military Cross in 1917. He joined the RAF in June 1918 and became a Flying Officer in August 1919.
He became Air Officer Commander 46 Group on the 16 September 1944.
He was promoted to Air Marshal and knighted in 1952 ; he retired in 1956 and died in November 1968.

Chapter 4

Arnhem

A rnhem also called 'Gelders Haagje' is the capital of the Gelderland province having gained its rights granted in July 1233. Between 1672 and 1674, and again for eighteen years beginning in 1795, it was ruled by France but liberated by the Prussian Army in 1813.

On the 10 May 1940, the Prussians, the same army that had liberated them over 100 years before, invaded and took over Arnhem. For the next five years it was the centre of destruction of the allies and Germany. Post-war it was evacuated for months while the residents returned to the ruins of the old city centre, with the Eusebius church destroyed and many houses badly damaged. The city was rebuilt quickly earning a fine reputation for the quality of their post-war construction. The church was rebuilt in reinforced concrete, and the large tower known as 'Miracle of Arnhem' was erected and can be seen today, it has the largest clockwork mechanism in Holland and from the top you can see over the area of Arnhem.

One of the monuments built in 1946 by Jacob Maris is for the Battle of Arnhem. It has no inscription but a bus stop near explains the battle. This monument, called a needle is surrounded by benches, and appropriately near the Airborne Museum.

At Oosterbeek, a Commonwealth War Graves cemetery, there were over 1,700 men buried after the war. These men were gathered in from all over their burial sites on the battlefield at Arnhem and re-interred at this cemetery. On the approach to the gate is the 'flowers in the wind' memorial. This marks the annual ceremony where the Dutch local children lay flowers on each grave. Of the 1,700, 1,314 are British Army casualties, plus 243 with unknown graves, seventy-eight RAF and eighty-one Non Commonwealth Foreign Nationals, one member of the Royal Navy killed flying with the RAF over Arnhem during the battle.

There are three holders of the Victoria Cross buried there:

- Captain Grayburn, VC of the 2nd Parachute Regiment. Killed 20 September 1944
- Flight Lieutenant David Lord, VC, DFC, RAF. Killed 19 September 1944
- Captain L. Queripel, VC, Royal Sussex Regiment attached 10th Parachute Regiment. Killed 19 September 1944.

Another Lieutenant Sergeant, John Baskeyfield of the South Staffs, is commemorated on the Groesbeck Memorial having no known grave.

Quite near the Oosterbeek cemetery is the excellent memorial to the Air Despatchers of the Royal Army Service Corps who fought alongside the aircrew of the Royal Air Force; seventy-nine paying the ultimate sacrifice.

Every year near the 20 September veterans come from all over and are welcomed by the Dutch people, a drop of parachutists, a few of them being veterans, make a drop in the area of Arnhem and a service of remembrance is held to remember those very young men who gave their lives in the cause of freedom.

The bridge at Arnhem that proved to be a 'Bridge to Far' is now known as the John Frost bridge in memory of John Frost whose men fought so hard and so courageously in an attempt to take it. The bridge has now been rebuilt and at the end of the bridges northern ramp is 'Airborne Plein Memorial' on this ramp is a plaque to Frost and his men. On the bridge a concrete shelter which was, during the battle, a pill box and damaged by PIAT fire and flamethrowers. Lieutenant Colonel Frost's old HQ overlooking the northern ramp area, is now a modern building but a wall plaque commemorates the fact. The building of the Arnhem Bridge started construction in 1932 and was completed in 1935.

On 10 May 1940 during the invasion of Holland by the Germans, the bridge was destroyed by the Dutch Army and blown completely off its pier at one end of the river in an attempt to slow down the advance of the Germans in their attack on the Western Front. It had been the target of the 207th German Infantry Division who, after capturing Holland, to use the original ship bridge that connected both parts of the town before the Arnhem bridge was completed.

In September 1944 only weeks before 'Market Garden' the Arnhem bridge was repaired and both bridges were used again, but only days before 'Market Garden' the middle sections of the ship bridge was removed. The Arnhem Bridge was finally destroyed in October 1944 by allied bombers. In 1945 when Holland was liberated a pontoon bridge was built at the spot where the ship bridge had been, and a bailey bridge was built near the destroyed Arnhem Bridge.

A link between Croydon in Surrey, and Arnhem began in 1946, both towns having suffered greatly from bombing and war with it seemed right that they should be linked.

In 1985 having been informally linked with each other it became formal and ceremonies were held in Arnhem and Croydon. The Mayor of Croydon was invited to the Battle of Arnhem service each year. Today the city of Arnhem has a population of some 160,000 people.

During the battle the Hartenstein Hotel in Oosterbeek, was the headquarters of the British Divisional Commander, Major-General R.E Urquhart. Today it is the Airborne Museum. Many things found and dug up from the battle, authentic film footage, true to life dioramas and an audiovisual presentation are preserved here, and is a wonderful tribute to the men who fought and died here, maintaining that their courage and dedication to freedom is not forgotten.

A memorial thanks to the efforts of Alan Hartley of the Down Ampney Association has now been erected at the Hartenstein to the aircrew killed in the Battle of Arnhem.

To his credit having raised the finance to build the monument, each year, and out of his own pocket he supplies the finance to insure and maintain the monument. Let's hope when Alan is not around the cause he began will be taken up and maintained.

Chapter 5

Operation Market Garden

On the 11 September, Montgomery contacted General Eisenhower and said, although he had the support of the War Office he would have to postpone 'Market' until the 21 September due to a lack of vital supplies. This spurred Eisenhower into flying to Montgomery's HQ to find out what he required, having found out he promised 1,000 tons of supplies to Brussels and said that the supplies promised to US 12th Army Group would be allocated to the 1st Army, this would enable support to be given to 30 Corps when the advance began.

British intelligence said the Germans at the time were in low spirits and morale, and that the area of Arnhem was inhabited by only a small number of troops and equipment. This was endorsed again on the 17th, but on the 15th the Dutch resistance informed the British that SS units had been sent to the Arnhem area, but for some reason the 1st Airborne Army were not given this information until the 20th, three days after the operation had begun. It appeared the German Panzer with tanks needed a resting area and Arnhem was chosen, General Browning had seen five oblique –angle, air photographs of tanks near the Arnhem area which confirmed earlier Dutch resistance reports of tanks. He had received this intelligence but chose to disregard the information and told General Urquhart commanding the 1st Airborne Division to take a rest and go on leave. The information that had come through was that the 9th SS Panzer Division resting at Arnhem heading to Zutphen, was laid aside without telling the men of the 1st Airborne.

But neither General Horrocks nor General Urquhart was aware that instead of SS-Recruits, they would be up against experienced SSPanzer –Grenadiers, this piece of ultra information had not been passed down to corps level.

The planning of the intricate details of the operation was left to a Squadron Leader D. Wallace and a Colonel John Overdorf. After the operation a message was sent back by a divisional commander saying that the timing and placing was superb.

The RAF had been asked to drop the 1st Parachute Brigade, by Major General Urghuart, Commanding the 1st Airborne Division, on to the Arnhem Bridge, with the minimum loss of surprise. They were to be dropped on both sides of the river as close as possible to the bridge, which was the last bridge before entering Germany and then straight down to the industrial area of the Ruhr. Urghuart was thought to be an unusual choice to command the airborne troops having never made a parachute jump or flown in a glider, and was prone to air sickness. It had been suggested that he take some parachute training, but when asked he said he was to busy preparing of the invasion of Europe, and in any case he was too big and, at 42, too old.

South of the bridges between the Neder Rijn and Waal Rivers was a belt of low-lying polder (fen) land with numerous deep ditches and few roads, very exposed and unsuitable for mass glider landings or for a rapid deployment. Four miles north of Arnhem, beyond a dense belt of woods, was a rough heath and dune land fit for parachute dropping and for limited glider landings, but not for mass glider landings.

But the RAF as in all airborne operations, were against this because of anti-aircraft on the run in and out routes. Also, although the area that would have been ideal as far as positioning, the ground was soft and bogie and would have been unsuitable for landing gliders. Bomber Command had been consulted on the aspects of anti-aircraft defences in the area of Arnhem and the crews reported back that it would be intense.

There was also a shortage of troop-carriers, the US and the RAF between them only able to muster 1,750, where as to get 35,000 men to Arnhem in one foul swoop would need 3000 aircraft. Of this number of men 20,190 would be parachuted in and the remainder by glider, plus 5,230 tons of equipment, 1927 vehicles, and 568 guns.

On 15 September 1987 Albemarle's arrived at RAF Manson, the thirty-seven gliders and airborne troops to be used had been there since 5 September for Operation 'Linnet' and 'Comet'.

In choosing the routes the following factors were taken on board:

• The shortest distance to targeted area with due regard to prominent land features.
• Traffic control in the air.
• Inner anti-aircraft artillery zone and balloon areas in the United Kingdom.
• Enemy anti-aircraft and searchlight batteries.
• Avoidance of 'dog-leg' turns over the sea.
• Choice of prominent irregular coast for making landfall.
• Shortest distance over hostile territory.

The main concerns were based on the airborne invasion of Normandy and southern France, the capabilities of the German Air Force and strength of the German anti-aircraft defences, and the transport crew on previous operations in scattering paratroopers across many miles of enemy countryside due to navigational errors.

The Luftwaffe day fighters posed a marginal threat to the operation; some 220 to 240 single-engine fighters were based within range of the targeted area. It is now known that 150 to 200 German fighter aircraft were assembled to operate against the airborne assaults on the first three days of the landings. But the ability to protect the transport aircraft from fighter attack was proved to be justified during the course of the operation.

However, the Luftwaffe night fighters posed a much higher threat with their experience against large bomber stream formations and being well equipped for this task as many Bomber Command crews would testify, much consideration was being given to the operation-taking place during the daytime.

Then the German anti-aircraft defences, which were known to be strong in the area of Arnhem intelligence, reported it getting stronger. With the transports and tugs flying in large formations at 100–150 mph, at low heights of 500 to 2,500 feet, and with no armour plating or self sealing fuel tanks, it seemed to be an anti-aircraft gunner's paradise.

Once again if the anti-aircraft batteries were to be restricted by air attack it would depend much on the operation being in daylight since they would be invisible at night.

The last factor was the navigation ability of the transport crews, particularly the inexperienced Americans, who had little if any experience of night time flying. The third factor for the operation-taking place during the daylight, although self-sealing tanks had been promised and although some arrived in the UK from America in September, they did not arrive in time for 'Market Garden'.

The routes to Arnhem were considered, one across the North Sea from Orford Ness, Suffolk, passing over Dutch Islands (Schouwen) a distance of 96 miles, 18 miles farther on and over the eastern end of the Schouwen Island. Then a turn towards the initial point, code named 'Ellis' and then 52 miles inland just to the south of Hertgenbosch, distinguishable by means of several prominent road and rail junctions. From 'Ellis' aircraft were to fly directly to the landing zones at Nijmegen, a distance of 25 miles, and Arnhem; 30 miles. A flight of some 80 miles over enemy held territory, the 38/46 Group gliders would fly 1,000 feet above the Americans.

The second a more southerly route skirting London crossing the coast at Bradwell Bay across the Thames estuary for 34 miles to the tip of the North Foreland, Kent. Then directly eastwards across the Straits of Dover to the Belgium coast, then a slight deviation took them around a salient of German territory to the initial point. Delos at the position where the route intersected the Albert Canal, at Delos aircraft then turned north-eastwards to the landing zones at Eindhoven, bisecting German flak concentrations at Eindhoven and Tilburg. This route would cut the time over enemy territory by more than half, this deviation was introduced on 16 September by General Williams to avoid a pocket of German troops who were holding out south of Scheldt.

The 1st British Airborne Division would seize and hold the bridges, road, rail and pontoon at Arnhem, with sufficient bridgeheads to allow the passage of the 2nd Army.

The 82 (US) Airborne Division would seize the bridges at Nijmegen and Grave, then the high ground between Nijmegen and Groesbeek, with the same object in view.

The 101st (US) Airborne Division would seize bridges and defiles in the Eindhoven area.

The decision was to use both, the 101st Airborne would follow the southern route and the US 82nd and the British 1st Airborne Army would use the northern route. Using only one route it was thought, would make the column too long and give the Germans chance to bring effective firepower against the rear part of the column. It would also cause the enemy to divert aircraft over a far greater area, using both also gave the flexibility to use the routes for reinforcements or re-supply lifts. Radar beacons and searchlight cones were to be used at the air formation assembly points and at the departure points on the English coast and where the aircraft started their North Sea crossings were also marked with Eureka beacons and light flashing code letters.

The town at Arnhem and the airfield at Deelen were both well protected by anti-aircraft guns. Because of the guns at Deelen being just north of Arnhem, slow flying aircraft such as the Dakota stood no chance if the approach was too near it during daylight, with this in mind the dropping and landing zones had to be well beyond the guns at Deelen.

Thoughts of the British and American dropping into swamps in Normandy came to mind.

A Coupe de Main introduced in the Operation 'Comet' plan to drop troops near Arnhem was abandoned, but incorrectly rejected, because the reports of anti-aircraft defences at Arnhem Bridge. The plan was for eighteen selected crews flying Horsas's from Harwell. The man standing by to fly the first glider was Staff Sergeant James (Jimmy) Wallwork who had landed with great skill the first of three gliders to land at Pegasus Bridge on the evening of the 5 June prior to the Normandy landings: Jimmy thought the idea not practicable and today glad it did not take place.

The Arnhem Bridge being much larger than the Pegasus Bridge and had a garrison of soldiers, where as the Pegasus was only lightly defended. The plan was for six Horsa gliders to be led by Captain Buchan of the K.O.S.B the famous whisky company and who made sure that a good store of whisky was aboard the glider. James would have had his No 2 pilot Stan Pearson who was a No 1 on the Normandy Coupde Main, also flying one of the three gliders that landed at the Pegasus Bridge as they were the only crew with the experience required and the other five would follow them down in line astern. He thinks now after sixty years that they would be the only ones with lights on, having been released at a height of 2,500 feet. They were to land on the riverbank at low tide, up the steps and over the bridge, the odds were so much against this that Jimmy feels now that they would have been the only ones to make the landing zone. He remembers that they actually loaded up and then it was called off at the last moment, and the next day it was cancelled for good.

The three fields chosen for the landing lay north of the railway lines through Arnhem to Utrecht, the furthest 8 miles from the bridge which was the whole object of the expedition. The fourth field was south of the railway and somewhat larger than the others, in this area the level rose above 20 metres, and in large clearings in a wooden belt, there were extensive, open form areas offering excellent D.Zs and L.Zs. The fifth and closest to Arnhem was near the small village of Wansborn and chosen as the place to which supplies were to be dropped after the landings. The lifts and drops would have to be done over three days, the 1st Parachute Brigade and 1st Air Landing Brigade and half the sappers and gunners and other divisional troops would go in on the first day, the remainder would follow on the subsequent two days.

As already reported it would need 3,000 aircraft to drop all 35,000 troops in one day but that was not possible as only 1,750 were available, this in hindsight was a crucial factor in the operation not being a success.

On 17 September, the first day, 16,500 troops would be parachuted in, 13,781 by glider, but it would be the 19th before all 34,876 troops were transported to Arnhem.

It was suggest that two shuttles in one day be made, but rejected by General Paul Williams USAAF, who was in command of US and British Transport to be employed on 'Market Garden'. The reasons for refusal was aircrew fatigue and insufficient time for aircraft maintenance. The RAF suggested flying the first lift before dawn allowing time for a second daylight mission. But because of the inexperience and navigational training for the US airmen, it was considered inadequate for such a task and so the decision was finally made to do it over three days with the main troops being dropped in the first two days. Many of the RAF pilots were ex-Bomber Command and were used to flying night operations and felt they could have flown a second lift at night on the same day. This would have meant two other parachute brigades with some signals support units this extra man power would have enabled the 1st Airborne Division to hold the Arnhem Bridge in strength but was turned down by Brereton.

The major decision of the operation was that it would take place in daylight.

Air Defence of Great Britain fighters would provide escorts and flak suppression on the northern route as far as the Initial Point Ellis, and Coastal Command would mount diversionary attacks outside the area and the routes of the airborne missions. The Ninth Air Force fighters would attack enemy flak and ground fire on the southern route between the Initial Point Delos and the landing/drop zones in the area of Eindhoven.

Second TAF aircraft would perform armed reconnaissance missions exclusive of the times that the 8th and 9th Air Force Fighters were in the area, this was to provide the most efficient and full cover possible between the Initial Points and the landing zones, but only a light cover over the North Sea.

The last parties added to 'Market Garden' was No 6080 and 6341 RAF Light Warning Units, mobile radar stations who worked with the ground troops and could direct night fighters on to German bombers approaching their area. They would be landed by glider and consisted of two fighter control officers and 10 or 11 radar and radio technicians, they would fly from Harwell as part of General Browning's Airborne Corps HQ. Wing Commander John Laurence Brown who had in 1941 been the senior controller at RAF Sopley and working with 604 Squadron, had been largely responsible for numerous enemy aircraft being destroyed for which he was awarded the MBE. He later became a senior controller in North Africa and at 'Market Garden' was put in charge of the whole operation.

If all went well 30 Corps under General Horrocks would motor 63 miles in two days and into the Ruhr, capture the factories in this area and the main source of Germany's aircraft, tanks and other war making material.

With the Irish Guards part of the Guards Armoured were Flight Lieutenant Donald Love, aged 28, and an RAF Fighter Reconnaissance pilot who was part of the air liaison team which would call in the rocket firing Typhoons of 2nd TAF when the breakout began.

If 'Market', the airborne side of the operation, and 'Garden', the 2nd Army follow through, was a success, it was said the war would be over by Christmas 1944.

Chapter 6

Sunday 17 September 1944

At DZ "X" six aircraft of 38 Group were to drop the marker forces of 21 Independent Parachute Company to set up ground aids. At DZ "S" Six aircraft of 38 Group were to drop 'marker' forces as above.

One hundred and thirty aircraft of 46 Group and twenty-three of 38 Group were to tow 153 Gliders; carrying elements of No 1 Air Landing Brigade.

Many support squadrons were out some time before the main armada to Arnhem; they set out and paved the way for the very first successful drop with the minimum of casualties.

On 16/17th September 1944, aircraft of No 1 & 8 (PF) Groups of Bomber Command bombed airfields at Hopsten, Leeuwarden, Steenwjk-Havelte and Rheiene and fifty-four Lancaster's and five Mosquitoes of 141 Squadron attacked flak positions at Moerdijk, between 8.30am on the 16th and 8.30pm on the 17th, 1,250 aircraft in total were despatched.

On the 17th, 112 Lancaster's and twenty Mosquitoes, of again 1 & 8 (PF) Groups Bomber Command, attacked German flak positions in the Flushing area and the proposed route that the transport aircraft would take. The force attacking the flak position at Moerdijk had slight fighter opposition but suffered no losses, apart from Lancaster's of 3 Group; Lancaster LM 169 of 90 Squadron and LM 693 of 115 Squadron collided over the target area and LM 693 crashing near Stryen, Holland at 2300 hours, both crews being killed.

On the 17th the US 8th Army Air force despatched 150 formations of B-17 Flying Fortress's to attack strong points mainly gun positions preceding the airborne operations in the Nijmegen and Arnhem areas. All attacks were made with 260-pound fragmentation bombs with the altitude of the attacks from 10,000 feet to 23,000 feet, the average being approximately 18,000 feet.

One hundred and seventeen different points were assigned, twelve US fighter escort aircraft were shot down attacking the flak positions from low level, unfortunately only forty-three of those 117 flak positions were bombed and suffered any real damage. However, the raid did disrupt the German anti-aircraft system throughout the day.

Seventeen Mosquitoes of No 464 Squadron of the 2nd Tactical Air Force were despatched to bomb and strafe roads and ferry crossings. Thirty-two Mosquitoes of 107 and 613 Squadrons from Lasham and from 21 Squadron, Thorney Island, took off to blast buildings in the Arnhem area, which housed German troops. Intense flak was en-counted in the Arnhem area and targets were attacked by a shallow dive from 800 to 1,500 feet with twenty-five-second 500lb bombs, two aircraft of 107 despatched were shot down.

The 9th US Army Air force bombed targets said to be housing German troops on the outskirts of Arnhem, one a mental hospital at Wolfheze. The secret German ammunition depots in the woods around this area.

The role of 198 and 164 Squadrons Flying Typhoon aircraft made attacks on the guns and defences around the bridge at Arnhem with rocket and cannon fire. Twelve Flak batteries were knocked out with only one gun left intact but this being bent and twisted.

As the attacks were near allied lines they had to be precisely mounted, the target was marked with red flares while the ground troops marked the perimeter with orange smoke.

The barracks at Arnhem were set on fire by Mosquitoes attacks, at Ede targets were attacked by fifty Mosquitoes, forty-eight Mitchell's and twenty-four Boston's of the 2nd TAF.

On the 17th three Mustangs and three Mosquitoes were shot down, with 141 Squadron strafing the airfield at Steenwijk from low level. Nineteen Squadron Mustangs took on fifty plus BF 109's and FW 190's over Emmerich, where one aircraft was shot down. Sixty-five Squadron lost two Mustangs in the same area, one to flak and one in a dogfight, one Tempest of 80 Squadron was also lost.

The support of No 83 Group 2nd Tactical air force under Air Marshal Harry Broadhurst, a veteran of army/air co-operation was second to none.

The weather on the 17th was good with the early fog, which had been forecasted, therefore not delaying the take off of the 359-tug/glider combinations. The wind was slight visibility, good and by 10.00am the few stratus clouds had lifted.

At eight British airfields and 14 US stretching, from Dorset to Lincoln, aircraft and crews were preparing for take off.

A message was sent by US General Lewis Brereton, who was commanding the allied force to all units before take off.

"You are taking part in one of the greatest airborne operations in military history. On the success of your mission today-on the navigation and flying skill and courage of the aircrew and the skills, courage and speed of the landing force rests the difference between a quick decision in the west and a long drawn out battle.

I know I can depend on you "God Speed to you."

The WAAF parachute packers at those airfields and at Credenhill, near Hereford packed thousands of parachutes. At Down Ampney the groundcrew preparations had started several days before. For a whole day, and in at great speed, they had started to fit the heavy steel rollers used for pannier dropping. But having fitted them to each of the 271 Squadron Dakotas they were then told to take them out and put the seats back for parachute dropping, patching the door catches with fabric and dope as a protection against snagging up on a parachute drop. However, they then had to put back the rollers and take off the parachute doors to open up the big cargo doors, this proved to be very tedious work and they grumbled that the powers to be should make up their minds. What they did not know was the 1st Airborne Division were anxious to prove that what the 6th Airborne had done on D-Day at Normandy, the 1st could do better.

The plan was the first lift to parachute the 1st Parachute Brigade consisting of 2,400 men and by glider the 1st Air landing Brigade minus two companies of the South Staffs Regiment and Divisional Troops consisting of 2,900 men.

All these bases were ready for take off by 09.00am with the first lift off from Fairford at 09.45am, with 190 and 620 Squadrons towing twelve loads of Pathfinder gliders to be landed near the bridges at Arnhem and Nijmegen.

Before entering the Horsa cockpit the all up weight would be reported to the tug pilot and that the glider was directly behind the tug and on the same heading and the nose wheel was straight. On entering the cockpit he would test the two release levers and check that the tow release control position was left in the fully forward position.

The check list before take off:

Flaps – Up
Air Pressure – Minimum 150lb and 200lb for operational flights.
Trim – Neutral
Altimeter – Zero
Brakes – Off

When ready for take off instruct the tug pilot would:

Take up the slack and then take-off when the glider starts moving, on take off keep directly behind the tug. At an ample margin above stalling speed pull off gently and hold near the ground until tug takes-off. When the tug was clear of the ground, climb gently to maintain a 'high tow', the low or high two positions varies from pilot to pilot although some found the high position more comfortable with less turbulence and the view of the ground was far greater.

They took off at one-minute intervals, circling Fairford at 2,500feet and 175mph, formatting into loose pairs. At 620 Squadron, six Stirling's were led by

Squadron Leader Richard Bunker, DFC, flying Stirling LJ 930. The six from 190 were led by their commanding officer Wing Commander G.E. Harrison.

In all nearly 200 troops, seventeen jeeps, seven lightweight motor cycles, a heavy motorcycle, seventeen trailers, sevenguns and a bicycle were despatched.

The glider drops were made at 12.40pm with six officers and 186 men of the 21st Independent Parachute Company under Major B.A (Boy) Wilson. Their objective was to secure the area and activate beacons to guide the approaching armada.

The Stirling had to be converted for parachute dropping, the exit aperture was a large coping shape hole in the floor to the rear of the fuselage. The men had never dropped from a Stirling before, at least four of the party dropped with a full, heavily laden kitbag strapped to their legs; they were the first to drop. It required only two despatchers, where as the Dakota required four, this was done successfully and without casualties.

The 1st Platoon had the task of marking DZ 'X' spelling out on a long strip 'X' and a 'T' for wind direction. No 2 Platoon had the task of marking LZ 'Z' for the glider landing, with support elements of the 1st Parachute Brigade, both laying parallel but separated by a belt of trees. No 3 Platoon marked LZ 'S', as soon as they landed they began to put out smoke signals and yellow marker beacons indicating to the planes, fifteen minutes behind, that this was the correct dropping zone for the parachutists, a 12 foot letter 'T', with each arm 100 yards long and made of white Hessian cloth, was laid in the centre of the landing zone: each point of the 'T' was to be prolonged for 500 yards by yellow smoke from the point of origin at 100yard intervals.

Major Wilson contacted the outlying platoons by radio and ordered them to release pigeons, which would carry the first news of the landings to the War Office in London. The message 'Landings complete unopposed'; One of those pigeons was called William of Orange, who had been trained by the Army Pigeon Service and bred by Sir William Proctor Smith of Brexton, near Kutsford. At the end of the war Sir William bought William of Orange 'out of service' for £135 pounds and ten years later it was recorded that the pigeon was still alive, but now to old for racing or breeding.

On 17 September 1944, the pigeon William was released at 4.30pm with an unimportant despatch and covered 260 miles, of which 135 miles was over sea, in four hours twenty-five minutes to its home loft. Its speed, 1,740 yards per minute and nearly 60 miles an hour, all the time showing great determination and endurance. For this feat the pigeon was awarded the Dicken Medal, the highest award to an animal and equivalent to the VC for humans. In 1965, the Dicken Medal awarded to William was presented to the Royal Signals museum. The pigeons were trained by the Army Pigeon Service and the Royal Signals, specialist pigeons trainers were used with the rank of Loftsman, this in the Royal Signals continued until 1946 when it was disbanded.

In 1940 the Royal Signals had established 150 lofts of which thirty were mobile. They were also used by the Royal Navy and the Royal Air Force. There were some initial problems with this when the pigeons flew only as far as the roof of a farm building but a few well aimed pebbles soon sent them on their long trip back to the UK.

At RAF Keevil, 620 Squadron provided six aircraft for the path finding mission followed later by another nineteen.

On the 17th the tannoy blared out at Fairford "Pilot Officer Fogarty and crew to flights." Two more from a 'A' Flight and three from 620 Squadron got a similar summons. The six were detailed as Pathfinders for a major operation in daylight, to a place called Arnhem. Three 190 aircraft led the procession; 'Red' Gilliard at the point of the first three Flight Officer Foggarty in EF916 to starboard, and the third to port followed by the three from 620. He climbed to clear the low cloud, with the port and starboard planes veering away from the leading plane momentarily to avoid collision as they passed through the cloud, and then re-forming on Gilliard.

Flight Sergeant Holden Foggarty's navigator had his own flight plan ready in case of necessity. Squadron Leader Gilliard's navigator was the key man, the rest followed with the other three Pathfinder aircraft in formation, followed by an immensely long line of towed gliders, Horsa and Hamilcar's, which at this time were only visible to the rear gunner in EF 916. Near Arnhem, Holden went forward and sat in the second dickey seat by Reg Foggarty, this was normally taken by another member of the crew who was now down in the nose, map reading. Reg would need help with the throttles if evasive action was needed, Ted the bomb aimer in the nose with his eye on the bombsight, gave the word, and the red light flashed on in the body of the Stirling followed seconds later by the green light. The paratroopers floated down to set up the 'Rebecca' –radar transmitters to guide the gliders with their 'Eureka' receivers to the Dropping Zone, it was just like another exercise and they flew back to Fairford having completed a textbook operation.

At 13.00pm the 1st Air Landing Brigade landed on Landing Zone 'S', at Reijers Farm, 134 gliders out of 153 that set out landing successfully, twenty-four landed in various parts of the countryside, twenty-two were recalled and were transferred to the second lift on the 18th. Five came down because of tow ropes breaking or the tug aircraft having engine trouble, and five ditched in the sea but were quickly picked up by the Air Sea Rescue launches, No 27 A/S.R at Dover, received a message that launch 2549 at Ramsgate had picked up six uninjured members of a glider, at 14.15pm they again received a message that H.S.L's 186 and 2549 at Ramsgate had picked members of a glider crew, 186 picking up four and 2549 nineteen. At 15.05pm Ramsgate Launches 127 and 169 had picked up twenty-four and seven respectably, No 24 A/S.R at Lowestoft were also detailed to cover the area being used by flights to Arnhem.

Launch 2687 at No 26 A/SR from Felixstowe saw a glider break away from being towed and started to glide until it ditched from which eight survivors were taken aboard, later another glider ditched again and eight survivors were taken on board, of which, three were injured. The men were given a change of clothing and a tot of rum; some were picked up so quickly that they were completely bone dry.

Seven survivors were transferred to H.S.L. 2557, Nine to H.S.L. 2572 and H.S.L. 2687, and two survivors were transferred to H.S.L. 2555. Launch was sent to the area of a glider seen to be on a different course to its tug, the glider was seen as a black dot on the water 6 miles away. Aircraft dropped smoke floats and patrolled the area until the launch arrived, at 13.30pm five British glider troops were taken aboard. The glider sank at 13.25pm, the crew of glider No 462 suffering from immersion in the water, minor cuts and bruises.

The 167 aircraft dropped 154 Horsa and thirteen Hamilcar gliders, carrying the Davison Tactical HQ to LZ-Z. The Hamilcars's carried heavy guns and Universal Carriers, these were to act as transports for the airborne troops, one aircraft on LZ ' S' and LZ' X' was damaged by flak. Two Hamilcars's carrying 17 pounder guns overturned in soft ground at LZ 'Z' and flipped on to their backs, three pilots were killed and a fourth wounded as were some of the passengers. The rest of the Hamilcars's landed successfully, one overran the LZ and hit a railway embankment damaging two Universal Carriers in the glider. Pre-operation, the greatest fear had been from flak and it was estimated that the losses of glider and tug aircraft would be up to forty per cent.

The Albermarle aircraft of 296 and 297 made the largest contribution in aircraft numbers despatching twenty-eight aircraft each, the other squadrons were only able to despatch twenty-five.

Wing Officer Blackhurst, later flying officer, was a wireless/operator air gunner serving with 296, which were normally based at Earls Colne but because it was out of range of the Albermarle, it moved to RAF Manston on the 6 September in readiness for Operation 'Comet'. Their normal role so far had been S.O.E operations over Europe, but from the 6th time was spent flying tests and overall familiarization with the set up.

On the 17th at 11.00am they took off in Albermarle P/V 1632, flown by Wing Commander Musgrave the squadron commanding officer, on this occasion they were towing an American glider the Wacco carrying US airborne troops to Holland. The weather was good and they flew at 3,000 feet, they found no opposition apart from ground flak position as they crossed the Dutch Coast was quickly despatched by US Fighters who were escorting them.

All went well and no problems at the DZ, apart from two gliders sitting on their noses.

The Albemarle was under-powered but had one advantage for glider towing, with its tricycle undercarriage out it went into a flying attitude even before it began to roll, the nose-wheel allowing full power to be applied rapidly because there was no torgue to offset. Its jump–hole in the floor was almost as bad for the noses of the parachutists as that in the Whitley, they been used in the invasion of Sicily, North Africa and D–Day.

Ken Frere joined 296 Squadron in August 1944 and on the 2 September time was spent moving towing Horsa gliders to Manston, to get as near Holland as possible. By the 15th all the aircraft and gliders were in place as they returned they saw masses of U.S B–17's on route to Germany.

The four Wacco gliders carrying the US signalling team was brought forward from the second lift the next day by the four extra Albemarle's. This had originally been five but in the morning of the 17th from a reserve unit, one returned as they were told they were not required but at the last moment they were, so the fifth missed out.

The main Manston force was made up of Horsas's carrying part of the 2 South Staffs, and anti–tank and light artillery.

Thirty-five out of thirty-eight gliders of the HQ of the 1st British Corps landed on LZ–N in the US sector near Nijmegen, one was lost over the UK, one in the sea and one over Holland. A further twenty-eight out of thirty-two towed by 38 Group, landed safely at 'N' and the six Adrian gliders also landed successfully.

In the UK twenty-four gliders made force landings in low cloud and turbulence, also a further fifteen over the sea or Holland. One glider a Horsa RJ 113 of D Squadron of the Glider Pilot Regiment, pilot Staff Sergeant L(Len).J. Gardner and his second pilot Sergeant R.(Bob) A.Fraser got caught in the tug's slipstream soon after take off forcing the cable to snap and the glider to break up over the village of Paulton in Somerset. Twenty-three soldiers, of which twenty-one were from No 2 Platoon 9th Airborne Field Company Royal Engineers and both glider pilots were killed in the crash, at 11.05am. This was only 30 minutes after taking off from RAF Keevil and on a north west course towards Gloucester to pick up squadrons coming from RAF Fairford and then to head out to the Severn and the Bristol Channel to form up, an explosion occurred in the Horsa over the village of Farrington Gurney blowing off the tail, it then lost lift and crashed.

The Horsa was being pulled by a Stirling LK 148 of 299 Squadron and taken off from RAF Keevil at 10.25am crashing at Double Hills, Poulton, Somerset. Today at Keevil where they had taken off is a memorial with the following inscription:

To the memory of two Glider pilots and twenty-one men of the 9th Airborne Field Company RE who were killed when their Airspeed Horsa glider RJ 113 of D Squadron GPR crashed in a field on Sunday the 17th en–route to Arnhem.

A poem was written by Ruby Bowell, 'A Paulton Nurse', who in 1944 attended the crash.

'They did not die in battle din of world renowned or a medal win. But they gave their lives for you and me that we and the whole world might be free; This is read each year by Peter Yeates granddaughter who had been reading it since she was 5 and is now 22.

The memorial is on land owned by the Prince of Wales, the CinC of the Army Air Corps, which previously was the Glider Pilot Regiment, and takes great interest in the Memorial which was was put up by sappers of the Royal Monmouthshire Engineers in 1979.

The men that died that day and had previously served in North Africa and Sicily are now buried in Weston-Super-Mare, Somerset. A Garden seat has now been installed at the cemetery to their memory by the Airborne Engineers Association with donations from the Glider Pilot Regiment.

Sergeant Walter Simpson who was flying in the rear turret of LK 148 was looking out of his turret watching the Horsa glider behind when suddenly it parted in the middle, the tow rope broke and the glider went down like a rock falling to earth. They turned around and marked the crash site then returned to Keevil and drove by jeep the 22 miles to the crash site, here it was horrendous with bodies and wreckage everywhere.

The pilot, Flight Sergeant Ken Crowther, said he never wanted to go back to Double Hills again but as he lived close to the area post-war he joined the Memorial Committee.

The remainder of the 9th Field Company in another glider went on to Arnhem, one of their jobs to seize the railway bridge. Of the eight officers and 200 sappers who left the UK for Arnhem only one officer a Major Winchester the commanding officer, and fifty-six sappers came across the river to safety, the remainder were killed or taken prisoner

Captain Eric O. Callaghan Royal Engineers was the No 2 Platoon Commander of the 9th Field Company Royal Engineers maintained that if he had been allowed to take the bridge as planned, the outcome at Arnhem may have been different. Their task was to remove the charges put by the Germans on the railway bridge which only failed at the last moment when the bridge blew up. His platoon had been depleted when a number of his men were sent to No1 Platoon in a failed task to seize the Wolfhenzen Hotel which was occupied by a large number of SS Troops. The men who had died at Paulton were part of this platoon and would have been used on the hotel operation, where as No 2 Platoon were given over to this task which meant the bridge party was seriously weakened.

Why did Horsa RJ 113 crash?

The official records of this crash are missing, said to have been lost in the blitz in London, but there are strong feelings that it was caused by a structural failure of the tailplane section. Also, that maybe the violent explosion and fire was caused by the explosives hamper going up when the glider hit the ground. It is known that many Horsa gliders had been parked at Netheravon out in the open for many months and some refurbishment had been done to replace or strengthen the tail assemblies.

A report by Wing Officer David T. Lewis the rear gunner of a Stirling of 299 Squadron, was flying just forward but close to the Double Hills glider. He said there was no explosion in the air, but he saw the tail suddenly come off the glider; it came down in two pieces and exploded on the ground, the Stirling carrying on with the tow rope trailing, it had a sobering effect on all five of them.

Ken Crowther the second pilot towing RJ 113 was convinced that a American Marauder aircraft crossing the flight path of the Stirling and glider caused a slipstream just before the crash which caused difficulty in flying the glider straight and level. However, Wally Simpson in his rear turret did not agree with Ken's theory and perhaps we shall never know what did happen to RJ 113 the first casualties of 'Market Garden'.

The tug aircraft had to have a reserve of power or the engines would overheat, the tug crew had to be as highly trained as those of a bomber crew with the contact between the tug crew and the glider pilots being very important.

General Browning was in a Horsa, flown by Brigadier George S. Chatterton. They took off from Harwell pulled by aircraft of 295 Squadron; the gliders from here carried the men of the headquarters carrying 154 men, twenty-one jeeps and nineteen trucks. In Browning's glider there were bikes, bazookas, bedding rolls, radios, and many other things associated with a command post. They landed in LZ-N and an Airborne HQ was set up in the forest some distance away on Groesbeck Ridge on the north side of DZ-N.

Also in Browning's glider was Wing Commander John Laurence Brown, MBE.

John came from Amersham and although a qualified pilot, his role in 1940 was a section controller. In 1942 he assisted the landings in North Africa and was able to establish quickly, radar cover all the way to Tunis. He had been the first RAF man ashore in the Sicily landings and also took part in the landings in Italy. He was then recalled for D-Day when he went ashore with the Americans but his LST went astray and got stuck on a sandbank and shelled for twenty-four hours before it could be re-floated.

He was awarded three mention in despatches, also the MBE, gazetted in September 1941. At the time he was senior controller at RAF Sopley and because of his pioneering work he was largely responsible for the destruction by 604 squadron of numerous enemy aircraft at night. When he left it had become the highest scoring mobile GCI with over 100 victories. The king visited Sopley in May 1941 and saw first hand the role of a controller, while he was there when

Brown was speaking to Squadron Leader John (Cats Eyes) Cunningham, who was flying at the time in a Beaufighter and on the tail of an enemy bomber. As the king left he was in time to see the enemy bomber fall to the ground in flames.

At the time of Arnhem he was a staff officer at HQ 38 Group and asked to provide a glider borne radar to fill the gap in radar cover of 2nd TAF, he chose the Light Mobile Defence and two were sent to hold the fort until the main radar could catch up.

The Germans had a JU 88 night fighter unit in the area of Arnhem, and required a 70 mile saline leaving the airborne forces beyond the existing radar cover. Therefore HQ 38 Group were asked to supply and train two glider borne Radar Units to be borne in Horsa gliders.

The twin units Light Warning Units, No 6080 and No 6341, with men from all units in the UK, most of which had never even seen the equipment they were to operate on, they were kitted out in army uniforms and time and time again loaded and unloaded the Horsa gliders. This was when suddenly Brown was told they would not be needed, he felt so determined that they were that he went to see Browning himself and the decision was reversed.

The four gliders carrying this equipment were due to arrive in the second lift, Monday the 18 September. John Brown was going ahead to wait for them, but when he went back to his glider to get his sleeping bag an ME 109 fighter decided to strafe the area and caught him out in the open, he was badly wounded and died the next day. To date he had taken part in every allied landing of the Second World War, and is now buried in the Grosbeak Canadian Cemetery about 7 miles from Nijmegen.

At Tarrant Rushton Wing Officer J.B. Mutton of 298 Squadron had an engine oil leak and the glider was cast off a mile east of Chilbolton airfield.

At Down Ampney forty-nine aircraft were airborne in thirty-seven minutes, at Bradwell forty-seven aircraft were airborne in thirty-nine minutes, and at Blakewell Farm thirty-four in twenty-three minutes.

Flight Lieutenantt Reg Turner of 299 Squadron and flying from Keevil in Stirling LJ 971,returned early with starboard outer engine trouble casting his glider off over base and making a successful landing. His glider, called 'Matchbox', was later taken by another crew.

At Down Ampney Wing Commander Booth in Dakota KG 545, led 271 Squadron with one of the pilots flying under his command, was Flying Officer Jimmy Edwards in KG 444. They carried the men of the 7th Kings Own Scottish Borderers and their fighting equipment.

Jimmy had trouble on take off when one of the engines started to play up developing a thing called 'boost surge' which meant the power fluctuated and was not picking up speed as quickly as it should, in the glider behind him were six soldiers and 5,000lbs of ammunition, somehow they got off the ground and passed over Cricklade church, lower than the red light on the top of it. He was wearing the newly issued flak suit over his uniform as instructed, but one of his crew decided he would sit on his and protect an important part of his anatomy. Over the landing zone he said farewell to his glider pilot Captain Joe Mills, whom he had got to know well over a pint of beer. On landing back at Down Ampney he had been in the air exactly six hours.

Major Joubert later to command 271, flew in KG 500. Pilot Officer Wilson in KG 512 had his glider flown by Staff Sergeant Nadin cast off when in the Oxford area after running into low cloud and the glider losing control.

On the 17th, Walter Wright was a navigator with 298 Squadron from Tarrant Rushton, Dorset. The route he flew meant him flying over his house in Ipswich and his wife out on a cycle ride in the countryside and also his parents who stood below and watched him and others go over. Walter's aircraft was towing a glider pilot, Staff Sergeant Denis Dean Daniels whom Walter had got to know very well during his time with 298 Squadron. In 1960, Walter and his wife paid a visit to the War Graves Cemetery at Oosterbeek and it was here they found Denis's grave, he was 21 when killed.

Air Marshal Hollinghurst, AOC of 38 Group flew in Stirling LJ 977 of 570 Squadron flown by Wing Commander Bangay the commanding officer of 570 Squadron who, sadly, was killed in 1951 when his Anson aircraft had engine trouble and in attempting to land at RAF Halton in bad weather crashed killing all aboard.

The Dakotas of 48 Squadron also based at Down Ampney were fitted with long-range petrol tanks to enable them to fly to the Dutch coast before the main tanks were switched on, somehow this did not work as the tanks ran out over the channel and the main tanks had to be switched on without haste. This was done with a hand pump to force the petrol through.

Flight Officer Blakney from New South Wales and flying with 217 said the operation 'was a piece of cake.'

Michael Moynihan of the *News Chronicle* flew in Halifax M for Mike that towed a Hamilcar to Arnhem. In the Hamilcar were two Bren gun carriers and five men, the airfield was sealed, sentries posted and the bus service into town cancelled.

On Sunday the 17th, the runways were amassed with Hamilcar and Horsa gliders in two straight lines.

The Hamilcar M (Mike) was towing was flown by Staff Sergeant Hill and Sergeant Openshaw, on it "The Undertaker and his Stiffs". They took off at 10.53am but at 12.15pm were behind time and decided to make "a lone wolf approach". At 1.55pm Staff Sergeant Hill said "This is it boys Ok I am casting off now. Thanks for the lift."

At 4.20pm M (Mike) arrived back at base.

William Troughton of the *Daily Express* flew in a Stirling P, for Peter, piloted by a 6 foot sandy haired Flight Lieutenantt Bill Gardner from Vancouver,

Canada. Who two years before had flown on the famous Augsburg raid in which Wing Commander John Nettleton was awarded the Victoria Cross. William (Bill) towed a glider and did not see any fighters, flak or form of opposition.

A Dutch Spitfire pilot reported that the Dutch people were flabbergasted at the sight of "Millions of Gliders and Tugs" and dived down to say 'Hello.'

The leading aircraft in front of P (Peter) had a few rounds let off at them but allied fighters soon swooped down and silenced them, he crossed the coast at 13.35pm right on schedule and saw one or two gliders ditch but soon picked up by the rescue launches. He then spoke to the glider pilot "Hello Robin we're getting in somebody's ruddy slipstream, sorry I'll go down a bit and get you out of it. Going down, going down, okay Bill we're all right ten minutes to go Robin good luck if I do not get a chance to speak to you again, see you in a week or so. So long."

The rope was cast off by the glider pilot Robin then he, and his twelve men, went away, Bill cursed the tug pilots in front who still had their tow ropes training behind them.

A reporter from the *Daily Herald* reported the Dutch people, in their Sunday best, coming from church with their mouths open at the sight above them. The gliders went down parking up, wing tip to wing tip in straight lines; just like cars in a garage.

Flight Lieutenant (Acting Squadron Leader) James Stewart was a pilot and flight commander with 570 Squadron. On the 17 September, in Stirling LK 555, he was detailed to tow a glider to a landing zone near Arnhem, on arrival he encountered a considerable amount of enemy anti-aircraft fire. Having released the glider and about to turn away for home, he observed that the gliders that had been released and were on there way down were being fired upon very heavily. Seeing this he deliberately turned his aircraft across the landing zone to draw the enemy fire, and in so doing his aircraft was extensively damaged by flak, his actions and determination undoubtedly helped several of the gliders to achieve a good landing. He was able to bring his damaged aircraft back to base, he had been a flight commander with 570 Squadron since January 1944.

570 Squadron was commanded and led by Wing Commander Jefferson from Broadwell. He found heavy mist over the airfield and bedded evil for the operation, despite this they took off on time

and the weather improved as they flew eastwards. The Dutch coast soon came in sight and a comforting sight of the Spitfire escort and then US Dakotas in formations of nine, carrying paratroops began to overhaul the glider stream.

When they crossed the coast they were confronted with a heavy concentration of flak from a coastal flak ship and a gun position on the tip of Schauwen. One aircraft was seen to go down in flames, this was soon confronted by two Mosquitoes who beat up the gun position and all was well from that area.

Around S'Hertogenbosch and the final run towards Arnhem, a burst of flak aimed at the leading aircraft of 575 Squadron exploded under the nose of the glider unfortunately killing the Pilot, Flight Officer Henry, outright.

The area was a carpet of aircraft, Halifax's, Stirling's, Dakotas's, Albermarles, Horsas and Wacos and what seemed to be thousands of fighters milling around.

On return many aircraft came back with bullet and shrapnel holes dotted over the fuselage and mainplanes but despite this it was obvious the Germans had been given a big surprise.

Ian Robinson had been in the Far East flying on Hudson's and then Dakotas training with the Ghurkhas dropping supplies and parachutists and then dropping supplies to General Wingate's Chindits. In January 1944 they were dropping supplies to troops of the 14th Army, which had been encircled by the Japanese forces in the Arakan peninsula, a fierce battle took part, which became known as the "Battle of the admin box". After four weeks the Japanese withdrew, it was described by General Slim, commander of the 14th Army, as the turning point in the Burma campaign. This should be recorded in the history of the airborne operations that they kept two divisions supplied from the air for three weeks.

In February 1944 they were told to pack their bags and they were on their way back to the UK, when they arrived in the UK they were posted to 48 Squadron and became involved in glider towing. On D–Day the 6 June 1944, they were one of the first Dakotas to drop paratroopers just after 1.00am on the 6th, that night they again returned to Normandy with a glider carrying troops and equipment.

Supply carrying and casualties followed up until the 14 September.

On the 17th they were issued with flak jackets, but very few wore them, they were in four parts with a quick release tag, designed so that in an emergency they would not fall off, so they just spread them out and sat on them. The glider they were allotted to tow had twenty-six men from the Kings Own Scottish Borderers. They were well down the line and so sat watching all the others in front being hitched up, they then moved forward to take up the slack on the tow rope for full speed for the take off, the glider becoming airborne behind the tug. Take offs were about every forty seconds and they got off at 10.05am, 271 Squadron tugs and gliders had gone off ahead of them. It was a beautiful Sunday morning as they climbed to the designated height of 2,000 feet, all the Dakotas and most of the Stirling's were towing Horsas and the Halifax's Hamilcars. The Americans were co-ordinating the parachute drop and were heading for Nijmegen with a total of 1,500 aircraft – a large number towing gliders. They were moving over southern England, all on the northern route, as they approached the Dutch coast, memories of previous experiences came flooding back. Flight Lieutenant Peter Smith, the pilot, and Ian had flown patrols on Hudson's with 59 Squadron in that part of the world. On one occasion they spotted a large merchant ship off Texel Island as they started bombing run, as they got close it was sitting on the bottom, it had already been sunk. Earlier, but still with 59 but flying Blenheim's, out of six sent none returned, all being shot down by ME 109's. However this time they had a fighter escort of Spitfires and Typhoons who were quietly going about their business of silencing ack- ack- batteries. Ian realising they would reach the LZ too early, asked Peter to reduce speed, when later he asked again Peter replied "If I reduce it any more we'll drop out of the sky." The cast off drill was that when they were at about 2,500 feet the glider pilot would pick his time and place to cast off, this he did and they then went to pick a spot to cast off the tow rope with the ground, soon full of gliders and men disembarking.

They had not seen any flak but aircraft of 48 who were ahead of them did encounter some flak opposition, they turned for home landing at 15.35pm.

In one church the vicar said a prayer as they went over for a safe passage in the cause of freedom.

On return to Down Ampney, Alan Hartley, an LAC who had joined 271 at Doncaster and on the 29 February 1944 moved with them to Down Ampney, near Cirencester, Gloucestershire, as well as glider towing, paratrooper dropping, air despatch, the dropping of supplies to ground troops they also brought casualties back from Europe. At Down Ampney there was a Casualty Air Evacuation Centre with a fully fitted surgical hospital. In all between 48 and 271, they were with ten Dakotas to a flight over three flights in each squadron, making a total of sixty aircraft. The noise around the area Alan describes as horrendous and he felt sorry for the 280 villagers living nearby. This was greatly swelled by 3,500 airmen and WAAFS, and when the bakery opened at 8.00am there was not even a crumb left by 8.15am.

On return from Arnhem on the 17 September, Alan asked the pilot of the aircraft he maintained, Pilot Officer Len Wilson, how the operation had gone. He said with the gliders going in and the parachutists dropping in their thousands it was the most spectacular sight he had ever seen.

Flight Lieutenant David Lord, DFC, was one of the 271 Squadron pilots despatched, he had new members in his crew one having gone on leave to be married and was replaced by a pilot officer, the son of Air Marshal Medhurst.

Flight Lieutenant Stan Lee was flying with the commanding officer of 512 Squadron, Wing Commander B.A. Coventry on the 17th and led twenty-two glider combinations to drop on a landing zone near Arnhem.

It was such an easy operation and they had no idea of what they could expect to face in the coming days. He had joined 512 as a wireless operator from 24 Squadron, a VIP Transport Squadron, flying members of the Royal Family around, war chiefs and war cabinet ministers. In August 1943 the DC 3, or Dakota, started to be used by 24 Squadron based at RAF Hendon. After assisting in the Sicily campaign they returned to Hendon to find that they were now 512 Squadron and in January 1944 moved to Broadwell, which after the comfort of Hendon was a shock to the system. They were now part of the newly formed 46 Group with 271 and 48 at Down Ampney and 233 at Blakehill Farm a mile or so from Down Ampney. They shared the field with 575 Squadron, to this was added 437 (RCAF) Squadron formed at Blakehill Farm.

Stan by now was the Squadron signals officer and when dropping parachutists the wireless operator acted as despatchers, standing by the open door at the rear of the Dakota on the inter-com to the pilot and controlling the jump according to the instructions given by the pilot. On D-Day, 6 June, 512 had dropped the 9th Battalion of the Parachute Regiment, 32 aircraft dropping 568 troops and in the afternoon of the 6th towing gliders to Normandy. The 9th Battalion later taking and destroying the Mervill gun batteries in Normandy and not far from Pegasus Bridge.

A Stirling of 196 LJ 502-D flown by Flight Lieutenant Hoysted, DFC, was also hit by flak after releasing its glider from 2,500 feet over Arnhem.

In addition to the 1,534 transport aircraft and 500 gliders, which executed the airborne assault, a total of 1,113 bombers and 1,240 fighters were flown in support of the operation. The Americans dropped, by parachute, the men of the 1st Parachute Brigade, who were flown in two serials with great accuracy, 2,279 men of the Brigade and Parachute Squadron of the Royal Engineers, plus sixty containers.

And so ended the first day of Operation 'Market Garden', a day with one exception, D-Day the 6 June, which had seen the largest number of allied aircraft take to the air during the Second World War.

The Guards Division began to roll towards Eindhoven but soon encountered German anti-tank guns after crossing the Belgium/Dutch border, in no time at all several Sherman tanks were knocked out and the column became bogged down. Only after help from RAF Typhoon fighter-bombers did the British succeed in crushing the German resistance, but because of this 'Garden', the ground part of the operation was behind schedule.

The Spitfires of 2nd TAF destroyed eight guns, four MET's, two barges destroyed and damaged six with two Spitfires lost.

On the 17th the Germans put up fifty fighters.

General Brereton had flown over the area in a B17 Flying Fortress until it was hit by flak.

The landings were from 500 feet above the DZ's or LZ's and out at 1,500 feet and back at 3,000 feet. The parachute aircraft flew at 140mph, the tug at 120mph and the Pathfinder at 150mph which was also the return speed for all aircraft.

The glider tugs were told to drop their tug ropes into pre-determined drop zones.

General Walter Model, later field marshal, was taken completely by surprise and had to move his headquarters to avoid capture.

On the 17th no less than 3,887 aircraft were despatched and 500 gliders airborne.

In addition to this 1,534 transport and tug aircraft of No's 38 and 46 Groups and US IXth Troop Carrier Command towed the gliders and dropped the paratroops, 1,240 fighters and 1,113 bombers were used in support, this was the largest number of aircraft ever to take part in any one operation with the exception of 'D–Day Normandy, 6 June 1944.

The number of parachute troops actually dropped on the 17th was 16,500 and subsequently a further 3,690 making a total of 20,190, the breakdown:

By glider	Total	13,781
Flown in by aeroplane		905
Total airborne troops in by aeroplane, glider or parachutists, who arrived safely..		34,876
The aircraft involved		240
Gliders despatched		228
Successful		221
Losses		Nil

A successful day so far.

Chapter 7

Monday 18 September 1944

The Second Lift

The plan for the second lift on the 18th was 126 aircraft, of the U.S.T.C.C, were to drop the main body of 4 Parachute Brigade to the DZ at "Y".

One hundred and sixty aircraft of 38 and 48 Group Aircraft, towing 189 Horsa, four Hadrian and fifteen Hamilcar Gliders carrying elements of No 1 Air Landing Brigade Group to DZ "X".

To DZ "S" sixty-two Aircraft of 46 Group towing sixty-two Horsa gliders carrying elements of No 1 Air Landing Brigade Group, and to DZ "L" thirty-five aircraft of 38 Group dropping supplies.

On the night of the 17/18 September 1944, forty aircraft of No 3 Bomber Command dropping dummy parachutists named Rupert, a figure made of sacking, with three draw strings on the legs, arms and head and weighed with sand and explosive devices to simulate small arms fire west of Utrecht. While similar operations were carried out near Emmerich in an attempt to divert enemy forces from the 'Market' area.

They were dropped from 2,000 to 3,000 feet between 20.50 (8.50pm) and 21.16 (9.16pm). This 'spoof' operation failed to achieve the desired result but did have some effect through the operation, where airborne forces were landing in small numbers at various points in Holland.

As the bombers returned to Holland there were signs of the weather changing for the worse with a forecast of fog, low cloud, and persistent rain over the channel in the area of the troop carrier bases, until midday on the 18th.. Because of the weather General Brereton decided to postpone the start of the second lift day from 10.00am to 14.00pm, however, aircraft were able to get off at 11.00am. On the 18th, because of a build up of dense fog over the western side of the southern route which it had been planned to be used, plans were switched to use the northern route which was clear. Both the US and British 38 Group would use the northern route with the tug towing crews of 38 Group flying at 2,500 feet and above the US Troop Carriers.

On the 18th the air armada would be 350 US Troop Carriers and 1,205 tug glider combinations. They would be escorted by sixteen Spitfire, five Tempest, and three Mustang Squadrons, a total of 277 aircraft added to 575 Mustangs, Thunderbolt, and Lighting aircraft from the 9th US Air Force, who it was planned would take care of any flak defences of route. The main problem as opposed to the 17th, was haze and low cloud resulting in the German gun defences being more effective and inflicting casualties on the incoming armada.

As with all good planning things do go wrong. In this instance because of a break down of communication, the fighter escort arrived at the designated rendezvous area to find no sign of the transport aircraft and returned to base. The consequences were that this left the transport aircraft over the drop zones without fighter cover, the troop carriers were given fighter cover by the Air Defence of Great Britain who sent 277 fighters but only for part of the way owing to lack of fuel.

On the 18th, 126 Dakotas of the US Troop Carrier Force, dropped the 4th Parachute Brigade and 208 aircraft of 38 and 46 Groups, delivered 189 Horsas, four Waco's, and fifteen Hamilcars carrying divisional troops at landing zone 'X'. The Hamilcars would again carry anti-tank guns also Universal Carriers and others carried Royal Engineers and ammunition.

One Hamilcar cast off early and landed in the UK after the aircraft had developed engine trouble. Another ditched in the Channel, again, after the tug, also having engine trouble. Both unfortunately had much needed 17 pounder anti-tank guns aboard, the remainder of the Hamilcars coming under heavy fire as they landed at LZ 'X'.

Four Spitfires of 345 (Free French) Squadron were shot down, three to flak and one lost 25 miles off Beachy Head escorting the transport aircraft back to base. Mustang's of 19 Squadron were attacked by twelve FW 109's near Rotterdam and one shot down.

At Landing Zone 'S' sixty-two aircraft of 46 Group were to release sixty-two Horsa gliders carrying elements of the 1st Air Landing Brigade. Thirty-five aircraft of 38 Group were to drop supplies at Landing Zone 'L' (Papendal) which had been marked by No 1 Platoon of the pathfinders which was eight-five per cent successful, No 2 Platoon went to LZ 'X' and No 3 to DZ 'Y'. Seven gliders cast off before reaching the English coast but were recovered and took off later in the 3rd lift, two gliders ditched in the North Sea, one breaking up on impact, and fifteen gliders were lost over Holland on route to the landing zone. Three had ropes cut by flak and three because of engine trouble with the tug aircraft, one glider shot down by light flak and machine gun fire, two aircraft were shot down and nearly all aircraft suffered some damage or another and aircraft were coming back with all manner of problems. Returning crews reported a Stirling crash and explode probably Culling, another on the ground, and another crash landed with the crew baling out with fuel spewing out of one of its tanks.

The *Daily Herald* recorded:

'The gliders filled the sky for 285 miles to rejoin the troops paraded out on the 17th aircraft of different types and fuel consumption setting out from twenty-five different airfields to be timed to within half a minute.'

The Albermarle's again took off from RAF Manston towing forty-two of the 275 Horsas, of which 257 reached the landing zone. Of the fifteen Hamilcar's, fourteen arrived safely despite the flak and small arms fire from German forces along the route to the landing zone. Flight Lieutenant Derek Boyer of 296 Squadron joined the squadron on the 26 October 1942, and had completed over twenty operations participating in every major airborne operation since the inception of 38 Wing, and many successful S.O.E operations to France and Norway. On the 18th, while crossing the island of Overflakkee on the inward route, he received a direct hit on the port wing with a fairly large calibre shell tearing a gaping hole between 3 and 4 feet across, when he was already flying below the safety speed of the Albemarle due to the heavily loaded Horsa on tow, he was further crippled by the loss of lift from the damaged wing, therefore being singled out as a straggler by further ground fire. The pilot continued undeterred for the rest of the route and delivered his glider to the right place, bringing his aircraft back without further damage; as a result in March 1945 he was recommended and awarded the Distinguished Flying Cross. At Down Ampney fifty aircraft took off in thirty-seven and a half minutes, forty-nine from Bradwell in forty-four minutes and twenty-three from Blakehill Farm in fourteen and a half minutes. The first of the four gliders carrying the radar equipment, chalk number 5001, and flown by Staff Sergeant John Kennedy and Sergeant 'Wag' Watson and towed by Flight Officer Spafford, RCAF, in Stirling LK 140 of 570 Squadron, took off and landed safely at the landing zone. The second, was flown by Sergeant Teddy Edwards and Sergeant Ferguson, was towed by a Stirling of 295 Squadron and despite machine gun fire was able to get their glider down. Sergeant Edwards was, in March 1945, also on the Rhine Crossing and awarded the Distinguished Flying Medal. Staff Sergeant 'Lofty' Cummings Chalk, Mark No 5000, was towed by a Stirling LK 121 of 570 Squadron and flown by Flight Sergeant Culling, who was shot down 20 miles from the landing zone. He and his crew were killed, but Cummings was able to get his glider down safely in a field near Zette, 7 miles short of the landing zone.

Staff Sergeant Harris and Sergeant Bosely had the tail shot off their glider leaving it out of control and although released by Flight Lieutenant Kingdon of 295 Squadron it crashed near Doodeward and all were killed.

Second Lieutenant Howard Coxon was flying with Staff Sergeant Cummings. On landing took charge of the party which included in addition to his own, six men and the two other glider pilots. Shortly after landing they were joined by the crew of another glider which had carried a serviceable jeep. One of the other glider pilots, 'Jock' Ferguson, had been badly wounded after coming under heavy enemy fire. It was now clear to Flight Lieutenant Richardson, the controller of No 6341 LWU flying with John Kenney, that the mission should be aborted and when he could not raise anyone on the radio all radar sets were destroyed by Sten gun fire and explosives.

On the 19th, on crossing the Nijmegen, Bridge Staff Sergeant 'Lofty' Cummings was killed by a sniper. At 190 Squadron things were anything but smooth; they were detailed to tug twenty-one Horsas carrying ninety-two men, jeeps, cars, guns, Bren gun carriers, trailers, and motor cycles. But only moments after take-off Pilot Officer Sellars had his starboard outer engine fail, he cast off the glider before landing again.

Pilot Officer Beberfield had his tow rope break just leaving the English coast and both tug and glider came down at Woodbridge safely, the records show that the glider had placed itself in the wrong position.

Flight Sergeant Herger of 190 Squadron was drawn into the slipstream of a Dakota, his glider rose and as he put the nose down to avoid the Dakota the tow rope snapped and the glider landed near Over Flakkee, Flight Officer Farren's glider landed some 25 miles from the L.Z. when the tow rope broke.

Flight Lieutenant Berridge of 299 Squadron had the tow rope break but landed at Marleston Heath airfield, when the glider was reattached to the tow line and took off to land his glider in Holland.

A crew of 575 Squadron were on their way to the landing zone towing a glider: in the glider was Lieutenant Colonel Thomas Haddon, the commanding officer of the 1st Border Regiment. On the 17th his glider tow rope broke and they had to land at Broadwell airfield.

Flight Officer Foggarty took, on the 18th, a tow rope to Woodbridge, an emergency airfield, which was almost as wide as it was long. His glider had cast off prematurely and made an emergency landing there.

Flight Lieutenant Reg Turner recorded in his logbook, for the 18th, operation completed successfully, moderate flak; In an aircraft of 299 Squadron were two senior army officers, Brigadier Monie and Lieutenant/Colonel Darling, who flew as observers. On return Monie knelt down and kissed the ground.

Pilot Officer McHugh, flying in Stirling LK 299 of 620 Squadron, was badly hit and damaged by flak but was able to get back to base and taxied to an area at RAF Keevil where the aircraft could be repaired.

Warrant Officer Blackhurst again flew on the 18th, from Manston in an Albemarle; at the briefing he learned that things were not going well. They took off at 11.45am towing a Horsa glider carrying troops and reaching the DZ without incident but then encountered enemy fire from the ground, the Horsa had cast off, he looked to see if it had landed successfully but owing to smoke he was not able to do so and set off back feeling he was lucky not to have been hit, as he left the scene it looked awful.

The debriefing was a very sombre occasion, all knew how lucky they were all to return and that something had seriously gone wrong. The next day 620 Squadron returned to Earls Colne and the Albermarle did not take any further part in 'Market Garden'. It would appear the main reason for this was that the aircraft was thought unsuitable for supply drops.

The *News Chronicle* correspondent, Michael Moynihan, flew in F-Freddie, towing a Hamilcar glider and sat in the co-pilots position. As they crossed the coast, puffs of smoke from flak came up but it was soon wreathed in smoke from a Typhoon rocket attack, ahead of them a Halifax of 298 which was hit by flak; and the wireless operator and navigator were wounded.

Stan Lee did not fly on the 18th but 512 Squadron did and was led by Second Lieutenant Smulaiu, with twenty-four aircraft carrying jeeps, guns, and supplies for the troops who had been despatched on the 17th. On return crews reported that there was heavy flak, despite this they had made successful drops. One aircraft was missing and many returned damaged.

Second Lieutenant Trevor Southgate, AFC, in Dakota KG 570 of 512 Squadron, took off from Broadwell towing a Horsa carrying a jeep, 6-pounder gun, and two army gunners plus two pilots. They ran into flak after crossing the island of West Shouwen from a flak barge sunk by Typhoons at 14.21pm, and only five to six minutes from the landing zone and at 2,000 feet. There were four to five loud bangs, and the Wing Operator, Flight Officer Joseph Parry, reported that the aircraft was on fire; the aircraft below the flight deck was on fire and it spread rapidly and was soon near the overload tanks within the main cabin. The aileron controls were also unserviceable, Flight Lieutenant Albert Saunders, the second pilot ,and Flight Officer Joseph Parry, the Wing Operator, tried to jettison the pilots escape hatch using an axe but with no success.

At 1,000 feet the order 'abandon aircraft' was given by Southgate and Parry. Bryant and Southgate went to the rear of the aircraft where he proceeded to remove the parachute door, it was then realised that Flight Lieutenant Saunders had not followed them to the rear. The aircraft was well alight at the main bulk head, the flames were licking around the fuselage tanks. They then realised that Saunders was trying to crash- land the aircraft as it was now far to low to bale out and braced themselves for the impact when the aircraft belly landed and swung violently to starboard and came to rest. On impact the fuselage tanks burst and Southgate was flung across the fuselage, Parry, went back towards the crew compartment to assist Saunders but was beaten back by the flames so they all ran around to the front and found Saunders still in the cockpit. But because of the flames it was impossible to get him out, however he managed to break the windshield. As he struggled to get out the front of the aircraft disintegrated, and he fell to the ground. He was very badly burned about the hands, arms, and face and had deep cuts over his right eye, and below his right ear he was also bleeding very badly. Two Dutch farmers approached and Bryant, speaking a little Dutch, was able to ask how close the Germans were, the Summers told them to go into the woods and hide. After a little while they returned and said it was too dangerous to stay in the woods and they should move at night-fall. Despite his wounds, Saunders was willing to make a 4 mile journey on foot to a new location. Here they were given dungarees to travel in and taken to a house in Dodewaard, where they stayed until night-fall and from there to a house in Andeelst, where they stayed for a week and were looked after by a Mr and Mrs Tuit. While there a doctor was sent for to tend their wounds and injuries.

On the 24th they made contact with a British armoured car who took them to Nijmegen where, at a Casualty Clearing Station, it was found Southgate had a dislocated shoulder and after an X-Ray revealed he also had a broken elbow, Parry had a broken ankle. Both Saunders and Parry were detained in hospital at Nijmegen the others were taken to Brussels where they arrived on the 28th and were flown back to the UK the same day.

Flight Lieutenant Bryant had joined the RAF in August 1940, he had been a bank cashier in civilian life, and Flight Officer Parry in January 1939 having been a cabinet maker. The Dutch underground had informed them that Glider 759 with its two pilots, jeep, and gun, had made a perfect landing a mile to the north of them and arrived at the landing zone with twelve German prisoners, the crew of KG 570 never met up again. Flight Lieutenant Saunders, for his great gallantry, was awarded an immediate Distinguished Flying Cross.

A crew of 575 Squadron were on their way to the landing zone towing a glider containing Lieutenant/Colonel Thomas Haddon, the commanding officer of the 1st Border Regiment. On the 17th the glider tow rope broke and they had to land at Broadwell airfield. On the 18th, again with the same Stirling and crew, they took off and over the enemy territory. The Dakota received a direct hit from a shell and the pilot Flight Officer George (Ed) Henry (RCAF) from Maintoba in Canada was killed outright. The navigator Wing Officer Bert Smith had been trained as a pilot in Belfast after joining the RAF on the 1 September 1939, when he arrived in the UK from Belfast he was put down as a navigator and posted to 61 Squadron Bomber Command, and later on Catalina Flying Boats with Coastal Command. He was then posted to 575 Squadron of Transport Command so he had in the Second World War served in all three commands, now flying with 575 and operating with Dakotas which needed a co-pilot. As the pilot was down he became a second pilot and not the navigator.

When George Henry was killed, the navigator Flight Officer McKinley and wireless operator Sergeant Fowler was peppered with shrapnel and Bert himself hit in the chest and arm, later, when the co-pilot took over the controls it was found also his leg. After they had got the dead Henry out of his seat, he turned the aircraft around and headed back to allied lines, with most of the tail and rudders of the aircraft shot away. A message came through from the glider pilot to say he was casting off but Bert told them to hang on and he would try getting them nearer allied lines which he did, they cast off, and landing safely he met up with allied troops later, on the 24 September, having crossing the Rhine, the glider pilot was soon captured and spent the rest of the war as a prisoner of war at Oflag XIIB. On return he stayed in the army until 1968, retiring with the rank of brigadier, some promotion.

Bert in the meantime, and without navigation aids, found himself over Dunkirk under severe fire power from the German defences, he headed out to the English Channel and landed at an American base; Martlesham Heath. By this time he had lost a lot of blood from his arm but received a lot of help and support from Sergeant Fowler who normally stood in the cockpit doorway smoking a cigarette and before landing would put down the flaps and undercarriage, which as usual he did on the 18th. At Martlesham they were taken into the sick bay and examined by an American medical officer who took out pieces of shrapnel with the aid of a bottle of whiskey, but it was not until Bert arrived back at RAF Broadwell and took his trousers off did he find his legs also had wounds; after the war Bert still had pieces of shrapnel in his legs.

Bill Fowler found his lighter in his top pocket was bent in half having been hit by shrapnel. At the debriefing Bert told the intelligence officers of the help and support Bill had given him in flying back to base and where Bert and Flight Officer McKinley, an American, were awarded immediate Distinguished Flying Cross' London Gazetted 31 October 1944 but for Bill nothing. The recommendation was dated 20 September 1944, and counter signed by the Air Officer Commanding Allied Expeditionary Air Force, Air Chief Marshal Leigh-Mallory on the 30 September 1944, and London Gazetted on the 31 October 1944. Flight Officer George Henry is now buried in Brookwood Military Cemetery, Surrey.

Bert was sent down to the BBC in London, which turned out not to be as easy as he had thought as they wanted him to read a script that they had compiled and had not seen before, he insisted that there were unacceptable changes made to it. When later he went to the Canadian Club where he was staying, he heard a broadcast by Winston Churchill, followed by his.

The No 38 Group Intelligence summary for D-plus1, said that 210 aircraft supplied the areas on the 18th, nineteen were unsuccessful, nine tow ropes broke, four had mechanical failure, one was missing, one hit by flak, one from bad loading and others had slipstream difficulties and fell into the sea. Reports of aircraft in distress, a Stirling with smoke coming from it, a second hit by flak and seen crashing and exploding, a third was seen burning on the ground, a fourth crash landing, a fifth hit by flak and one member of an aircraft seen to bale out, a sixth was seen with its starboard tank leaking and a Dakota was seen going down and four chutes were seen opening.

Ian Robinson took off again for the second day in KG 395. He was down to be the first off 26, of 48 Squadron aircraft airborne at 11.00am but his aircraft was delayed and did not get away until 11.30am, the delay was caused by the load of the glider ahead of them not having arrived despite the glider being ready to hook up. When he was 30 miles into Holland he saw a four engine bomber, probably a Stirling, overtake them towing a giant Hamilcar glider. As it came level the whole back end of the glider broke away with its contents spilling out, there was no flak at the time so the reason was a mystery. He carried on and delivered his glider to the landing zone and arrived back at 17.10pm.

Flight Lieutenant Jimmy Edwards was again operating with 271 on this occasion take of was without incident. As he climbed away from Down Ampney he made a tighter turn than normal and found himself being pulled about the sky by the glider he was towing; this contained a jeep and two trailers, plus men. He soon found that the problem was one of the front bits of the tow rope had got on the wrong side of the glider's nose wheel, Jimmy asked the glider pilot if he could cope and the reply was 'yes although we have got the controls almost upside down'; Jimmy knew they could not possibly fly for four hours like that but they would not hear of turning back so Jimmy eased the throttles slightly and when the rope had fallen away from the nose wheel he took up the slack and without breaking the tow rope, they rejoined the stream, the trip was then onwards, as Jimmy reported, nearly as easy as on the 17th he landed back at Down Ampney after six hours of flying.

Pilot Officer Len Wilson was asked by Leading Aircraftsman Alan Hartley, who looked after his aircraft, how it went, he said a fantastic sight with gliders flying in, with different coloured supply chutes to indicate ammunition, food, clothing, medical supplies and the remaining paras. Alan asked him if he could go with him the next day, Len said "No problem. When you put the pins in tomorrow, jump aboard," the flight sergeant chief was happy with this as there was nothing to do once the aircraft had taken off. The pins were the locking pins on the undercarriage which prevented it being raised while stationary on the ground, the last job for Alan was to remove the chocks; the famous saying "Chocks Away" from the wheels. Take out the pins with their long red streamers to show them to the pilot and then place in a box just inside the open door frame, as they flew without any doors being fitted.

Flight Lieutenant David Lord, DFC, towed a glider to LZ 'S' piloted by Staff Sergeant Rye, DFM. On route Lord had a problem with the starboard engine but he pressed on and was a great source of encouragement to Rye, which was a difficult trip.

At 233 Squadron Flight Lieutenant Jenkins in KG 589 came back with slight damage. And KG 420 flown by Flight Lieutenant McIlraith, RNAF, came back with his navigator. Wing Officer Phillips, having sustained a cut over his eye.

At 570 Squadron they had three losses; Pilot Officer Charles Culling and his crew in LK 121, had been hit by flak and crashed in flames in the area of Kesteren, he was aged 29 and came from the Birmingham area. Sergeant Vincent Williams in his crew was only 19 and came from Bolton. Also in the crew was a Corporal John Coleman (RCAF) age 26 and from Montreal, he was on the ground staff and had asked if he could go as an observer on the operation. All the crew were killed and are buried in Holland.

Flight Lieutenant Dennis Liddle flying LJ 913, was hit by flak and crashed landed at Schaersbergen, and he and his crew were taken prisoner. They were thought to have crashed after being hit repeatedly by anti-aircraft fire in the area of the DZ, but he pressed on and dropped his load of supplies on the DZ, the aircraft was seen to crash land to the north-west of Arnhem. In 1945 he was awarded the Order of the Dutch Bronze Lion, in the recommendation it stated he had flown twelve operations and was a deputy flight commander with 570 Squadron.

Balmer RCAF came from British Columbia, Canada and was on the 18th flying LJ 594, he took off at 14.30pm to drop supplies to Arnhem. In the region of Stampersyat his aircraft was severely hit by flak, it caught fire and he gave the order to bail out, Flight Sergeant Archer, Sergeant Crabb, Pilot Officer Blight, Sergeant Ireland and Flight Officer Keay, all bailed out but by this time they were to low for the remainder of the crew to bail out so he told them he was going make a crash landing. Flight Officer Bomb, at great risk to himself, strapped Balmer into his seat using his arms as a strap, he thought that if he did not do this Balmer would be killed on landing. He landed the aircraft in a grass field and was badly bruised and shaken but otherwise unhurt, and Flight Officer Bombrun and Sergeant Kempton were also okay. Driver Bridgeman sustained a dislocated shoulder and Corporal Barker had a serious head wound. Sadly, Balmer later learned that Barker had been taken to hospital at Roosendaal where he died, he was aged 31 and came from Braintree, Essex.

Balmer was taken to the house of a Catholic priest, Pater Raseroms, who spoke English. From his house he was taken to the house of a W. Campagne in Roosendaal where he stayed for three days, on the 22nd Father Raseroms came back, and took him to Oudemboosh and the Central Police Station where he was dressed in the uniform of the Dutch police, and by a policeman, taken on the back of a motor cycle to Breda, this had been organised by the Chief of Police whose name was De Geir. He was taken to a large shop owned by Mr. Wiete who also lived in the store, he had closed it in order to accommodate allied forces who were evading capture in the area. During the day he was joined by the rest of his crew and a Lieutenant Arnold, Staff Sergeant Quick, Technical Sergeant Broga, Lieutenant/Colonel Kembs, and Major Cannon, a crew from a US Dakota. They were joined by Sergeant Fitzpatrick who had been taken prisoner and escaped at Breda Railway Station. Here they stayed until the 3 October when they were dispersed to different places as things were becoming difficult at the shop with the Germans coming in for supplies.

Balmer and Sergeant Crabb were taken to the home of a family by the Breda underground chief, here they stayed for nine days until the 12 October when Balmer was moved to the home of a J.W. Verstrepen also in Breda where he stayed until the Polish troops entered Breda on the 31 October.

Flight Sergeant Kirkman's LK 560 had crashed when his port engine lost power on take off.

At 48 Squadron one aircraft flown by Flight Officer Albert Lavoie (RCAF) age 24, failed to return. He and his crew are today commemorated on the Runnymede Memorial as having no known grave, this was apart from one Australian an all Canadian crew.

Again, the fighter support played their part. Sixteen Typhoons of 2nd TAF, attacked gun positions in support of the army on the ground with good effect, and 2 MET's and barges were shot up. The German's, on the 18th, put up 100 to 125 fighters, increasing their fighter strength by fifty per cent.

The air officer commander of one of the airborne groups sent the following message:

"You are about to take part in one of the largest airborne operations.
It transcends in importance even that launched on D–Day itself.
It is an operation vital to the outcome of the complete battle.
    Success may mean all the difference between a rapid decision in the west and a protracted winter campaign.
    The operation so relying implicitly on us to drop them in, supplies at the right place and time.
    The many instances of your courage and determination what I have seen during the last few months, makes me confident that no matter what the odds may be you will deliver the goods.
    May the good fortune which attends the brave be with you, Good luck."

On the 18th the following were employed:

Aircraft employed	210
Gliders	175
Successes	186
Aircraft Lost	3

So far all had gone well and losses were light, the hope was that this would continue. But would it?

Chapter 8

Tuesday 19 September 1944

The Third Lift

The plan for the third lift was; to DZ "K", 114 aircraft from the US TCC dropping the main body of No. 1 Independent Polish Parachute Brigade Group. To LZ "L", forty-five aircraft of 38 Group to tow thirty-five Horsa gliders carrying elements of No 1 Polish Independent Parachute Brigade Group, plus ten Hamilcar gliders carrying elements of the 878 (US) Aviation Engineer Battalion. To LZ "V", and 100 aircraft of 38 Group and sixty-three aircraft of 46 Group, to drop 163 re-supply loads.

The situation on the third day was extremely serious and enemy resistance was increasing. It was decided to postpone the dropping of the Polish Parachute Brigade on zone 'K', south east of the bridge, that is apart from the thirty-five gliders carrying equipment and other elements of the Polish Independent Brigade, with the day's air activity was being devoted to re-supply.

Although weather reports indicated that conditions might be better on the northern route, it was decided to use the southern route in order to avoid using the same route on three successive days. Over England the weather was unfavourable with extensive area of low cloud which grounded gliders detailed to transport the Polish units from the Grantham area by aircraft of the United States.

The take off was again delayed until the afternoon and, on the glider mission, seven broke from tow ropes. Two in cloud over the sea and, although flak was not severe probably owing to the weather, one glider was forced to ditch with a shot away tow rope. Another was shot down, while both pilots of a third aircraft were hit but managed to reach the landing zones and land successfully in the area of the landing zone where the flak was much heavier.

Because of communications failure with fighter bases on the continent, an aero was made in the timing at the rendezvous, consequently there was no fighter escort for the airborne missions. One hundred and twenty seven Spitfires of Air Defence of Great Britain and one Mustang squadron of the US 8th Air Force arrived at the rendezvous but, finding no transport aircraft, assumed that the operation had been cancelled and returned to base.

The ninth air force neutralised flak batteries between the turning point on the route and Arnhem, but somehow the details of the instructions did not arrive with them until the afternoon of the 20th.

The 2nd TAF flew only fifty-nine missions in the area on the 29th and 115 of the 139 US Ninth Air Force fighters that did fly were forced to abort their missions due to low cloud.

Despite the weather, several formations of the Luftwaffe aircraft made strafing and bombing attacks on Arnhem and air raids, mainly by FW 190 and BF 109 aircraft becoming a regular occurrence for the men on the ground from the 19th onwards, more than 425 ME 109's were encountered, the US Army Air Force claiming twenty-three destroyed and losing nine.

Mosquito Squadrons had attacked rail routes to Arnhem and Walcheron during the night in an attempt to delay reinforcements getting to the Arnhem area of the battle.

The last of the glider operations transported the Polish Independent Parachute Brigade to zone "L" and of the thirty-five Horsa's despatched, twenty-eight released successfully, the landing ground was covered by enemy fire and some of the loads were lost when gliders were burned out. A glider was seen to break away from its towing aircraft until it ditched at 14.03pm, but when rescue launch 2687 arrived, the glider was found to have smashed to pieces and six survivors were clinging to the wreckage, they were taken aboard the search vessel and a search was made for the 1st pilot but no trace was found of him. Another glider ditched and survivors were picked up by HSL 2631.

Ten Hamilcar's were also despatched along with the Horsas, carrying the Polish Brigade and the 878th US Aviation Engineer Battalion to landing zone "X". Seven glider missions, in addition to those planned, were flown: but only two reached the zone, three of these had become available owing to failure on previous missions.

In the afternoon of the 19th, 163 aircraft of 38 and 46 Groups flew into the area by way of the southern route, this was the first large scale re-supply mission. Despite intense and accurate flak, they were able to carry out the drop, with some commendable accuracy. Forty-five aircraft dropped supplies on the dropping point and five on zone "S". The remaining fifteen aircraft, five Dakotas and ten Stirling's, were lost and no fewer than ninety-seven damaged by flak.

The courage and determination of these crews were remarkable, flying into intense anti-aircraft fire at 1,000 feet and, without exception, maintaining accurate courses until their loads were safely released. Communications with base was at this time impossible and there were several reasons for this, sometimes partial and often total failure to communicate where the frequency was unsatisfactory when it clashed with that of a powerful British station. On the first day, the 17th, heavy interference as well as technical failure caused difficulty in communications. On the 19th it was possible to receive but not to transmit, this is because the sets were surrounded by woods which created physical interference and screening. All the low powered sets became unserviceable as the battle increased in intensity and on subsequent days, the injuries to wireless transmitter personnel, the effect of blast and the destruction of battery charging sets thoroughly disrupted all communications.

The only method left to avert useless sacrifice was to attempt to attract the attention of the aircraft to a new zone marked with white ground strips. A Eureka Beacon set upon a tower nearby, but owing to the weather, the exact time of the drop was uncertain and during this interval the enemy "strafed" the area where the ground signals were displayed.

The Eureka Beacon could not be left on indefinitely as the batteries would have been exhausted, and although Verey Lights were fired the attempt was in vain. The new supply dropping point was indistinct from the air being obscured by trees, and those on the ground had the mortifying experience of watching nearly all the supplies, 350 tons, fall to ground held by the enemy.

Landing zone "V" had been in enemy hands for some time and, because of the communications failure, it was impossible to inform the supply aircraft of the RAF, and it is said that as much of the food dropped at "V" was handed over to the starving Dutch by the Germans, at least some of the food went to a good use. And when the wind changed some of the parachuted supplies were blown into British lines.

An extract from the 1st Airborne Division War Diary reads: 19th Arnhem September 16.30 hours. Re-supply dropped on re-arranging supply dropping point (V), which was in enemy hands, yellow smoke, yellow triangles and every conceivable means were used to attract attention of pilots and get them to drop supplies within our lines, this had limited success.'

The crews of 620 Squadron had only eyes for the arranged dropping point and little else with the amount of flak coming up at them. At 12.10pm the first Halifax squadron took off with 298, towing ten Horsas, with the five Hamilcar's due to be despatched were stood down. One Hamilcar, towed by a Halifax of 644 Squadron, however was despatched, this had been used on the 17th but had broken loose.

The weather over the Channel deteriorated slightly then improved over the continent but with persistent haze visibility was poor. It was in Holland that the weather deteriorated with lifting fog and bad visibility, nearly all the aircraft were hit, although in many cases not seriously.

On the way in aircraft were subjected to a terrific barrage of medium and light flak added to by small arms fire, the aircraft receiving the same treatment on the way out of the landing zones from enemy gun sites.

Halifax LL 305-2P-A flown by Pilot Officer Conville, was hit in the tail and dived towards the ground, he then went into a climb but in an attempt to hold the nose up the tow rope snarled under the strain and the Horsa went straight into the ground.

Because of the communications problem, it was not until 17.30pm on the 19th that HQ in Holland and the UK received the news of the situation in the north of the Rhine.

Nearly all the crews that had operated on the 17th the first day, operated again on the 19th.

Congratulations were sent to all 38 Group stations by the air officer commanding of 38 Group:-

> "The success of the airborne operations carried out during the past forty-eight hours is a reflection of the skill and determination of your aircrews. Please convey to them my most sincere congratulations on their outstanding achievement. I should also like to congratulate the maintenance personnel who by their endeavours have kept us at one hundred per cent strength during the operations."

A signal was also sent by General Williams, commanding the US Ninth Troop Carrier Command via HQ 38 Group:-

> "Reports on your mission today indicate a magnificent success and outstanding contribution to an early victory. My congratulations to each member of your command who shared this accomplishment."

Flight Lieutenant Stan Lee was operating on the 19th but felt that Dakotas were not the best aircraft for supply dropping. The Stirling and Halifax's could load containers into the front bays but with the Dakota it had to be carried inside the fuselage and pushed out through the main door of the aircraft. The supplies, Lee he remembers, went in wicker baskets or pannier as they are known, each with its own parachute with static line hooked to a cable that ran along the ceiling of the fuselage to the baskets. On the 16th in Stan's log book, it showed that they were packed with ammunition and medical supplies. Normally they carried in the crew of four despatchers of the RASC but on the 19th they carried five. Once inside the aircraft the panniers were lashed down to stop them rolling about, the main problem was getting them from the flight deck to the door at the rear and over the rollers, not an easy task even when the aircraft was flying straight and level let alone in turbulence. The other obstacle was the two long range fuel tanks just behind the crew door, so getting to the exit was difficult.

The Dakota was not that suitable for daylight operations as it had a restricted view to the rear and no armour plating for protection, where as the Stirling and Halifax had manned gun turrets, self sealing tanks, armour plating and a good all round visibility, plus being able to fly the drop zone at top speed. The 'Dak' flew low and slow, it also had to fly straight and level so that the despatchers could manhandle the panniers from one end of the fuselage to the door in quick time, in order to get the supplies out over a very small dropping zone.

On such missions it was usual to fly with the flight deck off or open and the navigator would stand between the two pilots. The wireless operator, standing behind the navigator looking out of the astro dome using the intercom was useless and so instructions were given by shouting. When the word came from the pilot, the wireless operator would relay the word to start dropping to the air despatchers in the back, along with much waving of arms in the vent they had not heard.

On the 19th 512 despatched fourteen aircraft and Stan was in the lead aircraft KG 392 flown again by Wing Commander Basil Coventry who commanded 512. When they reached the Belgium coast the visibility became very poor and patchy with the sky massed with 'Daks' plodding along, very soon they were being attacked by flak and there was no sign of the pre-arranged fighter escort. At this time they were flying at 1,500 to 2,000 feet and progress was painfully slow.

As they started to get further north Stan saw Stirling's being attacked by enemy fighters and soon realised they were much more vulnerable and tempting a target, the four engine bomber being a greater prize than the little 'Dak'. When they arrived at the DZ, aircraft from different squadrons were flying in formation and in three's, the drop zone was 'V' on the north western outskirts of Arnhem and about one and a half miles from the railway station. They were now down to a 1,000 feet and passing over the top of the bridge that the operation was all about, Stan remembers feeling surprised that it looked exactly as on the photographs shown at the briefing.

Suddenly, as he looked out of the astro dome an aircraft on the starboard wing tip and in close formation was on fire, upon which Stan shouted to Wing Commander Coventry and grabbed the Aldis lamp to warn the other aircraft that he was on fire but then realising he must know as the fire was so large. The 'Dak' was about 20 feet away and Stan became alarmed that the aircraft would go down and take them with it. The flak was still coming up from the drop zone and in the direction they were going, they could see men on the ground and that they were Germans, they later learned it had never been in the hands of the allies as they had not been able to get that far. Having seen this drop was cancelled, the aircraft soon moved smartly to port followed by the crippled Dakota, they were heading for the area they had been on the 17th when towing a glider. This area looked like it was still in the hands of the allies so they made a 360 degree turn and started a drop run, the other 'Dak' staying with them.

As they turned, Stan felt the other 'Dak' was right above them and that the fire had now spread over the whole engine nacelle and past the training edge of the wing. It soon became obvious that the pilot was leaving the decision on where to drop the load to them and he would follow, Stan wondered why he did not try to crash land, as being less than 1,000 feet he could have got down quickly, but no he just stuck there and Stan's eyes were glued to him. Finally they dropped the panniers followed by the panniers from the other aircraft. Stan could see the shapes of the men at the door of the doomed Dakota and the pilot in his seat, for a moment he thought they would make it. Stan was certain now they had made a drop, they would crash land, when suddenly something came out of the other aircraft, a white chute, the panniers had coloured chutes so it must be a member of the crew who had bailed out. The 'Dak' then faltered and started to descend then fold up with the two wing tips coming up to meet each other and as they touched the starboard wing separated and fluttered down with the rest of the aircraft diving into the ground upside down. Stan, on reflection, feels that this 'Dak' took most of the attention and because of this they took a lot less than they would have otherwise. The fire on the ground was like a beacon in the sky for the flak gunners, they had noted the identification of the aircraft and reported its crash position at the debriefing, and apart from the fact it came from 271 Squadron, they knew no more until months later when Wing Ccommander Coventry told them that the pilot had been awarded the Victoria Cross.

An official group report stated:

"During the drop, flak was intense. Ground reports tell of one Dakota aircraft of 46 Group which, after being hit on its first run–in and with its port engine on fire, made a second run–in through "fearful flak"; the crew could be seen throwing out the panniers from the burning aircraft before it went out of control and crashed, a Stirling aircraft of 38 Group was likewise seen to complete the dropping of its supplies, although one engine had been hit, before the crew bailed out, this could well have been Lord."

Flight Lieutenant David Samuel Anthony Lord, was born in Cork, in Southern Ireland on the 18 October 1913. His mother was from Cork his father was a warrant officer in the Royal Welsh Fusiliers and when his battalion was posted to India, David was to spend the first part of his education there. When his father was posted back to the Fusilier Depot in Wrexham he spent the next few years growing up in North Wales, when he left school he became an assistant in a chemists and also tried his hand at writing short stories, he did try a career as a freelance journalist but this didn't work out. In 1936 he set off for London and very soon realised he wanted to learn to fly and joined the RAF on the 6 August 1936. One of his first duties in the RAF was to line the route in London for King George VI Coronation in 1937. He was promoted to Corporal in August 1938 and took up flying training on the 6 October. On the 5 April 1939 he received his wings and was promoted to Sergeant in August of that same year. On 1 April 1941 he was promoted to flight sergeant and warrant officer on the 1 October 1941.

After training he was posted to 31 Squadron in India and served with them in Burma, India, Iraq and the Western Desert. Whilst with 31 Anthony was given the nickname "Lumme", this was because it was the strongest expression he ever gave to his feelings. When in Burma he was employed in supply dropping to Wingate's Chindits, carrying officials, wounded and evacuating women and children, often with the babies on his lap as he flew the aircraft, he also wrote short stories and played the piano.

He was given a commission on the 12 May 1942 having been promoted from warrant officer and at the time he was still with 31 Squadron in Burma. On the 16 July 1943 he was awarded the Distinguished Flying Cross in the recommendation that it stated he had flown 732 hours and thirty minutes and served in the Western Desert. In 1941, he was shot up by two ME 110's, but despite bullets grazing both sides of his head, the navigator having been shot in the back and one passenger killed, he made a successful crash landing and he and his crew and passengers walked 10 miles to base. His Distinguished Flying Cross was presented to him in 1944 at Buckingham Palace by the king. He had also been awarded a mention in despatches, he was not keen on publicity over his award and gave it to his mother, and told her 'I did not win this,' at the time he appeared to be worn out and needed a spell off flying.

On 12 November 1943 he was promoted to flying officer and, on the 12 May 1944, to flight lieutenant. Having arrived back in the UK at the end of January 1944 he reported to 271 Squadron at Doncaster, later moving to Down Ampney in Gloucestershire. During the D-Day landings he flew paratroopers to the Caen area and came back with his aircraft badly damaged. On 1 September 1944, he was awarded a King's Commendation for Valuable Services in the Air.

On the 18 September from Down Ampney with 271 Squadron, he flew a Horsa glider to landing zone 'S' and had his tail plane and rear fuselage hit by flak. When the take off was delayed, David Lord went out for a run, as keeping fit was important to him having given up smoking because he felt it would affect his eyesight.

On the 19th aircraft took off from 271 Squadron carrying sixteen panniers of food and ammunition supplies in each aircraft, to troops at DZ 'V' near Arnhem. Flight Lieutenant Lord was flying KG 374, with a crew of three and four air despatchers of the RASC, because of the weather on the continent navigating was by dead reckoning through thick cloud. As they broke through the cloud into thick haze, Lord was engaged by very heavy gun fire and, when the starboard engine was set on fire, he instructed the second pilot to attend to the switches for the starboard engine. He asked if anyone had been hit and was told everyone was okay and then asked the navigator, Flight Officer Harry King, the distance to the landing zone; the reply three minutes. In the operation book for 271 Squadron it shows McDonnell in the crew as navigator but he at the time was on leave getting married so this was later with a pencil changed to show King in the crew. He then announced to the crew that the troops on the ground were in such need of these supplies that he was going to drop them. By this time the aircraft was burning furiously, he dropped down to 900 feet and immediately became the centre of attention from the ground gunners and it was astonishing that he was not blown out of the sky. On reaching the landing zone he gave the routine signals to the despatchers and maintained a straight and level flight and then after the panniers had been despatched gave the signal for despatching to cease. He was then told that because the rollers had jammed, two panniers still remained in the aircraft, Lord immediately gave the order for the crew to stand by as he was going to make a second run over the dropping zone. He then circled to the left knowing that any minute the wing would collapse and joined the stream of supply aircraft, giving the signal for the dropping to commence, he was shortly after told, the last pannier had been despatched which took eight minutes, during which time the aircraft was under intense low level fire from the ground, he then gave the order to bail out but made no attempt to leave the controls himself. By now they were down to 500 feet, perhaps he had the idea of crash- landing, but before he could even consider this the starboard wing collapsed when the fire in the starboard engine reached the petrol tank and the aircraft fell to the ground in flames.

When Harry King reached the rear of the aircraft he saw the flames from the burning engine flashing past the windows of the aircraft. After the two delayed panniers had been dropped, King out on his chute, and Ballantyne, helped the despatchers to put on theirs when suddenly King was thrown out of the exit door and had no memory of pulling the ripcord but suddenly landing heavily on his back only seconds after leaving the Dakota. It was nine minutes by his watch since they had been hit, he had been thrown out about 500 to 600 yards north of the dropping zone and near a farm with a tall water windmill pump.

Major Jackson of the Army Air Corps was watching the re-supply mission and saw a Dakota with one engine on fire come into the dropping zone. He expected because of the fire, to see the crew abandon the aircraft but it made a complete circuit in the face of intense flak of all calibres and drop its load right on the target. Suddenly there was a bright flash from the aircraft and pieces seemed to fall off it and then it dived to earth in the vicinity of Wolhegen.

Major Jackson with a Lieutenant Tomson, who also saw the act of gallantry, said the pilot had ample time to abandon aircraft but remained at the controls and carried out his duty, upon which time it was too late for him to get out. A Captain Casomervik of HQ 1st Airborne Division also saw a Dakota on fire, which everyone was watching, then made a left turn and came around again through heavy gun fire to drop further supplies which had not been dropped on the first run in. For some days the act of heroism by this Dakota pilot and his crew was being talked about.

In leaving the aircraft Harry King had lost his shoes, as he lay on his back in a field, he looked at his watch, it was 3.16pm, nearby was a farmhouse which, apart from some cows seemed deserted, so he decided to make for it and obtain better cover, but he was driven back with bullets flying over his head, he was certainly in 'No Man's Land'. A few minutes later a glider also from Down Ampney, came into the field which distracted the German gunners and this was his chance to make for the farmhouse, and then to a grounded glider which was commanded by a Captain Elliot.

On one of the airborne troops that had been killed on the glider, Harry found a pair of boots which fitted him perfectly. The glider was opened then the jeep and equipment were unloaded and, after burying the dead soldier, they moved off towards Wolfheze. Here they made contact with a Lieutenant Colonel Smythe who was commanding the 10th Battalion Parachute Regiment. By this time Harry was armed with a Sten gun but at 7.00pm on the 19th the SS, supported by Panzer tanks over ran the battalion, and by the 20th those that remained were taken prisoner. By about midday seventy parachutists and Harry were marched along a sandy track by the railway towards Ede and made to sit down, many of the men were so tired they just fell asleep.

He awoke to hear voices, angry German voices. They had found an unexploded bomb by the railway line and wanted it moved and quickly. It was a 120lb bomb, the type used by fighter bombers, it had been dropped too low for it to detonate. A Captain Brown of the Royal Artillery and the Senior British Officer present said he would deal with it and took Harry with him. He made the plunger secure by tying it to the fin with his tie and then dug it out with bayonets borrowed from a German guard and dumped it in the Enka Silk Works. Harry had been a pre-war policeman and remembered being on duty at the Enka Silk Works in Lancashire in the 1930s during industrial unrest, and here he was now putting a bomb in the Dutch factory yard.

From two fellow officers who were on the train with him, Harry learned how they had seen his aircraft come in burning and dropping the supplies, followed by the starboard engine exploding and the plane spinning in, they had also seen him come out, fall out of the wreaked aircraft as it came down.

After being in transit probably Dulag luft for about two weeks, he was taken to Stalag Luft I at Barth on the Baltic Coast, here he met Flight Lieutenant Chalk, DFC of 299 Squadron who had also been shot down at Arnhem, Chalk was the rear gunner of a Stirling bomber dropping supplies and agents to the Dutch Underground Movement. He had posed as a paratrooper to avoid being handed over to the Gestapo, at the PoW camp German doctors discovered that he had fractured bones in his body and internal injuries from his heavy fall. Major Joubert SAAF flying with 271 Squadron had also seen Lord crash on the 19 September.

Major-General Urquhart, CB, DSO, sent a message from HQ 1st Airborne Division, to Air Marshal the Hon Sir Ralph Cochrane, KBE, CB, AFC the air officer commanding of Transport Command.

> "I well remember an incident in which a Dakota aircraft flew into our area with one engine well alight. It dropped some of its panniers and then circled very slowly to come in again to drop what remained. Its fate was certain from the time it first put in an appearance. The flak through the whole of the re-supply mission was heavy and became heavier. It was quite amazing that any of the planes escaped without some damage.
>
> I would only be too pleased to try and get any further information for you, which would be of assistance. I, personally, have no hesitation in suggesting that, in the circumstances, the pilot of this plane should be awarded the Victoria Cross."

He attached the two letters sent by Major Jackson and Captain Casomervik. "I daresay there is not a survivor of Arnhem who will ever forget, or want to forget the courage we were privileged to witness in those terrible eight minutes. Major-General Uruhart, CB, DSO."

Group Captain Howie the station commander at Down Ampney at the time remembered writing up the citation for David Lord's Victoria Cross. A parachute major possibly Jackson, had gone into his office after Arnhem and said, "We must find the wreckage of the Dakota, as the pilot must be given the VC," he having seen the whole incident at Arnhem.

In June 1945, Harry King was flown by the now Lieutenant Colonel Joubert commanding 271 Squadron, a brigadier, colonel, and a major, all from the Airborne Forces, all of whom had seen the Dakota crash, to a landing strip near where the Dakota had crashed. He took them to the farmhouse and the field where he had met the glider party, also in the party, Group Captain Howie the station commander at RAF Down Ampney, here they found the burnt out Dakota in an adjoining field, all that was left, a twisted frame with the two engines buried deep in the ground. In the party was Flight Sergeant Green who with him had the maintenance records of Dakota KG 374, when the engine plate had been cleaned with a wire brush the number was established, making without doubt KG 374.

This was followed by the sad part of the visit, Dutch workmen who began digging, discovered the seven bodies from the Dakota, each man was identified by Harry and later re-buried at Oosterbeck War Cemetery. The Dutchman who owned the farm had removed from the wreckage the bodies of Lord and

Medhurst and buried them in his front garden, the site was Reijers Camp, near landing zone 'S' and administered by No. 37 Grave Registration Unit under a Captain Grant.

Harry had, post-war, taken Lady Medhurst to see her son's grave, but Air Marshal Medhurst would not come as he was fed up with the whole waste at Arnhem. Harry had received a letter from the air marshal asking him what happened to his son's aircraft.

The recommendation for his Victoria Cross was submitted to the king by Lord Stansgate, the then Secretary of State for Air, on the 7 November 1945. During 1945 the Air Ministry had three Secretaries of State, Sir Archibald Sinclair, the Right Honourable Harold MacMillan and Lord Stansgate.

In result David Lord was awarded a posthumous Victoria Cross in the *London Gazette* on the 13 November 1945 and presented to his family on the 18 December 1945. His brother Francis was also a Dakota pilot with Transport Command and awarded the Air Force Cross, his son also David received a mention in despatches serving with the Royal Navy as a helicopter pilot during the Bosnian campaign.

Besides David Lord and Harry King, the other members of the crew were Pilot Officer Richard Edward Hastings Medhurst, born at Fulford Vicarage, near York and the son of Air Marshal Sir Charles Medhurst, CB, OBE, on the 19 December 1924. He joined the RAF in 1941 and his training was undergone in Canada, and Arizona in the USA, he returned to the UK in 1944 and was posted to 271 Squadron, he had replaced Flight Officer Ager as second pilot to Lord.

Flight Officer Alec Forbes Ballantyne born in Fife, Scotland on the 21 September 1919, he joined the RAF in December 1939 and was posted to 271 Squadron at Doncaster in 1943.

The four despatchers were:

- Corporal Philip Edward Nixon born in Oldham on the 23 June 1915, and joined the army in 1940. Became a physical training instructor then a non commissioned officer installation commander despatcher with 223 Coy RASC, 63 Air Division Company Coy.
- Driver James Ricketts was born on the 11 April 1917 in Newcastle-Upon-Tyne, and joined the army in March 1940.
- Driver Arthur Rowbotham was born near Manchester in May 1917 and moved to Oldham in 1925, his name is on the Cenotaph perched 1,300 feet above sea level in the Pennines.
- Driver Leonard Sidney Harper was born on the 20 June 1915, and joined the Army in 1943, he came from Harlington, Hayes, Middlesex.

Harry King said "The army boys in the aircraft were magnificent, the plane was on fire and the flak the worst he had experienced in four years of operations, yet these boys carried on doing their job coolly following out the orders of the captain. It's a great shame that those despatchers did not even get a posthumous mention in despatches."

Flight Lieutenant William Pearson flying KG 368-AY also of 512 Squadron, was badly damaged by flak over the DZ including parts of the control surfaces, having made one run he again made a second one through even heavier flak to ensure the remaining panniers were dropped. On returning to base he had no hydraulic pressure, and subsequent inspection of the aircraft it revealed the aircraft was riddled with bullet holes, it was his twenty-seventh operation and 130 flying hours. For his actions he was awarded an immediate Distinguished Flying Cross.

Flight Lieutenant Jimmy Edwards was not operating on Arnhem on the 19th but instead transporting a 5,000lb load of petrol to Belgium, but because of bad weather he was not able to get into Brussels but was able to get to Lille and deliver his load and arrived back at Down Ampney before dark.

Flight Lieutenant Lord was not the only casualty from 271 Squadron on the 19th.

Pilot Officer John (Len) Wilson in Dakota FZ 626, took off at 12.35pm but failed to return.

On the morning of the 19th Alan Hartley stood waiting to go on the operation but when Len Wilson came over and said that another Dakota on their flight had developed a trimming fault but all Dakotas available were required for this operation, he being the senior pilot decided to take FZ 626. He asked another pilot who was taking Wilson's regular Dakota, to take Alan as he had promised, but when the pilot came over to the 'Dak' Alan recognised him as a peacetime officer who was always turned out in full dress officer's uniform and insisted on being saluted on every occasion. So Alan retracted his request to go on the operation using the grounds that permission had been withdrawn, he waved off Len and never saw him again.

The Dakotas for this operation had been ordered to fly at 500 feet and 120mph and in a straight line for two minutes, in broad daylight and with no escort. The outcome was that at the DZ the 'Daks' were swamped with flak guns and every possible machine gun that could be mounted even on orange boxes, and from every angle they met horrendous firepower.

Alexander (Lex) Roell was born in France in 1925 but during the war he with his family of mother, three brothers and two sisters lived in the northern periphery of Arnhem. On the 19th a German anti-aircraft unit took up position along the Bakenbergse Weg under a tree with four, 200mm guns 20 yards apart. The German military told Lex and his family to stay indoors, if possible in the cellar, because when the guns opened up the noise would be deafening. Later a German soldier came in and told them a plane had been shot down and the house was on fire, the pilot showing the highest bravery in that he tried to crash his aircraft on to the gun-batteries but failed by a margin. The pilot had pulled the plane away from the DZ and was hit by a flak gun and badly damaged, he then attempted to wipe out the gun who had fired upon him and to prevent it firing on the 'Daks' following him. As he aimed his aircraft at the gun battery the three parachutes were seen to leave the aircraft, Wing Officer Len Gaydon the navigator, the three air despatchers on board were Driver V. Dillworth, who having been wounded ended up in hospital, and Driver W. Jenkins, both becoming prisoners of war.

It would appear that Len must have been hit in the initial attack or in the dive and slumped over the controls, as suddenly the aircraft swung to port, slicing the top of the tall tree which the guns were below, hit Lex's house and crashed into the back garden. Alexander and his brother Eric buried the members of the crew who had been killed in the crash. Two were lying near an open plot of ground about 10 yards ahead of the wreckage, probably Len who was 32 and the second pilot Flight Sergeant Herbert Osborne aged 23. A third member was also found, Flight Sergeant Reginald French the wireless/operator age 24. The last was still in the wreckage and would have been the third despatcher Lieutenant Corporal James Grace age 28, the fourth despatcher, Driver Richard Newth age 35 was taken to hospital in Arnhem but died of his wounds on the 23rd and was buried in the grounds of the hospital. All those killed were later re- buried at Oosterbeek, Len Wilson was aged 32 and came from Cottingham, Yorkshire.

This information of what had happened was given to Lex by members of the German gun battery. Up to the time Lex died he was still trying to get Len a posthumous award of the Victoria Cross.

The tree for many years after the war was a point of reunion and remembrance for veterans to place wreaths. For some time it was under threat of being cut down but now it has been given a conservation order so that it will remain. In 1984 Len Wilson's wedding ring was found in the area where he crashed and sent to his widow.

Flight Lieutenant Hollom in KG 488 took off at 12.33pm and successfully dropped thirteen of his sixteen panniers on the correct DZ, the remaining three were dropped on LZ 'S' which is what Wing Commander Coventry and the last two panniers of David Lord's were able to do. The port engine and starboard main plane were hit by flak when over the DZ, but he was able to climb to 5,000 feet. As he did the oil pressure and temperature of the port engine fell and the engine finally seized up. Despite this he was able to maintain height and get to B56 (Brussels/Evere) where he made a successful landing without any injuries to his crew.

299 Squadron provided seven combinations and seventeen aircraft for re-supply on the 19th. The tug combinations were briefed to release their glider on the same LZ as on the 17th, LZ 'L' and the re-supply aircraft to drop on DZ 'V' only a mile and half between them.

Only one aircraft failed to deliver its glider Pilot Officer Rowell when his glider was caught in slipstream and released near Ostend. All the supply aircraft were successful but not without losses.

Pilot Officer Bayne RAAF flying EF 267 made a crash landing at Leur, near Wiehen, and he and his crew were taken prisoner.

Flight Officer Harold Hancock flying EF 322 took his Horsa glider in on three engines having been hit by machine gun fire over the battle line in Belgium, which punctured the oil system, and he had to feather the propellers. Not being able to maintain speed with a loaded glider he lost contact with the main stream, he encountered much opposition from the enemy flak and the aircraft was again hit and damaged in the starboard elevator. He finally reached the landing zone and the glider was cast off from a height of 1,000 feet, and made a successful landing, he was on return awarded an immediate Distinguished Flying Cross.

Wing Commander Peter Davis, the commanding officer of 299 Squadron flying Stirling EF 319-5G.N and, before being hit himself, saw a Stirling in a steep dive and crash -landed on the southern bank of the Rhine. The aircraft was also from 299 Squadron. Flight Officer Geoff Liggins in LJ 868-R had taken off from Keevil at 12.45pm carrying twenty-four containers and panniers.

At about 4.00pm and having dropped the supplies successfully, they were hit by light and heavy flak and the port wing was set on fire. It went into a dive and Walter Simpson in the crew remembered the plane dragging its tail across the north bank of the River Rhine, lifting, then catapulting across the water, coming down on the southern side. Walter was thrown to one side of the fuselage and the wireless/operator Sergeant Runsdale crashed into him and lay across him. The aircraft, which had broken in half and was on fire, had landed in the river behind the church at Oosterbeek. The two air despatchers, Lieutenant Corporal Prior and Driver Braid along with Walter were unhurt, Runsdale and the flight engineer Sergeant Gaskin were hurt and unable to get out of the aircraft so Walter went back to get them out. He then realised Flight Sergeant Crowther was also missing so he went back in and got him out. The pilot and navigator Flight Sergeant Humphrey, were rescued by Prior and Braid, Liggins was in great pain and given morphine by Braid. At 20.00pm Dutch civilians arrived, with them, a lady doctor and two nursing sisters, the wounded were taken to a barn for immediate first aid treatment, here they stayed until the 20th. The whole time they were under sniper and 88mm cannon shellfire being aimed at the stricken aircraft while the injured men were carried on makeshift stretchers made out of ladders and an open cart to the vicarage in the village of Driel where they were tended by a Mr Hendrick, a first aid man, and Cora and Reat Baltussen. Mr Hendrick had a special pass issued by the Germans which enabled him to carry out his duties, and so he could tell the Germans that the wounded were too ill to move, although in fact much of the dressings were

'Window Dressing', about sixty to seventy evacuated civilians were also there, the Germans were looking for them in the village.

For the next three days, Prior, Braid and Simpson were hidden in a drainage tunnel let into the riverbank. The food they had was from Walter's air box and twenty-four hour pack from the aircraft's dingy, it contained Horlick tablets, sweets and chocolate, but they had no water and going down to the river would mean exposing their position to the German patrols in the area. But as it happened it was not a German patrol they heard but a friendly one.

A farmer came and brought someone who could speak English but all he could say was that the British were expected on the 23rd. He came from Driel and said that the people there were nervous. It was not unexpected as five had been shot a few days ago for helping evaders. The British arrived on the 21st but owing to a lack of transport they had to stay there until the 24th.

On the 21st a Polish patrol got into the village and a fought with the Germans with the result being the Polish had to retire leaving behind a Polish doctor to treat Liggins and the other injured crewmen. Sadly he had to amputate part of Crowther's foot due to gangrene setting into his heel, he had also broken both arms, a fractured skull and shrapnel wounds.

Walter had watched a parachute drop which would have been the Poles of the 1st Polish Parachute Brigade Group who had been dropped by the IX US Troop Carrier Command, later they came across a Polish patrol who took them to their headquarters where they met Polish General Sosabowski and a few British officers. They also watched the re-supply drop to zones occupied by the Germans, and one flight of Stirling's dropping wide and west of the dropping zones which also went to the Germans. A British colonel asked if there was any way of signalling to the aircraft not to make drops into DZ's that had not been taken by the allies, to say the least the Polish general was 'hopping' mad.

On the 22nd a patrol of the Durham Light Infantry got to Driel and the Germans evacuated it but it was shelled continuously and the vicarage had three direct hits and the Polish doctor wounded. On the 24th they were able to get to the medical centre where the wounded in the crew were being looked after, Geoff Liggins had burns to his hands and face, he had also injured his back in the crash landing. Flight Sergeant Humphrey had a badly cut left leg, Wing Officer Rugsdale had a broken back, and Sergeant Gaskin a broken leg. On the 24th the wounded were taken by ambulance to Nijmegen and put into a Casualty Clearing Station, all three, Briad, Prior and Simpson were taken by jeep to Nijmegen and stayed there for two days. When they were taken to the Reichswald Forest for three days under canvas, it was here that Walter wrote to his parents to say he was safe and trying to get home. From the forest they ran the gauntlet on a transport column down a 2-mile corridor known as 'Hell's Highway', only the previous day only three out of twenty-seven trucks had got through, the others having been shot up by the Germans.

They finally arrived in Brussels and MI9. On the 28th Walter's parents had received a letter to say he was missing, on the 29th he arrived back home in the Coventry, he was only 20 at the time. After his pilot, Geoff Liggins, visited his old airfield at RAF Keevil and had given his version of events, Walter was recommended for the Conspicuous Gallantry Medal (Flying), an inappropriate decoration as all the action was on the ground. In keeping with this, the air officer commanding of 38 Group deemed the Military Medal a more fitting award, this was approved and London Gazetted on the 27 March 1945.

Sadly, in 1955 Geoff Liggins was killed a in car crash and Walter had now passed on but not before, along with his Military Medal, he added having been an active member of the St John's Ambulance the Serving Brother of the Order of St John. It would appear his first aid career started at Arnhem. I wonder over the years how many people have asked him how a rear gunner in the RAF came to be wearing the Military Medal which was an award mainly awarded to the army and action on the ground.

Not long after Peter Davis had seen Liggins go down, he himself was hit and the aircraft set on fire. A 20mm shell had hit the aircraft in the bomb bay where petrol canisters were attached to their parachutes which were ready to be dropped. When flying at 1,000 feet the order was given by Davis to bail out. The Stirling came down flying in a south east direction in a young wood with 6 to 8 feet pine trees and 500 yards away from the sand base of a new highway to Germany being built at the time. A German anti-aircraft unit consisting of at least two 88mm guns and four 20mm guns, had taken up a position on the Bakenbergse Road that morning, declaring it out of bounds for military territory to civilians. It would appear to be the same battery as the one that shot down Len Wilson.

Wing Commander Davis, DSO, was killed in the crash, as was the navigator Flight Lieutenant Freddie Mason. Also a passenger from Group HQ, Squadron Leader Wingfield and one of the air despatchers Driver Richard Ashton of 63 Company RASC were all killed. The other despatcher, Driver Showell, bailed out and was taken prisoner, Flight /Lieutenant Lovegrove ,the co-pilot, bailed out and landed on the roof of the Cafe'-Restaurant 'Rustwat' which absorbed his too high landing speed and softened his landing. The roof was damaged, dented and tiles broken, he evaded capture and got to Eindhoven where was flown back to the UK in a Dakota after evading for five weeks in Holland. Having been helped by a number of people including Arend Timens, the son of the local policeman who happened to be at the cafe' at the time and saw him sliding down the roof to the ground with his parachute behind him. A decision was made to hide him in a haystack in the backyard of his house, 100 yards from the 'Rustwat'. This was risky as nearby, billeted, was some SS soldiers who had been there since the start of the battle. Four days later Lovegrove was moved to a safer place wearing civilian clothing with a red cross marked on one of his arms, he rode on a girls bike into Arnhem, accompanied by two guides also wearing red cross's on their arms. The bike was never returned and post war he was still in the bad book's of the girl's father for having taken her bike without his permission, he offered to pay for the damage to the cafe roof, which I am sure was declined.

Henk Tiemens saw the Stirling on fire, flying low, and a man standing in a large door behind the wing, he had a khaki uniform and is thought to have been despatcher Driver Shovell. Flight Lieutenant Chalk, the rear gunner, bailed out and landed amongst the Germans who took him prisoner. Auld the flight engineer also bailed out and landed near the DZ at 'Bornsheve', as did Flight Lieutenant Francis the wireless operator, who was also taken prisoner.

On the 10 June 1946, Her Majesty Queen Wilhelmina of the Netherlands decided after a recommendation by the Foreign Minister of Affairs Mr Sukker and the Minister of Defence Mr Scholling, to award the Bronze Cross to Flight /Lieutenant Chalk, DFC, Sergeant Auld, and Flight Officer Francis, but for Squadron /Leader Lovegrove, there was nothing. In the same submission was Flight Lieutenant Harry King, of David Lord's crew, and Flight Officer, later Flight Lieutenant Francis, the signals leader of 299 Squadron who had almost completed his second tour. Sergeant Auld had stayed with the air despatchers successfully delivering the supplies, and Flight Lieutenant Chalk had continued firing on the enemy ground positions until he was finally ordered to abandon the aircraft by his captain.

Wing Commander Peter Davis who gave his life to get his crew out of the stricken aircraft, was 28 and came from Harpenden, his brother Henry also died on active service. Previously he had flown a number of operations with 299, from Sicily in July onwards, when he took over 299 it was classed as the worst squadron in 38 Group and by the time of his recommendation for the Distinguished Service Order it was now one of the best. He had been recommended for the Distinguished Flying Cross but this at the direct wish of the air officer commanding of 38 Group, Air Vice Marshal Hollinghurst, was upgraded to the Distinguished Service Order, the recommendation was counter signed by Air Chief MarshalLeigh-Mallory on the 14 August 1944.

He is today buried in the Oosterbeek War Cemetery along with Squadron Leader Cecil Wingfield age 31, Flight Lieutenant Frederick Mason age 25 and Driver Richard Ashton aged 29. All having been originally buried at the site of the crash.

Flight Lieutenant Charles Slack of 575 Squadron was flying Dakota KG 388 from RAF Broadwell when his aircraft was hit by flak, crashed and he and his crew were killed. The names of the despatchers was thought to be Driver James Bowers, Driver William Cross, Driver Robert Hodgskinson, and Driver George Weston, all of 63 Coy RASC.

Lex Roell remembers a man bailing out and being shot by one of the guards of a mobile flak battery and being buried as a paratrooper in front of Alexander's house, and later as an unknown soldier being buried at Oosterbeek. This still happened despite the fact that Lex had sent explicit identification after the war to the War Graves, as to the identity of the man. It would appear that he was an air despatcher and not a paratrooper and came from Charles Slack's aircraft. All four of his air despatchers have no known grave but are on the Groesbeek Memorial, where as Slack and his crew are buried in Oosterbeck. The mystery air despatcher was in fact Robert Hodgskinson age 33, in some records is spelt Hodgkinson. This was changed on the Groesbeek Memorial due to the research by Alexander (Lex) Roell. When he became ill it was taken up by Eric Pepper who has devoted a great deal of his life to research on Arnhem, not only to the RAF and the air despatchers, but also the Troop Carriers of the US Transport Command. It would appear Robert had been shot through the heart by Germans guarding the flak battery.

Twenty minutes after the action, an excited German came into the house carrying the soldiers belongings including his ID tags, opened a small booklet and said 'One dammed American, they shoot on farmers.' When Lex looked over his shoulder and only for fraction of a moment to read it, he saw Sheffield, followed by York. It would appear he had read York as New York, thus thinking he was an American, then with his brother Eric they buried the fallen soldier about 30 yards from the road and in the fields opposite their house. On his battledress the flash RASC but all the belongings had been taken away by the Germans, his beret was red and he had the RASC cap badge which at the end of the war was used for identification purposes. It was size seven and a half, he had dark blonde hair, a long receding forehead and a perfect set of teeth, but it was not enough evidence for the War Graves Commission that the grave of an unknown soldier at Oosterbeek was in fact Robert Hodgskinson.

Flight Lieutenant Reg Turner was again operating and recorded in his logbook; 'Enthusiastic reception committee organised by the Germans who put up a big show of flak.'

Wing Officer Prowd, flying Stirling EF 248 from RAF Keevil, was hit by flak and crashed north west of Arnhem, he and two members of his crew were taken prisoner. The remaining member of his crew was killed and another Flight Officer Reginald Gibbs, RCAF, was wounded and taken to Communal Hospital, Arnhem, but died of his wounds on the 21st. He was originally buried in the grounds of the hospital but at the end of the war buried at Oosterbeek. Driver William Chaplin one of the air despatchers was severely wounded but died on the 11 November 1944, he was originally buried in the Reserve Lazarett at Granau, but is now buried in the Rheinberg War Cemetery. Driver Frederick George Smith age 33, has no known grave but is remembered on the Groesbeek memorial.

They had taken a passenger on this operation; air mechanic 2nd Class Leonard Hooker of the Fleet Air Arm at HMS *Daedalus* who came from West

Drayton, Middlesex. He was part of the ground crew at Keevil with many fitters from the FAA serving with the RAF.

Flight Lieutenant, Acting Squadron Leader and Flight Commander Clifford Potter of 295 Squadron, was hit many times on the run in but was able to drop his supplies, although, his homeward journey was made on three engines. When he could not maintain height sufficiently to reach base he force landed at an emergency landing strip at RAF Woodbridge, he had carried out twenty operations and a total of 216 flying hours previously with Bomber Command and been awarded the Distinguished Flying Cross in November 1944.

Group Captain Wilfred Surplice, station commander at RAF Harwell, led thirty-three Stirling's, seventeen from 295 and sixteen from 570, he also carried twenty-four containers and four panniers. When 100 miles from the DZ his aircraft was severely damaged by anti-aircraft fire and petrol, part of the cargo was found to be flowing through the fuselage, despite this he carried on and discharged his supplies successfully. Sadly Group Captain Surplice was killed on the 3 November while on a mission to Norway, and is now buried in the Oslo Western Civil Cemetery, Norway.

Squadron Leader John Gilliard of 190 Squadron, flying Stirling LJ 939, was hit over the DZ and came down at Park Bilderberg, Oosterbeek. The navigator Flight Officer Reginald Lawton heard the order to abandon aircraft and when the aircraft was at 1,000 feet, bailed out and landed in the woods near Oosterbeck. Squadron Leader Gilliard was killed, as was the rear gunner Flight Officer Norman McEwan, and the two air despatchers, Driver Denis Breading and Frederick Taylor both aged 21. They were reported by Lawton as being killed in the aircraft, the flight engineer Flight Sergeant C Byrne, bailed out but was injured on landing and taken to hospital at Arnhem, Squadron Leader F Royle-Bantoft from HQ 38 Group, also bailed out and survived.

Once on the ground Flight Officer Lawton took cover quickly as he was surrounded by machine-gun fire and two heavy flak batteries that were firing at a nearby aircraft. He decided to wait for darkness when he crawled for about two hours towards the river. At about 21.30pm he managed to make contact with a patrol of the 1st Airborne Division who took him to their artillery battery near Oosterbeck, it was here that he met Squadron Leader Royle-Bantoft and the next day the bomb aimer Flight Officer Cullen. They stayed here until the 25th when orders came to try and cross the Rhine, Flight Officer Cullen and Lawton crossed in an assault boat and then they parted.

Flight Officer Lawton was taken to Nijmegen and stayed there until the 28th when he went to Louvain. On the 29th he moved to Brussels and flew home the same day, Flight Lieutenant Whitfield of 48 Squadron based at Down Ampney, complimented the glider pilot Staff Sergeant Melrose whom he towed to Arnhem on the 19th. They flew through clouds flying blind over the sea and Belgium at 300 feet in very poor visibility, all the while Whitfield taking evasive action. Melrose offered on more than one occasion to cast off when he thought Whitfield was in trouble. He was not perturbed by seeing several Horsas and numerous Wacos going down in flames, although his own glider was damaged. He finally identified the landing zone and warned that he was casting off, he then cast off and landed successfully, Flight Lieutenant Whitfield was later awarded the Distinguished Flying Cross.

In 644 Squadron, Pilot Officer McConoiles had the tail of his glider shot away and it went down out of control, and Flight Lieutenant Tomkin had the tow rope shot away by flak.

Michael Moynihan of the *News Chronicle* flew with Flight Lieutenant Don Lee in M-Mike, he reported the weather being bad, and due to low cloud visibility down to 400 feet to drop his glider which safely got down at 14.15pm a crowd gathered around the glider and the pilot stood on the wing and waved.

Acting Squadron Leader Arthur Hudson of 570 Squadron had his aircraft LJ 944 severely damaged by accurate light flak just before the DZ, but completed the mission and, despite losing the use of two engines made a successful crash-landing behind allied lines at Ghent. He and his crew apart from Flight Sergeant Wood got back to the base within twenty-four hours, at a time when the squadron was in dire need of every skilled man. On the 4 June 1945 he was recommended and awarded the Distinguished Flying Cross having completed twenty-one operations and now a flight commander.

Flight Sergeant Wood was taken by the Dutch resistance to Ede on the 27th, here they gave him civilian clothes and used the code name 'Telephone'. They were taken to a chicken farm in the village where they met the leader of the group known as Bill who had been a sergeant major in the Dutch Army. He had a ieutenant Joliffe of the Royal Army Medical Corps contact another unit in a nearby chicken farm south of Nederwoud, which was under the command of a Captain King. They were then taken on bikes and gave him what information they had, which he then passed on to London. Flight Sergeant Wood stayed here for five days and helped lay out a DZ for the resistance people in the area north east of Amersfoort, on the Apeldoorn road. In due course they received containers, pigeons and comforts for the troops. On the 4 October he left carrying a roll of film showing the depths of the waterways of Rotterdam, wrapped around his ankle. He was then, with the help of a guide, taken across the river Rhine and on the other side met two guides who had crossed the Rhine at 15.00pm in a dinghy and in full view of two German soldiers who were watching them. Later he and others were moved through Tiel to a barge on the river Waal, the sailor on the barge panicked and ran off so they pushed off and reached the southern bank where the German put up Verey lights but did not open fire.

Various trips followed in cars until on the 6 October the resistance took them to the Guards Armoured Division at Nijmegen, who in turn sent them to 30

Corps by jeep and then on to Eindhoven where they were interrogated by officers of the Royal Hotel. One was Major Airey Neave, MC, who had some years before escaped from Colditz Castle, he took them to the SAS who interrogated him about crossing of the Rhine and information as to locality of invaders hiding in west and north of Arnhem, he then proceeded to Brussels.

Flight Officer Alexander Campbell of 512 Squadron was hit over the DZ by 20mm and small arms fire which badly damaged one wing, the ailerons, one engine and wounding one of the air despatchers. The loss of power and the damaged ailerons made turning a difficult and hazardous procedure, but with great determination and courage he made a second turn over the DZ and dropped all his supplies. Despite the damage and loss of power he got the aircraft back to base and carried out a successful landing in very poor visibility, he was awarded the Distinguished Flying Cross.

Flight Sergeant Ray Hall flying Stirling LK 170 of 295 Squadron was hit returning from a re-supply mission and crashed in German held territory near the house of Mr F.B. van Rie of the Commune of Aardenburg. The whole crew with one exception, Sergeant Alfred Wheeler an air gunner who is buried in the Adegem Canadian War Cemetery, are on the Runneymede Memorial, Driver Harry Simmonds was hoping to fly with his friend Norman Enderby, so it was great shock to find he had not returned.

Flight Officer Lynus Pattee flew Dakota KG 401 'AF' of 48 Squadron, he took off from Down Ampney at 12.35pm, 25 miles from the Belgium coast he lost sight of the formation and was forced off course to make way for two Stirling's towing gliders. They were underneath the cloud and then climbed through it to 4,000 feet north of Ghent, and after crossing the enemy lines, was forced to weave and deviate from his course to avoid enemy flak. The DZ was small and surrounded by woods, and because of poor visibility he did not see the DZ until he was right on top of it. They approached at 1,200 feet and dropped supplies at 15.35pm, as they quickly pulled away the aircraft came under intensive enemy fire. The tail unit was hit and the rudder seemed to be jammed, the port aileron was hit about 2 feet from the end, and the port engine was hit and the starboard auxiliary tank pieced and drained except for about 35 gallons. All the gyro instruments were unserviceable, the pitch controls, rudder and aileron trim and port engine boost gauge broken, the fuselage had been raked by machine gun fire, and it was at this time that the air despatcher Driver Herbert Davis was mortally wounded. To get out of the fire line, Pattee put the nose of the aircraft down and to the left, managing to level out with the help of the second pilot, Pilot Officer A.C. Kent at 800 feet. The wireless–operator, Flight Officer F.J. McIntyre was at the rear of the aircraft administering first aid to the wounded Davis, at this time three bullets went through the seat he had vacated. They managed to get to 1,500 feet but were again hit in further attacks from the ground and a hole shot in the port wing near the roundel and had several hits on the under part of the fuselage. The observer Wing Officer T. Fenwick was saved by his flak suit stopping several bullets that came through his seat. After levelling off at about 700 feet they were met by another salvo from the front, they were now able to see the enemy gunners quite plainly and hits were made in several places on the bottom of the fuselage, hits on the cross feed valve and a piece taken out of the starboard leading edge. Having somehow got to 1,700 feet they were hit again by comparatively light flak which hit the aircraft in several places, the leading edge of the fin was hit near the top whipping off the radio aerials.

Driver Davis had been hit in both thighs and was bleeding profusely. Lieutenant Corporal Wilbye Whittaker the non commissioned officer commanding the despatch crew, had to think quickly to leave Davis and despatch the panniers, he also had to rally his crew who were badly shaken. He did this so well that all the panniers were despatched on one run in, despite being hindered by a bar falling on the conveyer it was in, the opinion of Flight Officer McIntyre, the best despatching he had ever seen, he had put a tourniquet on Davis's legs and kept a tight hold on it while they went through a heavy pounding from below. Pattee left his seat to inspect the fire in the rear and decided they would stay airborne as long as possible, he could not close the starboard engine and stay airborne as he applied the starboard engine fire extinguisher without throttling back. This did seem to do some good but still the fire would not go out, again they were hit by shells which hit the bottom of the fuselage in the area of cockpit, with a consequence smoke got into the cockpit, the fire increased in intensity, the intercom was destroyed and the electric circuits broken. Again Pattee went to look at the fire fearing an explosion but stuck to his decision to make for allied lines, Wing Officer Fenwick told him they had 12 miles to go to the Albert Canal. The fire increased and there were puffs of smoke and flames in the cabin around the bulkhead door and the wireless operator's seat. More hits came on the aircraft and a square foot of the fuselage floor was cut out, the firing stopped as they dived to the left, Pattee seemed to think that the fire fooled them and they thought they were going down. As they crossed the Albert Canal there were two explosions which lifted the aircraft 50 feet, this was the last time they were fired upon. Pattee now thought it would not be long before the aircraft exploded and he gave the crew and air despatchers the opportunity to bail out, he would stay with Davis and crash land the aircraft. After some consideration it was decided they would all stay.

An area ahead was chosen, the throttles were cut, the nose dropped and they went into a dive so it was necessary to open the throttles again, upon which they now had quite a good speed, Pattee was able to put the tail down in a small patch of hedge like trees before an open field which acted like brakes, the touch down was gentle with the tail swinging towards the starboard about 60 degrees. The crew got out quickly and carried out the injured Davis. They had come down on the edge of Kessel at about 16.10pm, in no time there were many Belgium's willing to help. Shortly afterwards a medical officer of Rear HQ 83 Group arrived and took the injured despatcher away, sadly he later died and is now buried in Ath (Lorrette) Belgium. Flight Lieutenant R.B. Auston, camp commandant of Rear HQ 83 Group, was soon on the scene and offered them assistance.

On the 30 September 1944, Flight Officer Pattee was recommended for the Distinguished Flying Cross, in his log book he had twenty-four operations and 156.45 flying hours. The recommendation dated the 18 December was submitted to ACM Conningham the air officer commanding in C 2nd Tactical Air Force on the 25 October 1944, and approved on the 28th. Also came the award of the Distinguished Flying Medal to Lieutenant Corporal Wilbys Whittaker, with the full story of his actions in the Dakota when it had been hit, being recorded that on return he was suffering from shock. He had also developed a bad stammer but immediately volunteered to go on another operational sorties, he was not allowed to do so. His award was endorsed by a letter from Flight Officer Pattee dated the 25 October, in which he said he was pleased with the leadership of Lieutenant Corporal Whittaker in the speed with which supplies were despatched and with his coolness and presence of mind throughout the ordeal. Also, on the same day, a further letter from Flight Officer McIntyre, both letters being sent to the Officer Commanding 223 Air Despatch Coy R.A.S.C, the recommendation was counter signed by ACM Coningham and finally by Field Marshal B.L. Montgomery commander in chief 21st Army Group.

Pilot Officer Christie Valentine Brock, RCAF, flew with 48 Squadron in Dakota KG 428, the radio silence after take off was broken a number of times by US pilots wanting their colonel to fire off red cartridges so that they could find the leader. As they approached DZ 'V' they found space around them full of puffs of smoke the size of footballs, 20mm light flak he thought they called it, when it hit the aircraft it sounded like gravel hitting a tin roof. Ahead of him two Dakotas were on fire, later he thought one could have been David Lord. Just seconds after giving the signal to the air despatchers, Driver Thompson, Olderton, Corporal Balcock and Lieutenant Corporall Bradley, one engine failed and seconds later the other engine spluttered and stopped. They had now in Brook's opinion a very heavy glider and with so little height nothing to do but crash land in an opening between trees. While 100 feet up came a rifle shot from ten o'clock to their glider which entered the port window and grazed Brook's left shoulder which felt hot like a branding iron, a second or so later and it would have been through his heart. He alerted the co-pilot Flight Sergeant Frank Fuller but still kept control of the aircraft. They slid over a single track railway and the nose of the Dakota only feet away from the trees, 12 inches in diameter. It was found out later the spur line from Wolfheze to Deelen airfield was built by the Germans. On landing, Brook and Frank escaped through a split on the starboard side of the cockpit which they squeezed through, there was no glass left in the windscreen by now and it was only a few feet to the ground. The normal exit was jammed with radio equipment and part of the supplies that they had not been able to despatch. The navigator, Wing Officer Anderson, and wireless operator, Wing Officer Fulmore, both RCAF, survived the rough landing but Frank did have a few cuts from flying cockpit glass.

The four despatchers had all been injured by the supplies on the roller conveyer, plus from flak and were seen to be bleeding. Corporal Balloch had been wounded in the leg, by a bullet in the left arm and a piece of shell in the left shoulder, and Driver Ollerton a broken leg.

The navigator maps were buried, with their revolvers in the woods, as they felt being unarmed if captured would be in their best interests. They spent the 19/20th in the woods and used the contents of their water bottles and lunch packs. On one occasion just as it was getting dark, two German soldiers came walking along the edge of the wood towards their concealed position laughing and talking to each other. When one handed his rifle to the other and walked into the wood stopping only a yard from them, a yard more and he would have stood on them. On the 21st they made contact with a forester named Gerard Bloem who took them into his care, and on 2nd October they were joined by a GPR pilot and an officer from the Parachute Regiment. On the 19 November, Anderson and Fulmore were taken prisoner but Frank Fuller escaped and was liberated on the 5 May 1945.

Thanks to the 'Rhine Crossing Group' – LEEK of the Dutch Resistance headed by Klass Heijboer of Groot Amersfort- forty-nine allied men were led to freedom. The first group out was on the 6 February, included Brigadier Hackett and Dr Lippy Kessel, who had operated on Hackett after he had been shot and allowed him to recover from his severe stomach wounds received on Sunday morning the 24 September, Brook got out on 17 March 1945.

Frank Fuller was told of an amazing plan for a mass escape of up to 100 men. The resistance had mapped out a route from Northern Holland, down to the Rhine, the route had been checked out and the risk worth taking. Dates were fixed and the forces on the southern bank of the Rhine would send amphibious craft across at a certain spot, at a certain time, and scores of Sten guns that had been dropped by the RAF.

The first job was to gather together the party from a widespread area to one mutual spot, which the resistance men did magnificently. They were all packed into a motor van and taken to a barn in a farm that had been chosen as the meeting place, the van stopped three or four times on route and the drive was questioned by German soldiers but somehow they kept going. In the barn were British and American airborne troops, RAF men, glider pilots, and even men from the Royal Navy.

In charge a British colonel who organised the marching formation of the party with Dutch guides. The main fighting men were the paratroopers with Sten guns who were positioned in the front, round the sides and at the rear of the party, in all about ninety men all in uniform. Those that had disposed of their original battle-dress were fitted out with a new one, that way they would not be shot as spies if captured, the plan to march for two days, rest for two days in selected hiding places and hopefully on the third night they should be at the Rhine and a crossing point, all went comparatively well. Although there was the odd incident with the front of the column being separated from the rear, and guns being fired accidentally. When they were forty-five minutes from the meeting point a German sentry challenged them, he was obviously shocked to hear a large body of men marching in what was a restricted area, there was a pause and he shouted again, then the roar of machine guns. German soldiers were everywhere and the paratroopers returned the enemy fire, upon which the Germans started to send up flares with the whole area becoming a battlefield. Frank and the other members of the crew had made contingency plans for such a happening, they shook hands and split up into two's and made their way to the meeting area on the Rhine.

Again on route they were challenged but kept running and Frank lost track of his companion and did not see him again until the end of the war. The Germans were now chasing Frank with dogs but after running for about an hour he dropped down exhausted in a field full of tall wet grass. He then saw very light red flares being fired from the south bank of the Rhine, this was the signal that the amphibious craft were crossing at this spot, and arranged for the pick up. When Frank eventually got up he was soaked to the skin and very still, it took him an hour to get himself walking again, and when he looked up at the sign posts he realised he was back where he started two months previously. He tried to contact the resistance again but was not as successful and many doors were closed in his face until he was taken in by the owner of a small cottage and given food and drink and allowed to dry out his wet clothes, but with Germans in the area he was told he would have to leave before dawn next day. He did this and was approached in the woods by a Dutchman, a local resistance fighter. The man in the cottage must have contacted them and taken him to a hiding place where there were several other RAF chaps. Two days later another member of his crew turned up, the second pilot but not the wireless operator, other members of his crew were eventually taken prisoner. For the next five months they evaded capture for a long time in enemy held territory and it was April 1945 when the allied army crossed the Rhine into Holland, and seven months after crashing, they were free.

Of the ninety men who set out in the march of September 1944, sixty were killed, wounded or taken prisoner. A few managed to make the appointed spot on the Rhine and the remaining twenty got to North Holland and joined the resistance.

Wing Officer Coeshott aged 23, and his crew, were killed when Stirling EF 263 of 190 Squadron was hit by flak and crashed.

Pilot Officer Hincks of 570 Squadron flying Stirling LJ 647, after being hit over the DZ made an emergency landing. He, his crew and AD's were able to evade capture and get back to the UK, but Pilot Officer Mortimore in Stirling EH 897 having crash landed, he and his crew were taken prisoner.

Pilot Officer B. Belberfield, RNAF, aged 23 of 190 Squadron, had run into cloud and the Horsa glider he was towing rapidly closed up on him and nearly put him into the sea. When, the tow rope broke and the glider went down into the sea, the three men aboard the glider were able to clamber aboard a dingy dropped by the Stirling.

Flight Lieutenant Losson, flying KG 338 of 48 Squadron, was able to get back to Down Ampney but when he landed and inspected his Dakota he found several bullet holes from ground-fire.

No 38 Group Intelligence Summary for D plus 2:

The object to re-supply, strengthen and capture another DZ at Arnhem, 144 aircraft engaged, 120 successful, ten aircraft reported missing. Many had delivered gliders before becoming casualties, operations no longer having the element of surprise, producing considerable stiff opposition from the enemy.

Again a most noticeable feature was the non-interference by the Luftwaffe which had been taken care of by allied fighter cover, crews reported flak opposition extremely active along the route to the DZ range, from small arms fire to 40mm, flak was also encountered along the River Waal.

The most poignant memory of Lieutenant Colonel M.St.J Parke, in charge of the Royal Army Service Corps elements in Oosterbeck, was at the time watching the supply aircraft coming over and dropping their containers in an area not yet under the control of the allies. They were met by a screen of flak and it was awe-inspiring to see them fly straight into it, straight into a flaming hell. We thought that some would not face it and would jettison their cargoes, in which case we should get them for they would fall short and therefore in our lines; but they all stuck to their course and went on, nor did they hesitate.

On the 18th six per cent losses, on the 19th eight per cent, and only seven point four per cent of the total number of supplies dropped reached the airborne division.

The men who served in the Second World War navy, army and RAF, came from all manner of backgrounds, but in a war this mattered very little, it's the comradeship, and the team building towards each other, particularly an RAF crew, that matters and keeps you alive. No story of the RAF's contribution to the Battle of Arnhem would be complete without the dedication and contribution of the air despatchers of the Royal Army Service Corps being fully highlighted.

On the 19 September Leo Disher of the Stars and Stripes Mediterranean received a grandstand picture of the landings at Arnhem from a fighter pilot.

> "The transports came in perfect formation, swung out from the coast to the target–some going and some coming. There was little opposition from German AA positions, which had been previously silenced. The paratroops dropped from their planes as if shot from guns, at times I could see as many as 400 in the air. Their many-coloured parachutes made a picturesque scene. Following up the paratroops I could see waves of big bombers towing gliders, which landed in a field much like cars parked in a garage alongside the other neat, straight rows. Everything was quite on the ground."

And so the end of the third day at Arnhem.

Stye Wade RAAF who was on the ground staff at Down Ampney remembers aircraft coming back hit and on fire but somehow surviving. As they approached the air field he could see smoke pouring out of the engines and when they landed many had large holes in the wings, fuselage and tail units.

All the ground crew would return to dispersal, armed with fabric and dope to patch the aircraft up, knowing, that one hundred per cent effort would be needed the next day. The midnight oil was burned whilst the riggers patched up the holes and this continued for four days. From Down Ampney they saw a Stirlings limping back to Fairford, another day a Stirling flying in the circuit firing red flares which meant they had wounded aboard, but it was coming in head on to the other Stirling's on an anti-clockwise circuit. To their horror they saw it collide with another Stirling and both plummeting earthwards in a black plume of thick smoke. The Dakota, Stye said, was just a big flying petrol tank, he had been offered a ride with Len Wilson but for some reason he did not go, as he said if he had gone he would have been up there without a parachute.

By now the Stirling losses were mounting up with ten being lost on the 19th. They had met flak and other enemy fire all along the route to Arnhem, small arms up to 40mm shells, and all along the Waal River were waterborne guns.

Aircraft Employed	144
Gliders	41
Successful	120
Aircraft Lost	10

Chapter 9

Wednesday 20 September 1944

The Fourth Lift

During the late afternoon of the 19 September, news of the situation at Arnhem was received at the Command Post, Eastcote. It was then known that supply dropping would be required for several more days and a new supply-dropping zone was therefore chosen. The location of this DZ, consisting of small fields about 1 mile south, was south east of the landing zone 'L', a road junction 200 yards west of the Hartenstein. The message of the 19th also stated that LZ 'Z' was still being held and so it was arranged for a supply drop to take place in new supply dropping point.

On the 20th came the fourth day of Operation 'Market Garden'. On this day, 38 Group despatched 101 aircraft, again in an attempt to re-supply the ground forces. From Fairford, thirty-four Stirling's, seventeen from 190 and nineteen from 620 Squadrons, from Harwell, thirty-four of 295 and 520 Squadrons, and from Keevil thirty-three Stirling's from 196 and 299 Squadrons. Added to this was one crew from 1665 Conversion Unit at Tilstock, it is likely that this crew had been posted in to a squadron as this unit was a training one for 38 Group.

From Down Ampney, thirty-two aircraft were detailed to drop 512 panniers containing badly needed food, the DZ assigned was 'V' along which 38 Group 46 Group despatched 163 aircraft.

On the 20th there was again wide spread fog and low stratus over central England which, by mid morning (11.30am) had lifted to 1,000 feet giving a strong visibility of 3 miles.

The route was as before the southern one, flying over the area of Eindhoven and Nijmegen which was still occupied by the allies; this began at noon flying in four waves which, it was felt, would reduce the flak factor. The DZ on this occasion was 200 yards east of the previous one, which showed the precision in dropping demanded of the crews.

The low cloud and fog had again grounded the aircraft assigned to transport the Polish paratroopers to Arnhem, despite this the aircraft were all loaded, warmed up and ready to go with the hope of a break in the overcast conditions which never came. The weather over the sea was down to 1 or 2 miles in ten tenths cloud and lasted into the afternoon.

Fighter cover was again promised by the Air Defence of Great Britain Squadrons, three Spitfires and three Mustang Squadron making a total of sixty-five aircraft, with the US 8th Air Force, forty-six P-51's being despatched. The first two waves of the four was adequately covered by a fighter escort but the last two were not because the majority of the US 9th fighters were grounded owing to the weather.

All but three of the thirty-three Stirling from 38 Group dropped their supplies safely on DZ 'Z' but once again as the day previous they fell into enemy hands. This was because, in the eighteen hours elapsing since the message had been sent to England concerning the taking of the zone, it had been re-taken by the Germans.

Of the 131 detailed to drop on the new supply dropping point, 122 were successful, although there were problems in marking the zone and maintaining the Eureka beacon because of the severe flak. When the Germans realised the location of the new site, they attacked the area in force and the divisional line was pushed back so that many of the supplies dropped fell into enemy hands, although a certain amount was salvaged under the cover of darkness. Of the 122 only thirteen picked up the Eureka and thirty-two sighted visual aids, but the results were certainly better than the day before, because of the flak each time ground signal was laid out it attracted mortar and sniper fire, the drop despite this was reasonably accurate but loses and damage to aircraft were heavy.

Jimmy Edwards on this occasion took Dakota KT 500, because there was no time to fit Treble Four with the necessary metal rollers. As he approached the dropping zone it was obvious things were not going well and the whole area of the landings was ringed with German guns, which were firing incessantly. He went down to 600 feet making him an easy target for the 88mm howitzers but the Germans were after the Stirling's and left the Dakotas alone, they were twice the size and much easier to shoot at, in minutes he saw several Stirling's shot down in flames and smoke, when he arrived back at base he was amazed to find that they had all got back. Squadron Leader Jouby was very pleased to have seen some action and told Jimmy that 271 were expected to put up another maximum effort again the next day, the 21st.But, as Jimmy had been flying for four days on the trot, he said he could not ask him to go again but Jimmy said if Treble Four is ready he would go, they thought so much of Jouby that they would do anything for him.

Flight Lieutenant Douglas Robertson, RCAF, of 190 Squadron, flying LJ 831, was hit by flak over the drop zone, and the aircraft badly damaged went into a steep dive. Recovery was only made with the greatest difficulty but assisted by bomb aimer Flight Lieutenant Roseblade, he flew away from the danger area and gave the crew the chance to bail out, however, his wireless operator, Flight

Sergeant Thompson, had been wounded and could not jump, so the whole crew stayed with the damaged aircraft, he went on to make a crash landing at Ghent. On the 24 September he was recommended for the Distinguished Flying Cross, later awarded. Flight Sergeant George Thompson, although wounded, remained at his post and continued to keep watch, transmit messages and make entries in his log until the crash landing.

He was recommended for the Distinguished Flying Medal on the 30 September. Both Robertson and Thompson were sadly killed on the 10 May 1945 when taking the Air Officer Commanding of 38 Group, Air Vice Marshal Scarlet-Streatfield, CBE, and thirty men of the 1st Border Regiment and 1st Airborne, to Norway. They are now buried in Oslo, Norway.

Flight Lieutenant Norman Roseblade was awarded the Distinguished Flying Cross in February 1945 having taken part in D-Day operations in June 1944 and on his second tour as a bombing leader.

Flight Officer Martin MacKay, who was flying a Dakota KG 423 of 48 Squadron, came under fire on his run up over the drop zone at a 1,000 feet and the starboard engine was hit. As the whole of the load could not be despatched during the first run-up, a second run up was made, in spite of a failing engine. When the aircraft was down to 300 feet he, having feathered the starboard propeller, set off for home and, gradually gaining height, brought his aircraft back to base, where he carried out a masterly single engine landing by night.

Wing Officer King was hit in the port main plane by two cannon shells.

On the ground Lieutenant Air Commander Roffer Eden, age 31, a member of the Radar Unit and dropped on the 18th, was killed when a shell exploded at Hartstein HQ, Oosterbeek while he was repairing a wireless in an attempt to make contact with outside air support.

An order came out that no passengers were to be carried, as they could not afford to lose anymore groundcrew who went as observers.

Flight Officer Dennis Hardwick had taken part in twelve bomber missions before joining 299 Squadron, and up to the time of Arnhem had completed a further twenty-one. On the 20th he was flying Stirling LK 118 and was flying in loose pairs in company with other aircraft from 299 Squadron, they had to fly at 2,500 feet and then lose height to a 1,000 feet over the drop zone with an airspeed of 140mph.

Over the DZ they came under severe enemy flak, after the bomb aimer reported the containers gone when the aircraft was hit in several places. The bomb aimer, Pilot Officer Karl Ketches on (RCAF) was killed instantly, also the flight engineer Sergeant White was wounded. The aircraft went into a sudden dive owing to the elevator trimmer control cable being severed by flak but Hardwick was able to recover control at less than 200 feet. Hits had also been made on the tail plane and the escape hatch. They had not dropped there supplies on the first drop because Ketches was not sure that they would fall in the correct place and was killed on the second run, hit by the only bullet to enter the Stirling. On return to base he was buried at Brookwood Cemetery, Surrey.

Although wounded, Sergeant White went to the rear of the aircraft and discovered a break in the cable but owing to this being close to the fairleads he was unable to rejoin them. So as to enable the pilot to operate the elevator trimmers control from the front cockpit, the engineer then cut one of the pannier straps and tied the loose ends of the control wire to the side of the aircraft. By pulling on these he was able to operate the trimmer tabs and to assist the pilot in controlling the aircraft, which made a safe landing at base. Despite this he had managed to drop twenty-four containers and four panniers.

On the 20th Ian Robinson was operating again and taking off at 14.15pm, he would be the first Dakota over the DZ, about seventy Daks from various squadrons were due to follow.

Unlike their operations in Burma, where they operated alone and had circled the small DZ several times to deliver the load, they now had to drop in one pass. Each pannier had a parachute attached connected to a rail on the roof of the aircraft by a static line, a hook on the static line moved along the rail as the panniers moved back, when pushed out, the line opened the parachute.

Over the DZ at 800 feet, they could see puffs of flak which meant the enemy was ready for them.

As soon as the DZ was identified, Ian went back to assist at the open door, when the green light came on the DZ, the panniers were pushed out by the RASC air despatchers who moved them towards Ian and Jimmy, another member of the crew. When the red light came they knew they had passed the area of the drop, the aircraft was now weaving to avoid the enemy gunfire and Ian went back to the front of the aircraft. The pilot reported, a Stirling flying close by had suffered a direct hit and burst into flames, as they approached the North Sea a Dakota ahead was seen with a large panel of its fuselage hanging down below the aircraft. They landed at 19.52pm and the damaged Dakota landed safely a short time later, they only had superficial damage but one of the bursts must have been close as it had blown away the radio aerial. Several other aircraft were heavily damaged and one returned on one engine.

Flight Sergeant Holden was flying again with Flight Officer Fogarty in EF 962, they found the fields around Arnhem were becoming as familiar as around Fairford. To starboard over the DZ area he saw five fingers of smoke rising vertically and through what could have been their air space, there was no obvious gun-site so it must have been well camouflaged. He shouted to Joe, at the rear that there was a ground target coming up on the starboard rocket guns and that it might be worth a shot, then came the rattle of four cannons which were hardly heard above the roar of the engines. They went in at 600 feet as containers began to drop ahead of them and from aircraft who preferred to drop from above, silently Holden cursed the crews who did not go down to the arranged height to drop. The bomb aimer Ted was looking down his bomb sight, there was five seconds to go for the drop and then said, not 'Bombs gone', but 'Containers Gone'. Reg Fogarty turned the aircraft around in a climbing turn, Flight Sergeant Holden using one hand to push the four throttle levers forward to full, and the other hand to push the four boost levers forward.

On the ground, funeral pyres, perhaps one being Squadron Leader Gilliard who did not return.

On return and thinking they must be full of holes all that could be found was a fleck of paint scrapped off by a bullet and a hole in an empty fuel tank with a high explosive shell lodged snugly inside with the vapour in the tank, it should in theory have gone off had it not been a dud. The rest of the squadron reported being attacked by FW 190 fighters and had the holes to prove it, they had not even seen a fighter leave alone been attacked.

Flight Officer George Cairns, RCAF, was flying with Flight Officer John McOmie in Stirling LK 556, but were shot down before reaching the drop zone and crashed in the Valsburg/Elst area. Before crashing they had jettisoned their supplies, on crash landing they were soon surrounded by Dutch peasants who told them that there were Germans all around and that they should go north with a view to crossing the river and joining up with the airborne troops at Arnhem. A member from the underground led them to small wood where they stayed the night, on the 21st they joined up a with another Stirling crew that had also been shot down. They had with them a reporter from the *Daily Telegraph* Mr Edmund Townshend on his first flight with the RAF. They stayed there all day and on the 22nd a priest told them that there were some British troops on a road close by. So they went out to the road and met a British recce convoy that were pushing forward, they advised them to wait for the British troops that were expected in two hours, they informed the British HQ by radio where they were.

When they did not appear they again went back into hiding and made contact with a farmer who was able to look after them. On the 23rd the farmer told them that British troops were in Valburg so they walked back and reported to the HQ and from there they hitch-hiked to Brussels arriving on the 25th.

Correspondent Edmund Townshend had flown with Flight Officer John Le Bouvier, aged 22, in Stirling EF 260 R for Roger of 190 Squadron. As they neared the drop zone they ran into heavy flak but somehow they were able to drop their supplies. The port motor was hit and on fire and the crew was told to put on their chutes; Edmund had been given two minutes on the use of a parachute before take off. He got into the escape hatch in the bomb aimers nose and then bailed out, when he hit the ground he was picked up by a Dutch family and taken to the Dutch resistance. The navigator, Flight Officer Tom Oliver, aged 30, who had been a policemen in the City of London before the war, played the Dutch national anthem on a harmonium in a Dutch farmhouse where they had been taken. It was here that they joined Flight Officer Mc Omie and all but one of his crew, Sergeant Clough, who had been killed in the attack. Omie went out dressed as a Dutchman in a cap, clogs and overalls over his uniform, riding a bike and making contact with British troops.

Two aircraft from 620 Squadron failed to return.

Pilot Officer McHugh, RAAF, aged 21 from Victoria, Australia, flying LK 548, was hit by flak and crashed at Vorstenbosch. The flight engineer Sergeant David Evans, found the flak heavy from flak barges on the Rhine and were almost capsized by the discharge of rocket salvos. As they approached Arnhem incendiary bullets ripped into the aircraft hitting the trailing edge of the starboard wing, with flames licking over the edge of the wing. Both David and the rear gunner, Sergeant Vickers, kept an eye on it until the fire had blown itself out. With his head in the Astro Dome, David saw a hole in the wooden casing of the Perspex dome right in front of his nose, looking down he saw that they had been straddled by cannon fire with a series of holes about 18 inches apart. The wing operator, Sergeant Eric Bradshaw, also 21, and the two Air Dispatchers, Lieutenant Corporal John Waring, of 398 (Airborne) Division Company, Coy and Driver Ernest Heckford only 19, were pushing a container basket out through the despatch hatch. As David continued to watch from the Astro Dome a hole suddenly appeared on the surface of the starboard wing where an 88mm shell had passed through one of the main petrol tanks. The fuel gushed out like a fountain of white spray, which in seconds became a roaring jet of flame, it was now obvious the trailing edge was also on fire.

In no time at all the mainspar was a roaring fire, David, as he described, took the aircraft fire extinguisher which had no effect so he clipped on his parachute and made his way forward helping the navigator Sergeant Hume remove his helmet. As they went down to the hatch, that the bomb aimer Sergeant Gasgoyne had already released, they were hot on each others heels and they bailed out, David went out head first and promptly knocked himself out when the parachute opened, he came too, being helped to his feet by farm workers.

Some time was then spent in identifying himself for the benefit of the Dutch resistance being virtually force fed with an over rich duck egg and a ride on the pillion of a scooter. He then met up with British tanks on their way to Nijmegen, followed by Uden where he found 'Jock' Hume and Nick Gasgoyne being treated for minor cuts by nuns of a nursing order, back to Northolt and finally back to base at Fairford in the UK was via Eindoven and Brussels. They found a new crew had taken over their billet and were given overnight accommodation in the station sick quarters, the next day they were visited by the Squadron Commander, Wing Commander Lee, who himself was later shot down.

Several aircraft of 512 Squadron were badly damaged.

Flight Lieutenant Matthews, flying Dakota KG 418, was hit by flak and crash landed, and Pilot Officer William Perry, DFM, aged 24 and flying KG 324, was hit by flak after dropping his panniers, crashing near a brick factory by the Den Bosch-Nijmegen road at Schayk, Flight Officer Alexander Campbell, flying KG 314, made two runs over the DZ before dropping his supplies. He had one engine hit, his aileron controls rendered inoperative and made a crash landing at Brussels in poor weather conditions, he was later awarded the Distinguished Flying Cross.

On the 20th twelve Stirling's were lost plus those already mentioned, the following also failed to return:

- Pilot Officer Davis of 190 Squadron, he and his crew crashed at Doorwerth.
- Wing Officer Tait RCAF of 196 Squadron, he and his crew crashed at Natuurbad, Doorwerth.
- Flight Sergeant Averill 196 Squadron, he and his crew all bailed out after the aircraft caught fire.
- Wing Officer George Oliver LJ 851 and known to the groundcrew as E-Elephant (Never Forgets) had taken part in the operation on the 17th and 18th but on the 19th were not required.

On the 20th it was a 12.10pm take off carrying twenty-one containers in the bomb bay. When they arrived at the aircraft the two army air despatchers, Lieutenant Corporal Shadbolt and Driver Jones of 63 Airborne Company, were waiting for them. In the panniers they discovered 50 gallon tanks of fuel, as they approached Arnhem there was a thump and the aircraft shuddered violently. Denis Royston the flight engineer left his duties to deal with the fuel supplies, as he stood in the astrodome he saw smoke and flames coming from the port wing between the engines, also one of the ailerons was not responding to the pilot's actions. They were now at the drop height of 250 feet but to bail out at that height was possible, the pilot gave the order to crash stations, from the pilot's comments! They knew he was having a problem controlling the aircraft, they hit a tree causing the aircraft to spin around and part of the wing from between the two engines had fallen off. Having got down okay, they knew that they were on the ground by the fact the bomb aimer's compartment had filled with turnips. They all got out and had no injuries and set off after a short rest into a wood half a mile away, but then heard the sound of feet and voices so they jumped into a ditch and the rear gunner George Gelinas, from Canada, pulled out his '38 revolver whereupon George Oliver told him to put it away. It was in fact allied troops and they took them back to their HQ where they were given the delights from a field kitchen. As they stood there a staff car went down the road out of which were coming cartons, they were told it was 'Monty' and that it was something he did often. The unit, the Royal Welch Fusiliers minutes before captured a village and were expecting a counter attack any minute, a sergeant said that he was going to see if he could salvage any of the supplies in the aircraft. When he returned he asked them if they knew what they had been carrying, they said petrol, he then said it was nitro and mortars, how did he know they asked him, he said it was the colour of the parachutes attached to the containers.

They were taken by truck and eventually reached a village called Verle, where they saw a small pub and decided to stop and have a drink. The man in charge was only too glad to give them a drink and also invited them in to have a meal with his wife and three lovely daughters, whereupon a huge leg of ham appeared. It was then arranged with the local headmaster that they would spend the night; the crew of six, two air despatchers and the driver of the truck, five in the pub and four at the headmaster's house. The next day they set of and reached a small airfield at Diest in Belgium, when they asked for transport to the UK they were politely told to lose themselves for a few hours as there was too many wounded for them to deal with at that time.

They set off for the local hostelry where they had a few drinks and a sort of sandwich.

When it came time to pay they asked the owner if he wanted the escape money all aircrew were given, or George, the rear gunner's, French Canadian dollars, he accepted the latter. However when George checked his change he found he had more money than he had given the owner. At Diest they were taken in an old Sparrow aircraft along with two stretcher cases to Brussels, here they sought out the town major's office and again were told to lose themselves for twenty-four hours. When they asked about a bed for the night they were told to go to the tramway at about 22.00pm (10.00pm).

They then set out to get a meal which, when served, looked marvellous but was too greasy to eat. The manager came over and asked what the problem was, when they told him he agreed and had served a completely different meal which was not only marvellous to look but also eatable, followed by several jars of ale. Again George paid in French Canadian dollars and as before ended up with more than he started.

The next day having all found a bed for the night, they met up and went back to Brussels airport and given a flight home to Keevil in an Anson aircraft with some of the walking wounded, at Keevil they were met by the whole station. The losses had been high and they were only the second crew to get back, after debriefing, a shower and a meal, they all returned to the mess bar.

The message that the Royal Welch Fusiliers had sent back on their behalf had not reached the UK and so the dreaded yellow telegrams delivered by boys on red bikes had been delivered to the next of kin. The next day they collected their kit which had been taken to the stores, went on to HQ and received a pass for seven days leave.

In 1994, Denis went back to the area of the crash and, with the aid of a metal detector, found bits of his aircraft. In 1995, he again went back, this time with his wife and met the farmer George, his sons and daughters, who had helped him and they in turn went over to the UK for a holiday, in 1998. Denis was presented with the axe from his aircraft, minus the wooden handle, which had burnt in the crash, much metal had been collected and was removed in fourteen cartloads.

At the end of the war, as in many cases, the crew parted company and went back to civilian life had a family and a civilian career. But in 1988, they again, apart from Les Steele the wing operator /air gunner, who had died in 1968, were again in touch. The pilot now in his 80's is in good health, but Jimmy Oates the navigator is bedridden, George the rear gunner they have now lost touch with again and Chuck Henderson the bomb aimer in Canada having been located by the Royal Canadian Mounted Police in 1990. It would appear Henderson did not want to relive what happened over 60 years ago, perhaps for him it was too painful and he would rather forget it.

Pilot Officer Marshall of 196 Squadron crashed-landed at Aslst.

Pilot Officer Neil Couper, RNAF, flying Stirling LJ 618 of 295 Squadron, crashed at Pfuifliijk having been hit by intense and accurate flak from the gun emplacements, mobile flak vehicles and flak barges on the river. The crew said it sounded like being inside a tin shed and bombarded with small stones, the aircraft suffered considerable damage and was full of smoke and the smell of cordite. At 500 feet and having released the supplies, they were hit a number of times and the aircraft set on fire. The order to bail out was given but as there was no response by the rear gunner or the air despatchers, the wing operator/air gunner, Flight Officer Ken Nolan, went back to convey the order in person to them, he found that to enable them to move about, the air despatchers had unplugged their intercom. Flight Officer Nolan shouted to them, helped them on with their chutes and opened the rear door. The rear gunner's turret had been hit, the intercom severed and the gunners leg was jammed and unable to turn his turret until the doors faced outwards, so he undid his flying boot; upon which he was then able to bail out backwards leaving the trapped boot behind. By now the engines were on fire and the cabin full of smoke, when Nolan got back to the cockpit the pilot was standing up at the controls and beating his chest, indicating he did not have a chute. Flight Officer Nolan found it under the navigators table, clipped it on him and then clipped his own on and bailed out through the front hatch, as he did the aircraft exploded and Coupar was killed and is now buried in Pfuiflijk. As he came down in his chute Ken could see he was coming down into a village but he landed into water and had to inflate his Mae West and swim ashore.

One Halifax, flown by Flight Sergeant Goldsmith of 298 Squadron, also crash-landed in the water and was helped ashore by a man who at first thought he was a German but when he soon realised Ken was English shook his hand, he then went away and came back with two bikes and they rode into the village of Druten, there he was taken into a shop and the living quarters behind the shop. The man's name was Allard van Mook and he took his flying boots and found the hidden evasion knife that was there to cut off the top of the boots and made them into a shoe which was much more comfortable and far less conspicuous.

When the Germans turned up he was hidden upstairs in a wardrobe but for some reason they did not come into the room he was in and after some while a priest turned up and said he learned English in Rome. Some while later he heard an engine outside and the door was flung open and instead of a German he found an officer of the Royal Horse Guards who said they must leave straight away in a scout car and off they went at great speed. When they reached the river bank he was transferred to a waiting tank that was about to shell a barge, ferrying German soldiers across the Waal River. He got on the tank and settled himself in the turret and they set off until they got to woods where they were met by Dutch people who took his hand and led him through the trees. He took off his RAF tunic and put on a civilian coat he had been given, when they came out of the woods he saw an inn opposite and was taken to the back door, as there were German soldiers drinking in the front. In the afternoon he was led again through the woods to another tank which took him to Nijmegen and safety. Post war he visited Allard van Mook and he in turn came to the UK and spent time with Ken.

Two Spitfires from 16 Squadron were also lost; Flight Officer Bastow and Flight Officer Brodby.

One Mustang from 315 Squadron crashed near Jutphass.

Flight Officer Bastow, aged 21, took off in a Spitfire of 16 Squadron from Northolt for a photographic reconnaissance and was detailed to cover the German positions in the Arnhem area, while over the target area he was hit by flak and crash landed in a glider park at Wolfheze, as soon as he got out of the aircraft he was being sniped at and he hid in the nearest ditch. After burying his parachute, harness and Mae West he found he was cut off and surrounded by German troops who had obviously seen him come down, so he remained in the ditch for three days.

On the evening of the 23rd, and during a thunderstorm, he walked through the woods west of Wolfheze to the outskirts of Wangeningen. On the 24th, as soon as it was daylight, he called at an isolated farmhouse and from there, with the farmers help, the remainder of his journey was arranged for him.

Sergeant Roy Titman was flying as an air gunner in a Halifax of 298 Squadron flown by Flight Sergeant Goldsmith. Just before reaching the target area they were hit by flak and had to crash-land, they came down 15 miles south of St Hlyolth in Germany and the aircraft was completely broken up. Roy was, after the crash, in a very dazed condition, and not receiving any reply from the rest of the crew he stayed by the aircraft for some time, until he saw about 200 yards away, lights and found a farmhouse. The farmer and his family were very friendly towards him, after an hour a car arrived, and the farmer and occupant of the car went to the wrecked Halifax and brought the pilot and bomb aimer Flight Sergeant Barns back with them.

On the 21st a French Padre arrived and showed them on a map where they were at that time, at about 9.00am, an American ambulance arrived and took them to 514 Dressing Station. They then went back for the three dead crewmen, Flight Officer Sheffield the navigator, Flight Officer Borkett the wireless operator, and Sergeant Day the flight engineer who had all been killed in the crash. They were then taken to No 93 Evacuation Hospital where they remained for four days.

On the 25th they were moved to No 52 Air Evacuation Hospital (USA), they strayed until the 28th and were then flown to Marseilles and No 388 Air Evacuation Hospital. It was here that Roy was separated from the other two members of his crew who were sent to No 43 Air PoW Hospital near Aix, remaining there until the 2 October when, via Lyons and Paris, he was flown home to the UK on the 5th.

Flight Lieutenant James Atkin of 575 Squadron was flying KG 327, when his aircraft was hit by flak and one engine put out of commission, in spite of this he carried on and completed the supply drop. He flew the damaged aircraft back to the UK and carried out a successful force landing, for this, and later The Rhine Crossing, he was awarded the Distinguished Flying Cross.

The intelligence report for No. 38 Group stated that there were eighty-seven successful drops, with 2063 containers, 325 panniers, three packages, two kitbags and one sack being dropped.

There were reports of rocket projectiles being fired from two different positions.

One crew was seen to be picked up by ASR Launch east of Ramsgate.

There was considerable bunching by the stream of aircraft which were converging on the DZ, all intended to squeeze aircraft out over a wide dropping area.

On the 20th a message was received:-

"Received last night three jeeps, five men, containers."

In actual fact there were six men and twelve containers, so that one man and three containers had gone astray. Another message came later:

"No oil sent with Jeeps. Send tonight or earliest rocket culprit."

On the 22nd another message as received:-

Parachute Drop following Horsa Glider landings.

Supply Drop to besieged ground troops.

An attempt to signal supply drop aircraft.

Supply Drop.

A successful drop.

Horsa cockpit.

On Route to Arnhem.

Supply Drop.

A Dakota aircraft towing a Horsa Glider.

A commemorative post-war airborne drop at Arnhem.

Ready For Take Off.

Wing Commander Bill Angell and crew stood before a Stirling aircraft, used exstensively at Arnhem (credit Bill Angell).

Wing Commander Bill Angell DFC and crew (credit Bill Angell).

Bill Angell DFC, right, and Group Captain John Herold M.B.E in attendance at a memorial to those lost at Arnhem.

Reunion of the men of the Parachute Regiment dropped at Arnhem (credit Eric Pepper).

The commemorative medal marking the 50th anniversary of Operation Market Garden.

RAF Down Ampney today (credit Alan Cooper).

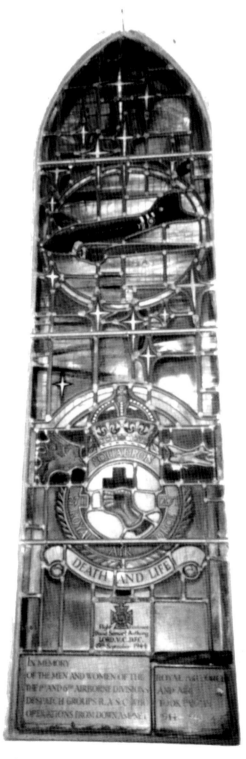

The stained glass window that serves as a memorial to those lost at Arnhem at RAF Down Ampney, Gloucestershire (credit Alan Cooper).

Another memorial stone at RAF Down Ampney.

Oosterbeek Cemetery, the final resting place of many of Arnhem's fallen men and women.

Grave stone of Corporal H.A. Austin, killed 21 September 1944, buried in Erith, Kent – grave re-furbished by Air Despatchers Association author Bob Baxter (credit Alan Cooper).

The final resting place of Flight Lieutenant Jimmy Edwards, Fletchling, East Sussex (credit Alan Cooper).

reconnaissance Picture of Arnhem.

"Congratulate 38 Group delivery six Jeeps. Large hatchets dropped to cut down neighbouring forest would have perfected operation."

This was sent to Flight Officer Brotherton, Wing Officer Oliver and Pilot Officer Shapley of 644 Squadron, and Squadron Leader Imber, Flight Lieutenant Northmore, and Wing Officer Smith of 298 Squadron; the crews that had made the drop.

Also on the 22nd Flight Officer Ashwell's crew of 644 Squadron will be pleased to hear that Moses "Received yesterday sixteen containers and two panniers."

Chapter 10

Thursday 21 September 1944

The Fifth Lift

With many aircraft lost and damaged the air supply organisation was stretched to the limit in aircraft, aircrew and air despatchers. But the men at Oosterbeek were desperate for supplies and another supply run was planned. The Stirling squadrons could only muster sixty-four aircraft as opposed to 100 on the previous day, but 46 Group were able to maintain the previous day's effort of fifty-three Dakotas. Two squadrons from the previous day were replaced, 512 for 233, and 575 for, the newly formed, 437 (RCAF), who for two days had been occupied in supply runs to Belgium.

The weather had improved in the morning over the UK, and in the afternoon over the continent, the southern route was used and instead of a long wave of aircraft they were despatched in waves of four to reduce the flak damage.

There was an express request from Oosterbeek to drop the supplies there, and all 117 aircraft were requested to make drops here. They would fly over two hours in four well-separated waves and again use the southern route.

The Polish Parachute Brigade were finally dropped south of the river, by Dakota's of the US 9th TCC, one Hamilcar was used with the 1st Polish Brigade, the same Hamilcar that force landed in the UK on the 19th. Again it had problems when the tow rope between the glider and tug snapped over Belgium and force- landed near Ghent, the new drop area was only 200 yards east of the one laid out on the 20th. However, very few air crew were able to see the Eureka beacon working from the roof of the Divisional HQ and men on the ground were trying to attract attention with the use of Aldis lamps. It is known that some navigators signalled the beacon but got no reply, the most successful was the Verey light smoke which thirty pilots saw.

Although ninety-one aircraft reported successful drops, very few of the supplies fell into allied hands. Out of 271 tons dropped only about eleven were recovered by those on the ground, and to whom it was intended.

The weather on the 21st was very poor with low cloud and haze which had a detrimental effect on the fighter escort who, up to this time, had kept the

German fighter at bay. The 2nd TAF which were in a good position and better position to appreciate the ground situation, were not allowed, under the orders of General Brereton, to fly over the target area while the re-supply was in operation. The first wave was well protected, and even the second, but the last two made their approach to Arnhem without any fighter protection at all. A situation, history shows the Luftwaffe took full advantage; it was to be the only time that the German fighter interception, in which FW 190's and ME 109's based in Germany, were successful.

Added to this, the flak defences were as strong and deadly as it had been on the 18th.

On the 21st reconnaissance aircraft saw twenty German tanks moving south from Arnhem and the Germans seemed to be establishing fresh defences, three PR missions were flown, Spitfire and Mustangs being used. 39 Wing and 34 Wing – 16 Squadron with high level Spitfires XI's were the eyes of the 2nd Army.

In all some 80 to 100 enemy fighters were waiting for the transporting aircraft. They were engaged by 137 Spitfires, Mosquito's and Mustangs of the ADGB, escorting the Stirling and Halifax bombers, and by some of the ninety-seven P47's and 51's escorting the Dakotas of the US air force. In all twenty of the enemy fighters were shot down, the fighters however were still able to get in amongst the Stirling's and Dakota's.

From Down Ampney twenty-five aircraft were despatched and supplies dropped on DZ 'V' (Warnsborn) where heavy and light flak was experienced. Here the Germans had placed 2cm and two 8.8cm guns on the very edge of the DZ and manned by two batteries of the SS Panzer Flak Ableitung 9.

Flight Lieutenant Beddow flying FZ 615 of 271 Squadron, reached the DZ easily and all panniers were dropped in the target area, but when turning his starboard engine and tail plane was shot up by flak, he attempted to feather the engine but it seized and the aircraft was flown on one engine at a height of 1,500 feet, between Schundel and Veghel the aircraft was again hit by flak and the fuselage damaged, but this did not affect the flight of the aircraft and safe landing was made at B 56. All the crew were safe and arrived back on the 22nd.

At the time of Arnhem and with 271 Squadron was Major Pierre Simond Joubert or 'Joubie' he was known. He was born in South Africa in 1896 and after service in the First World War in South, West and East Africa, he transferred to the Royal Flying Corps and gained his wings in the last few months of the war. After the war he flew mail and other civilian flying roles but was still on the reserve with the South African Air Force. Although perhaps too old for aircrew service in the Second World War he volunteered and in June 1940 was re-commissioned in to the South African Air Force, for the first years of the war he was assigned to ferry duties, he wore the khaki uniform of the South African Air Force with army ranks.

In 1943, and now in the UK, Joubert again met up with the RAF and was based at RAF Uxbridge as a ferry pilot. He then trained on Wellington bombers but it was not a bomber squadron he was posted to but a Transport Command Squadron 271, part of 46 Group, as a flight commander on the 29 February 1944. His crew was the same for the whole of 1944; Flight Lieutenant Ralph Fellow, Flight Lieutenant David Grant, and Flight Sergeant David Butterworth. With his crew he followed an intense few months of training, consisting of towing gliders, dropping paratroopers, supplies, and on odd occasion leaflet dropping over France.

His first major operation was D-Day in June 1944 in 'Operation Tonga' when they towed men of the 3dr Parachute Brigade to Normandy, his aircraft KG 500 was one of seven glider tugs carrying twenty men and a variety of equipment, jeeps etc. They were to drop at Gonneville near Caen, however only one of the seven gliders dropped landed on LZ 'V'.

Despite the entry in the operation record book for 271, stating the operation was a great success when in fact very few of the total ninety-eight gliders had landed undamaged on the correct LZ's and twenty-seven glider pilots were killed. In September 1944 he was awarded the Air Force Cross and only weeks later he took part in the Arnhem operations.

On the 21st twelve crews from 271 dropped 192 containers of ammunition and food. On arriving over the DZ, Joubert saw the Dakotas ahead of him dropping their panniers from 2,000 to 3,000 feet. Because of this rather high height for supply dropping, it meant many aircraft were having to take evasive action and he saw one pannier hit the main plane of one of the aircraft, one of the air despatchers came up to him and said that fighters were attacking a Dakota to the rear of them, at the time they at 6,000 feet and flying into scattered cloud. Below he saw another Dakota attacked and burst into flames, putting the aircraft into a dive, he waited for the fighters to attack, his wing operator Flight Sergeant Butterworth who was in the Astro Dome, gave him the positions of the fighters and warned him to prepare to take evasive action, somehow he was not hit and reached a solid bank of cloud where he remained. It was well after he had passed south of Nijmegen before he saw the first allied fighter support, from there on it was without incident, in all he saw three Dakotas going down in flames.

Pilot Officer Frank Cuer of 271 Squadron flying KG 340 'The Saint,' dropped his panniers on the DZ at 4.00pm and was turning away when hit by a 20mm flak in the fuselage and port engine and the petrol tanks burst into flames. This cut off the RAF aircrew from the despatchers and smoke and flames were rushing through towards them so Flight Sergeant Jim Bayler from Australia, closed the cabin door and opened the overhead escape hatch, the order to bail out was given by Frank Cuer and out went Jim and Flight Sergeant Bert Tipping the wing operator, followed by Corporal Slade one of the dispatchers. The aircraft seemed to be under control and they landed near Heteren and were looked after by a Dutch farmer and lady doctor who dressed their burns and gave them a meal. They were there for a few days when other members of crews shot down started to arrive, one, a Sergeant Robert Percy from Wing Commander Harrison's crew of 190 Squadron, was unconscious and in a bad way. Followed by Flight Officer Beck who was shot down on the 23rd with 570 Squadron, he had a compound fracture of one leg and shrapnel in the other, also from his crew Flight Sergeant Wheatley and a man they only knew as Ron from 48 Squadron, who was also very ill.

When a German patrol turned up, and although, the Dutch doctor told the Germans the men were too ill to move, they took Ron away and said they would be back for the rest and left a guard on the farm. When a Polish Para troop force turned up they said they could not help but it did get rid of the German guard, then came a patrol from the Hampshire Regiment who later sent stretchers for the wounded and carried them back to the first aid post. Sadly, Percy died on arrival and is now buried in Oosterbeek. They were taken by ambulance to Nijmegen and then on to No 15 Field Dressing Station, Flight Officer Beck was transferred to No 3 Casualty Clearing Station.

Bert and Jim contacted an intelligence officer of 111 Wing, where they had a bath and changed into clean clothes and were given a meal. The next day they were taken to B 56 air base and were flown to Northolt in an A.T.A Anson; they wished to state that the Dutch people helped them in every way possible.

On the 25 September 1945, Private Heywood one of the air despatches on the Dakota, received a letter via the War Office from the parents of Wing Officer Anderson, the navigator who was killed along with the Pilot Officer Cuer, he told them that a stream of tracer bullets came through the floor and the plane burst into flames, he clipped on his chute and bailed out, as he came down he saw the aircraft break in half and crash on the outskirts of the village in a mass of flames. On landing he broke his ankle and was taken prisoner, and he was repatriated on the 23 April 1945 and learnt that another member of his despatch team Driver Robinson, had evaded capture and got back to the UK. Another despatcher Driver George High was killed.

Corporal Slade, later lieutenant sergeant, in charge of the despatch team, had loaded up the aircraft overnight and it was their second trip to Arnhem. He also got a letter from Mr Anderson and replied on the 2 October 1945, and remembering that for some reason Pilot Officer Cuer had only arrived at the aircraft ten minutes before take off having replaced the crew who had been assigned. Wing Officer Anderson had explained to Slade the route, Margate, Ostend, Antwerp, Nijmengen, and then Arnhem and then he told them there was ten minutes to go and to stand by ready to drop on the DZ. This was the last time he saw him and ten minutes later the supplies were dropped on the DZ, then the port engines and body were hit by 20mm shells, and the petrol and tanks burst into flames. They were at 700 feet at the time and everything seemed to happen at once, the communication door in the Dakota jammed so he ordered his team to bail out, three made it; Robinson was wounded but made it back via the Dutch underground. As soon as Corporal Slade's chute opened he followed the direction of the stricken plane and saw it crash near a school or church wall in a small village about three quarters of a mile north of the Rhine.

Mrs Iris Tipping, Bert's wife, received a telegram on 23 September saying he was missing from operations on the 21st and a letter would follow, this came on the 23rd from the commanding officer of 217 Squadron. On the 30th she received another telegram to say he was safe and well, and on the 1 October another telegram to say he was back in the UK, he had been helped by a Geertje Slootweg of Heteren, Holland, she and her husband now live in Canada, Jim Bayley sadly died some years ago in Australia.

Flight Lieutenant Mott, KG 516, having despatched his panniers, was hit in the tail by tracer fire which did not interfere with his flight, but at a position between Uden and Nijmegen he was attacked by two FW 190's. The first came from above astern and the rudder and elevator controls were shot away, both engines were dead, as he began to descend he was again attacked by an enemy fighter and raked from beam to astern, the last burst setting the cockpit panel on fire. The order to bail out was given and the navigator Flight Officer Wells was first out followed by the three despatchers, the co pilot, Flight Lieutenant Parker, a fourth despatcher, the wireless operator Pilot Officer Kennedy and then Mott whose chute partially opened before he was able to get out of the escape door and was slightly damaged on the tail plane.

They landed 2 miles west of Uden and the aircraft crashed 2 miles southwest of Uden, where two men of the Royal Corps Signals picked up Mott and one of the despatchers. Then Flight Officer Wells and Pilot Officer Kennedy were contacted, they then proceeded to Uden and discovered that Flight Lieutenant Packer had been taken to Veghel by a Dutch policemen. Flight Lieutenant Mott and Pilot Officer Kenney went to examine the wreaked aircraft and found it to be total write off, they then went back to Uden and then on to Vehgel where they found Flight Lieutenant Packer. Here they spent the night and on the 22nd contacted a Colonel Oxley who suggested they move to Brussels and advised them to hitchhike as it was the best form of travel. This they successfully did and reached there at 19.00 (7pm) and found the three missing despatchers waiting for them, they were then flown back to Down Ampney on the 23rd.

Captain Colin Campbell South African Air Force, flying Dakota KG 346 of 48 Squadron, having been damaged by flak attempting to crash land, came down at Dingle Flats, 3 miles southeast of Bradwell Bay. Five bodies were recovered from the sea, only one was identified as Flight Officer John Mudge the navigator, the condition of the others made burial at sea necessary, two others must have been located later as Flight Officer John Garvey and Flight

Sergeant John Anderson, who along with Flight Officer Mudge, are all buried in Brookwood Military Cemetery. One of the dispatchers, Driver Sleet, has no known grave and the other three were buried in their home towns, one despatcher Corporal Austin, is buried in Erith, Kent, not in a Commonwealth War Graves Commission grave but in the family grave which after over 60 years was in poor condition. But not being under the wing of the CWG they are not responsible for its upkeep and so the Air Dispatcher's Association took this on board and made sure it was brought up to an acceptable standard, and maintain its upkeep.

Flying Officer Samuel Finlay, RCAF, in Dakota KG 404, dropped his panniers from 800 feet, although there was a considerable amount of gun fire over the DZ he was untouched, but as he turned he saw the first fighters coming from the north of Eindhoven. His dispatchers had already told him they had seen two Dakotas shot down. Flight Sergeant Grasy went into the Astro Dome and saw no less than six fighters coming 5,000 yards behind the Dakota.

On hearing this Finlay dived into the cloud and Pilot Officer Rice, the wireless operator, took over in the Astro Dome. He saw three Dakota's, each with an engine on fire and about eight fighters milling around for the kill, two broke away to attack KG 404 which was then 4,000 to 5,000 yards ahead, and 2,000 feet below them. One flew off but the second came into the attack from the port quarter and began to close in. Finlay was now taking instruction from Rice and taking evasive action to avoid the fighter's fire with hits registered on the lower starboard side of the fuselage, presumably by a fighter they had not seen. The auxiliary tank caught fire as a result, and the starboard wing and whole of the fuselage aft of the cockpit was on fire. The starboard motor was put out of action and the port motor showing signs that it was about to stop.

Flight Officer Finlay gave the order to the air despatchers of 223 Company to bail out, it transpired that because the fire was too much for them they had already bailed out and were picked up by the 7th British Field Dressing Station. One of them, Corporal Matthews, had been wounded in the fighter attack. Driver Backler of 223 Airborne Company tried to get to the door to jump but could not get the door open because the aircraft rubber dinghy was burning in the doorway, so he did the only thing open to him by rolling out on the roller runway which was used to roll the supplies out of a Dakota. He then went out head first and fell several hundred feet before pulling the rip cord, after making a good landing he was surrounded by Belgium's who seemed pleased to see him. The crew then went to their crash positions, Flight Sergeant Gray behind the bulkhead at the rear of the navigators department, and Pilot Officer Rice braced himself against the armour plating to the rear of the pilot's seat, Finlay and the second pilot, Pilot Officer Walsh stayed in their seats in the cockpit. At 1,000 feet with smoke in the cabin and their vision obscured for some seconds, the aircraft was set to crash land in a field but within 500 yards of the touch down and just as the vision in the cabin cleared, a fair sized tree was seen ahead of where they were going to land. They hit the tall tree and the nose of the aircraft caved in, the windscreen shattered and one large branch pierced the cockpit forcing Finlay's rudder pedals back to his seat spraining both his ankles very badly.

The Dakota came to rest in a turnip field with most of the aircraft on fire, they escaped through the upper emergency hatch and the rear door, not knowing that the air despatchers had already gone, Pilot Officer Walsh went back in to call them but the intense heat drove him back out.

They were picked up by the 58 Light Anti-Aircraft Regiment of the 11th Armoured Division under a Captain L.S Smith and given first aid for their injuries, then handed over to the 7th Field Dressing Station where they met up with Corporal Matthews and the other three air despatchers. He was treated as an air evacuation casualty and the others transported to B 56 where they were flown back to Down Ampney by Senior Lieutenant Wheatley-Smith of 48 Squadron.

On the 30 September, Samuel Finlay was recommended for the Distinguished Flying Cross by his commanding officer, and approved on the 18 December by the Commander in Chief Second Tactical Air Force, Air Marshal Conningham.

Flight Sergeant Webster in FZ 620 of 48 Squadron, saw two Dakotas ahead of him hit and crash as he approached the DZ with a load of panniers at 1,000 feet. He carried on and after dropping them all he was hit by flak aft of the cabin; he did a sharp turn to the left, opened the throttles and started to climb. The port wing was then hit and a large hole torn near the trailing edge and small holes appeared in both wings, he now found it impossible to straighten the aircraft out and the cabin began to fill with smoke, and flames began to appear aft of the cabin. Seeing the situation was hopeless he gave the order to bail out, opened up the engines to their maximum boost and trimmed back, he left his seat, unclipped his flak suit, grabbed his chute and made his way to the rear of the aircraft. By this time the flames were licking up the side of the aircraft and it was full of smoke, when he got to the rear door four had already gone and the others including himself soon followed. After jumping he got caught in the slipstream and commenced to turn over and over in somersaults, he then pulled what he thought was the ripcord but after falling some distance he realised he had pulled the cloth handle instead of the ripcord. When he did pull the actual rip cord the chute opened instantly, he experienced a terrific jerk, although he was the last to leave, he was, because of his free falling, the first to land. He dropped into the Rhine near the northern bank and after discarding his chute and inflating his Mae West he began to swim for the southern bank where several civilians were waving and shouting to him. Despite the strong current he was able to reach the bank and was pulled out by a youth who it turned out belonged to the Dutch Underground movement, he then saw Corporal Conquest of his air despatchers and they were both taken to a house and given a change of clothing, hot drinks and sandwiches.

There they were warned that the Germans in the area were searching for aircrew and when Webster looked out of the window he saw seven of them go by on bikes. They were, at dusk, taken to a barn and he met up with his wireless operator Sergeant Ruston, the navigator and the other three air despatchers. They spent the night in the barn but got very little sleep because of the incessant fire from big guns and machine fire, at 4.00am breakfast was served by a Dutch youth, with hot milk and pancakes and later baskets of apples, pears and plums. At 8.00am they were told a British armoured car had arrived and they were taken to it, the officer in charge told them to go to a farmhouse on the road to Valborg where they would meet ten other aircrew and that they were to wait there for four tanks to arrive. The ten, were seven aircrew, two air despatchers and a war correspondent, when they decided to walk to Valborg and report to the British troops there. As they walked along the road a civilian came along on a bike and where as they normally waved and cheered, he said nothing. Later they were told by other Dutch people that he had gone to get the Germans, they also told him that in Driel there were 2,400 British troops but when they were in sight of the town a sniper opened fire and a bullet came very close. They were taken into a farmhouse and again given a meal fit for a king, eggs, plenty of fruit, pears, apples, grapes and later a hot meal.

The next day one of the party, a Stirling pilot, put on overalls over his uniform, wore a trilby hat and went scouting along the road to Valborg. He returned to say that the 2nd Army were in command of the town and they set off with Dutch guides for the town of Valborg. Half way along they met the British moving up to take Elst. When they arrived in Valborg they were given food and felt quite safe until the Germans decided to shell the town and a shell that landed near, killed and wounded some of the soldiers nearby. They decided to leave and got a lift on a lorry to Nijmegen, here they were looked after by 30 Corps and given ample champagne and rum to make up for the shortage of blankets. The next day they were taken by truck to Driest and then a truck to Brussels, where they were flown back to Down Ampney by a Flight Officer Smith and his crew. The Dutch people had been, apart from one, marvellous to them, but that there RAF uniforms were often confused with Germans ones which caused a certain amount of embarrassment all around.

Wing Officer David Webb flying KG 579 also of 48 Squadron was hit but not seriously after dropping his supplies. His aircraft had been hit by cannon fire which at first they thought was flak and flak evasion action taken. Then a FW 190 fighter was seen flying past the starboard side and Pilot Officer Clarke got into the Astro Dome to give the pilot evasive instructions and saw no less than fifteen FW 190's on the port quarter. Coming into attack on the starboard quarter there was another ten FW 190's starting to peel off to attack. It has to be said that by the actions of the pilot and the instructions from Clarke only four hits were made but which resulted in a fire breaking out underneath the centre section of the wings, another hit was made and the Astro Dome shot away. At the time Clarke had ducked down to indicate to the pilot to go into a steep dive, a two second burst by another fighter resulted in a fire in the starboard engine and the aircraft into an even steeper dive. The air despatchers and the wing operator bailed out on the instructions of Clarke who yelled at the pilot that the aircraft was on fire, upon which the pilot waved back as if to say thanks for telling me. Pilot Officer Clarke who had been wounded in the legs made his way to the rear door pulling himself along by means of the fuselage ribs owing to the steep angle of the dive, he was able to get far enough out of the door and the slipstream did the rest. As he was making his way to the door more hits were received on the Dakota by the fighters. On the way down by parachute, six FW 190's remained and strafed them, killing, it is believed, the pilot and co-pilot Flight Sergeant Denis Plear. Clarke was able to avoid this by swinging violently in his chute and evading the fighter's fire. One fighter passed within 2 feet of him and he could see the pilot laughing, it also caused his chute to collapse but it opened again at about 500 feet from the ground.

After he had landed safely the fighters came in, and as he rolled away he saw cannon hits about 5 to 6 yards away, he then saw a girl waving at him from a farmhouse 200 yards away. She took him to another farmhouse where he met up with an air despatcher who was also slightly wounded and first aid was given, again by Dutch Red Cross workers, who dressed their wounds. They then heard that four other parachutists had landed, he was taken to one spot where two despatchers were found. One, Lieutenant Corporal James Pilson, was seriously wounded and subsequently died, and another wounded no less than nine times, after fifteen minutes the fourth air despatcher arrived also wounded in the legs.

Clarke got some Dutchmen to intercept transport and a British ambulance arrived and took the wounded survivors to Grave. Here was the body of Wing Officer Gordon Birlison the wireless operator who was riddled from head to foot with bullets, he had come down in a tree and as he hid there it would appear the fighters had strafed him. It was in the village of Zeeland they had come down and were taken from Grave to Eindhoven where they spent the night at St Francis hospital just outside the town. On the 22nd they hitchhiked to the Escant Canal where they were picked up by a RAF Regiment officer in two jeeps, who drove them to 30 Corps. From there they were taken in two staff cars to Brussels and Pilot Officer Clarke was brought back to the UK by Flight Lieutenant Alford of 48 Squadron. Pilot Officer Clarke reported that two of the FW 190's were shot down by a Spitfire.

Flight Officer Wills, RCAF, flying Dakota KG 417, was hit from above by supplies dropped by another aircraft, the wing dropped off. He crashed north of Driel, everybody on board being killed, including, the only officer air despatcher, Lieutenant Herbert Edwards of 223 Airborne Company.

Squadron Leader Duff-Mitchell, AFC, crash landed at B 56 Brussels in KG 350, having had his oil and fuel pipes severed.

Wing Commander William Coles, DFC, AFC, the commanding officer of 233 Squadron, had taken part in most of the Arnhem operations and on the 21st his aircraft KG 559 was hit over the DZ in both wings and elevator, making the aircraft very difficult to control. Despite this he made a second run over the DZ to drop the remainder of his panniers and was again hit a number of times, he flew the aircraft back to Brussels where his aircraft was declared a write off. Unfortunately one of his air despatchers, Lieutenant Corporal Ronald Clements of 800 Airborne Company, was pulled out of the aircraft without a parachute as the containers were being released near Ravnestyne, he was pulled out with a pannier which caught in the tail plane, he is now buried in Ravenstyne. Wireless operator Flight Officer Sharper was wounded in the right thigh.

On the 15 October 1944, Wing Commander Coles was recommended for the Distinguished Service Order, this was approved by the Commander in Chief 2nd Tactical Air Force on the 18 December. William Coles went on to be Sir William Coles, KCB, KBE, DSO, DFC*, AFC, he was also awarded the US Distinguished Flying Cross.

Charles Hamilton also of 233 Squadron, flying KG 566, was shot down by fighters and he and his crew were killed.

Wing Officer Russell KG 586 of 233 Squadron, crash landed at Bennekom and he and his crew were taken prisoner.

Flight Officer Michael Ades KG 399 was shot up by flak at 4,000 feet and came down near a gunpowder factory at Arendonk, near Brabant. He and his second pilot Flight Sergeant George Dorville were killed and buried by men of the 2nd Monmouthshire Regiment near Arendonk, but later re-interred at Valkenswaard Cemetery. The remainder of the crew survived; Flight Officer Dyer, RAAF and Flight Sergeant Hickey, AFM, evaded capture and arrived back about a week later but the four air despatchers were taken prisoner. One of them Driver George Woodcock, of 799 Airborne Company, died on the 27 February 1945 as a prisoner at Stalag 12a and is now buried in the Berlin War Cemetery, Brandenburg, Germany, a special plot for those who died when prisoners of war.

All the supplies were dropped and a course set by navigator Flight Officer Frederick Dyer, but just afterwards they were hit by light flak at 4,000 feet and caught fire. Addes decided to try and crash land but before he could do so the aircraft became a mass of flames with both engines on fire, so Dyer and Flight Sergeant John Hickey, the wireless operator, bailed out. Dyer landed at Hoogemiede, near Brabant, and hid his flying kit in a drain, a farmer nearby took him and Hickey, who had also landed nearby, to his farm. From the 22 September to the 2 October they were hid in a barn and nearby woods, the farmer, H. Valckx, and his family, brought them hot food and drinks three times a day.

On the 2 October 1944, the British overran the area and they were helped by 'B' Squadron, of 53 Reconnaissance Regiment, to Brussels.

John Hickey from Lancaster had been awarded the Air Force Medal in 1944 for his work in training before D–Day; it said yes as a wireless operator he had been an excellent example to other people on the squadron. Frederick Dyer came from South Australia and was 23.

For 437 Squadron things were not any better.

Squadron Leader Robert Alexander, DFC, RCAF, flying Dakota KG 387, after dropping supplies climbed to 7,000 feet above the haze that persisted in the area of the DZ.

Flight Officer John Rechenuc, who was in the Astro Dome, was told by the pilot to go to the rear to see if there had been any damage, he reported back that there was no damage. He then went back to his radio seat to record what he had done, then they were hit and Bob Alexander was wounded with his head and arm bleeding badly, he slumped over the controls and did not move again. The starboard controls were shot away and the engine ran away at a very high pitch. Then came a second hit, this time the navigator Flight Officer William McLintock, and the second pilot were hit and wounded, and Flight Sergeant Andrew McHugh, on hearing the metal striking, stood up, but as he did a bullet lodged in his back and he fell face downwards in the aisle. Then there came a succession of about seven bursts and the aircraft was on fire from stem to stern. Recenuc then went over to McHugh to see how badly he was hit, McHugh stood up and gave the order to bail out. In the meantime McLintock had taken over the controls and given the order to bail out, they put on their chutes and made their way to the back of the aircraft where the three air despatchers were lying on the floor of the aircraft in pools of blood with no sign of movement from them. The fourth air despatcher, Lieutenant Corporal Jones, was putting on his chute. By this time the tail of the aircraft was a mass of flames, John Rechenuc bailed out and McHugh pushed the air despatcher out. The Dakota did a half circle to the left and disappeared behind a clump of trees in a dive, all that could be seen after that was a great big puff of black smoke from where the aircraft disappeared, this was at Vetchel, 22 miles south of Hertogenboasch. John Rechenuc made his way to an American hospital, where the Americans told him there was nothing left of his aircraft and it was a waste of time going back to it, also they were expecting a German attack that night.

He had seen McHugh being taken into the operating theatre having landed in the Wilhelmina Canal and got out by the Americans, the same Americans who had manned the anti-aircraft battery, which had opened up on the German fighters.

He was later in October, recommended for the Distinguished Flying Medal; this was approved in December 1944.

Sadly, Alexander and McLintock did not make it and are remembered on the Runneymede Memorial, only Lieutenant Corporal Jones of the four despatchers survived, the other three died and are buried in the Bergen- Op- Zoom Cemetery. He had been taken on a wheel barrow to 'Zonehove' Children's Sanatorium at Son, being used as a hospital, by the 101st US Airborne Division, this was the same hospital that McHugh had been seen by John Rechenuc.

From here McHugh was taken to a dressing station at 'Kindengarten' and then to the RAF Hospital in Brussels, he had two bullets in his back and burns to his face.

Lieutenant Corporal Jones was, in November, made a member of the Caterpillar Club. He had suffered multiple wounds to the left shoulder, left forearm and right leg.

Flight Lieutenant Anderson flying Stirling LJ 833 found that there was no fighter escort and none waiting for them over the DZ. He was hit by flak over the DZ and then approached by enemy fighters. One engine was hit and stopped quickly, followed by the wing catching fire. The order was given to bail out, but before they were able to do so they were down to 500 feet. Flight Lieutenant Anderson decided to crash land, but right in the flight path was the village of Batenburg. If he crashed on the village most of the houses and farm with thatched roofs would have caughtt fire, somehow Anderson managed to clear the village and crashed in the middle of the River Maas. The fuselage broke off and the aircraft began to sink, but thanks to the help of the villagers three of the crew were saved. The remainder, including the gallant Anderson went down with the aircraft and were washed ashore days later, the two men who had bailed out were also killed.

Flight Sergeant George Orange the bomb aimer and Sergeant Alfred Smith after ditching were able to swim ashore and were met by Dutchmen on the shore. One of the despatchers who was badly wounded but had managed to swim ashore with them, was looked after by a local doctor who said he would be okay, but sadly it was learned later that he had died.

They were given a boat and rowed across the river, on the other side they made contact with forward patrols of the 2nd Army; they were then sent to Brussels on the 22nd and flown to Croydon over night of the 22 /23 September.

Senior Lieutenant Richard Cleaver, DSO, flying with 570 Squadron, was hit in the DZ and badly damaged with the main plane catching fire, despite this he carried on and returned to base. Two aircraft of 271 Squadron were employed on shuttling wounded back to Down Ampney and on the outward journey taking stretchers and blood.

The mission was not a success by the 123 aircraft of both 38 and 46 Groups. Much of the supplies dropped went to the Germans, and twelve aircraft were shot down on the DZ, the first time the enemy fighter forces had really been seen to an effect.

The Americans made a drop south of the River Rhine but 2 miles west of the area planned, seven aircraft failed to return. The glider operations for the American Airborne Division, was however a success, with the landing of the 325 US Glider Infantry Regiment at Grave.

On the ground, the 1st Parachute Brigade under Lieutenant Colonel Frost, who had been holed out in an area around the bridge without any re-supply and against strong opposition, was overcome. The Guards Armoured Division had tried to advance along a 9-mile road from Nijmegen to Arnhem, but were held up by enemy anti-tank defences and the countryside around the road not being suitable for tanks.

The men on the ground had tried to attract the attention of the transport aircraft with yellow triangles to let them know where to drop the supplies but failed.

Jimmy Edwards was flying his favourite Dakota KG 444, "The Pied Eyes Piper of Barnes", obviously named because Jimmy was born in Barnes in 1921. He took off at 13.11 (1.11pm) the weather was hazy with poor visibility but improved towards the DZ with one hundred per cent cloud over the Dutch coast. He began flying the Dakota in 1943 and remembers that you could do anything with it, pulling a Horsa glider over four hours to Arnhem, dragging it out of tiny grass airfields it took anything you could throw at it. It was virtually impossible to stall and once you got up to 100 feet you could put the Dak into George the automatic pilot and sit back. When approached by a fighter it proved to be very manoeuvrable with the drill to fly straight and level until the fighter committed its attack and then turned sharply towards it. This way the fighter could only get a short burst before passing over or under and then had to start all over again.

On the 21st this happened no less than several times before the fighter decided to come in from the rear. The wings and fuselage were raked by explosive bullets none thankfully hitting the petrol tanks, and it was only when through the loss of hydraulic oil, his 'variable – pitch' propellers went into fully fine pitch and lost all power, he had to crash land. He had successfully dropped his panniers on the DZ, turned away climbing to 7,000 feet and he told his wireless operator Bill Randall to get the sandwiches and coffee flask, when suddenly there was tremendous noise and the aircraft shook violently. Edwards at first thought they had been hit by flak when he saw, as he described them, the ugly snout and yellow spinners of an FW 190, who again raked them with bullets. He said many years later that he knew they were German as they had dirty great swastikas on the sides of the fighters.

It was here that the engines went into fine pitch and Jim gave the order to bail out, the second pilot, Alan Clarke, and Harry Sorensen, promptly complied with the order and went out, they were later taken prisoner. Jim then collected his chute and put the aircraft on automatic pilot and promptly ran down the aircraft to bail out of the open door, but he pulled up sharply as he saw lying by the door, the four air despatchers. When he asked them why they had not bailed out, he was told they couldn't as they had been wounded in the legs, on hearing this he threw down his chute and ran back to the cockpit. However he could not see through the cockpit window as it was covered in black soot and oil after one of the engines caught fire. At 6,000 feet the aircraft went into a steep dive but somehow he regained partial aileron control, and when 100 feet from the ground he held off too reduce speed. They passed over a village with its numerous haystacks and he shouted out to the crew "crash landing", one of the despatchers came forward, it was then that Jimmy knew the aircraft was on fire as the cabin was well alight. When he stood up through the escape hatch he rested on his forearm, the other hand still on the control column, by standing on the seat with his head out in the slip stream he crash landed the Dakota Treble 4 into a small wood, the saplings broke his speed, which stopped the aircraft breaking up.

As he hit the ground the nose dug in and catapulted Jimmy out of the top hatch and on to the ground, where he was joined by Bill Randall who had stayed in the aircraft. The aircraft was up at an angle of twenty-five degrees, with the despatcher having been thrown from one end of the Dakota to the other, but although shaken he and Jimmy were able to get out of the door. Jimmy picked himself up and warned the others to take cover in the trees, as he felt the FW 190 might make a strafing attack. He had just got to the trees when the fighter came in and opened fire but after a short burst the firing stopped, it was assumed he had run out of ammunition. They all assembled and crawled into a belt of larger trees where the Mae West's were buried. Randall had a sprained ankle sustained when he jumped out of the doomed aircraft, and the despatcher Corporal Deridisi had flesh wounds, but was able to walk. Jimmy had severe burns to his face and ears, his ears looking like cockleshells and the reason after the war why he always wore his hair long to cover his ears, his left arm was also scorched. The other three despatchers who had failed to get out of the aircraft perished in the flames. As they started to set off they heard voices and through the trees came a man and women, at first they thought they were Germans, but no gun fire came their way. They went towards them and found the man to be a civilian. Jimmy asked them where the Bosche was, the women thought he was the boss and she waved towards the man.

Jimmy thinking she meant the man was the Bosche, nearly opened fire with his revolver but when he dispersed a few people who were watching the man asked them to follow him. The woman was his daughter, they went through the woods for about twenty minutes when finally, in a corner of the wood, they settled and the man said he would go and fetch bandages and food, he returned with his wife carrying food and drink and then began to dress their wounds. Then three young men turned up, one had a white hankie made from parachute silk with the letters A.M on it, this he waved to them as a sign of good faith and that he would help them as he had other British airmen in the past. They then took their pistols on the basis that they needed them more than they did. Before dark a doctor like Jimmy who spoke French was able to converse with each other, They were then taken to a house where the doctor re-dressed their wounds, he put soothing ointment on Jimmy's face and bound up his face with cotton wool and bandages, the sight of which the Dutchman, whose house he was in, laughed.

The nearest British troops were at Grave so it was decided to take them there on the back of an old cart horse, but seeing the state of Jimmy's face they decided to use a cart pulled by the horse. After the doctor had gone a Roman Catholic priest turned up who spoke some English and, with the aid of their escape maps, he showed them the way to Grave, their current location being St Antonis. They were loaded on to a two wheel cart and taken to a farm and a bed, where they slept until 6.00am, at 8.00am a large car drove up which was driven on a gas generator principle and they all got in. They drove to Grave with two men on the front mudguard and one on each step and went straight to No 186 Field Hospital. By now the despatcher was finding it difficult to walk due to his ankle and thigh wounds he was found to have, so he was left at the hospital. Jimmy and Bill Randall were taken by ambulance to No 163 Field Ambulance Staging Post, Oldenrode, and after examination sent in another ambulance to Bourg-Leopold where they were given further treatment. They were, again by ambulance, taken to No 86 British General Hospital at Diest where Jimmy became a stretcher case and was kept in hospital. Sergeant Randall was taken by ambulance to St. Pierre Hospital and the No 55 MF Hospital Brussels and put to bed; here he stayed until the 24 September when he was flown home to Down Ampney by air from Brussels, Evere.

At the first Field Hospital the bandages on Jimmy's face were taken off to relieve the pressure and replace it with the proper dressing and a bag of lint with holes which had been cut for his nose and eyes. He was given an injection of penicillin, a sedative and, on his battledress, labels saying what treatment he had been given. Bill's ankle was strapped and then they were taken to the General Hospital where Jimmy's burns were found to be worse than thought.

After a few days here Jimmy was then taken to Brussels and a special burns ward, here he stayed until the 27th when he was flown back to Down Ampney. For eight days he had been reported missing and on his return he learned that 'Lumme' Lord had been killed on the same day, he had been shot down and been awarded a posthumous Victoria Cross.

Jimmy was recommended for the Distinguished Flying Cross on the 1 October 1944, which was approved on the 18 December by Air Marshal Coningham, Commander in Chief Second Tactical Air Force, this was approved by Secretary of State for Air and the king. He received an immediate Distinguished Flying Cross to add to his King George V Jubilee medal which he had received in 1935 as a chorister at St Paul's Cathedral. When he joined the RAF, and under 'square bashing', he wore the ribbon of this medal which his drill corporal took some umbrage, obviously not himself having a medal.

Because of the nature of his burns Jimmy was sent to RAF Wroughton, near Swindon and then on to RAF Ely for further treatment.

Flight Lieutenant Reg Turner had served with 120 Squadron stationed at Iceland in 1942/43 and had made three attacks on U-Boats, one of which was credited as "sunk" on the 15 February 1942, h was awarded the Distinguished Flying Cross in 1943.

On the 21 September 1944, and now with 299 Squadron, he made his third trip to Arnhem. He was flying LK 545 T-Tommy as part of the 117 aircraft flying supplies to the troops around Arnhem, carrying twenty-four containers to be dropped near the Hotel Hartenstein, Oosterbeek. The journey to the DZ had been a quite one, that is until they crossed the Rhine over the DZ, when heavy and light flak opened up followed by enemy fighters who were waiting outside the DZ area to catch aircraft coming in. At this point they had no fighter cover, due to this they were able to attack in numbers. When the air cover arrived later the enemy fighters were dealt with. While over the DZ the tail of Turner's aircraft was hit by flak and caught fire but continued on course until the fire got out of control and crash landed successfully, no one was hurt in the landing and all the secret equipment on the aircraft was destroyed.

Soon Dutch peasants came and welcomed them, they told them where they were and that the British troops were coming and then took them to a house. Here they were fed and made contact with the underground who took them to an army contact for crashed aircrew, a guard was put on the crashed aircraft. They were then sent to 30 Corps, via Grave, where they were given a lorry and driver and one armed escort, then taken to Eindhoven where there were various RAF and Army Airborne personnel. At one point they were stopped by a Military Policeman who said that only priority transport could go through Veghel as the situation there was unstable, when warned by civilians that German Panzers were approaching from about a mile to the east. So, as considerable traffic had passed towards Veghel, Reg with his party decided to go on. On the way, beyond Mariaheide, they met an army officer with three Bofor guns who was set on going ahead to prepare an ambush against anything he could find. Reg warned them about the Panzers coming up behind them but he disregarded this and went straight towards them, he later returned with one Bofor gun trailing behind his jeep, he had lost two guns and all his ammunition trucks and with about twenty-five men on the jeep and foot, he asked Reg to help and advise him, so they returned to Mariaheide where they set up a gun position by the road and Reg took charge of his spare troops, they were spaced out to observe an all round defence and a spotter Corporal Sproston was sent to the church steeple.

The Germans opened up with machine-gun from a point they had now reached, to which

Reg and his party replied with machine guns and two rounds of Bofor but with no effect.

At this point Wing Officer Harvey, and Air Despatcher Brackman of Reg's crew, decided to evade on their own and left the party along with Flight Sergeant Hartman, Flight Sergeant Greenwell, and Flight Sergeant McQuiggan of Wing Officer Azouz's crew of 196 Squadron, they went to a house in a village. Again civilians told them Panzers and 300 SS Troops were 5 miles south east of their position, the church tower spotter returned to say two tanks were coming up on their left flank from the north east. The army Bofor officer said he was going back into Veghel in his jeep and asked Reg to take charge of his surplus men in the lorry he had been given by 30 Corps. When they were all aboard he passed them, towing his Bofor gun and one full crew behind his keep, he was not seen again, before they reached Veghel they were ambushed by machine gun snipers and the lorry was hit and turned over into a ditch. All the men aboard fell out on top of each other, upon which Reg told them to get into a ditch as quickly as possible and to make sure they had their weapons with them: four men were killed and eight injured in this incident. Reg was crushed and for a while unable to use his limbs and stayed in the upturned lorry with Corporal Clemont Sproston, his air despatcher. The men were all bunched in the ditch so Reg shouted an order to them to open out and take up a defensive position, the snipers had the lorry covered and whenever Reg tried to get out of the lorry the Germans riddled it with machine gun fire. He was able to jump out when there was a further exchange of fire and the Germans threw over two grenades, none of which hit them. Then they again opened up with machine-guns until Reg saw someone put up a white handkerchief which one German acknowledged upon, Reg shouted several times to take it down. Another party in the ditch who had not seen the handkerchief opened up on the Germans and it soon came down. Two American other ranks joined them from a field and said the situation was confused, and soon left. They now had very little ammunition and were not certain of the German snipers positions so decided to lay low and quite to prevent further casualties, the enemy fire then stopped. An army sergeant made a recce but was unable to make any contact, so Reg decided to evacuate the men in small parties to a farmhouse in the evening. Here he remained with the sergeant until nightfall when they assisted the wounded in, at the farm the wounded were bedded down and a guard roster set up. There was much activity outside and Reg could hear Germans about, being short of ammunition and not being certain of the sniper positions, the order was to keep as quite as possible and no firing other than being discovered or directly attacked. Flight Sergeant Segwick of Reg's crew left during the night.

Under heavy shell fire they remained there all night and the next day, and the farm was the only building in the area that was not hit, despite much heavy fighting going all around no one came to the farm or knew they were there. When the Guards Armoured Division came through, Reg contacted a tank who sent a radio message for an ambulance to be sent to pick up the wounded. The army troops were left in charge of the sergeant who took them to Veghel, and Reg took his RAF party back to 30 Corps HQ where they stayed overnight, the next day they were sent to Brussels.

From his crew he had Flight Sergeant Price the navigator, Sergeant Moss the wireless operator, and air despatcher Corporal Sproston, plus Lieutenant Corporal Day, an air despatcher from Wing Officer Azour's 196 crew.

Flight Lieutenant Reg Turner, DFC, was recommended and awarded the Military Cross, London Gazetted on the 13 July 1945, and Corporal Clemont B. Sproston 253 RASC, the Military Medal, Gazetted 5 April 1945. In Sproston's recommendation, signed by Montgomery, it mentioned that he was put in charge of a forward observation post and directed fire of the Bofors gun with great effect. Lieutenant Corporal Day was also recommended and awarded the Military Medal.

Wing Officer Azouz of 196 Squadron, took off from RAF Keevil at 10.20am and after dropping his supplies, having arrived twenty minutes late owing to engine trouble when hit by flak over the DZ, but got away and rose up to 4,000 feet. Here they were attacked by five German FW 190's, the tail and both wings were on fire and when Azouz gave the order to bail out everyone answered except for the rear gunner Flight Sergeant Peter Bode, Spitfires. Thunderbolts then appeared around them and covered their descent. Flight Sergeant Hartman, the bomb aimer, having bailed out, landed by a farm near Wijchen and sprained his ankle. The farmers came out and took him in and a member of the underground arrived and took away his parachute and Mae West, they said they had seen him bail out of his aircraft.

Two padres who had turned up at the farm took West to a house where he met Flight Sergeant McQuiggan, an air despatcher Lieutenant Corporal (probably Day), and a rear gunner from 620 Squadron (Probably Flight Officer Scanlon's crew LK 127) and Flight Sergeant Murray who was badly wounded. A recce car arrived in which he met up with Flight Sergeant George Greenwell and Sergeant Turner from his crew, they were taken to Grave where he left the wounded air gunner and on to 30 Corps HQ, where they joined Flight Lieutenant Turner's party next day.

As Hartman and Flight Sergeant Greenwell were hurt and Flight Sergeant McQuiggan was assisting them, they decided to go into a house and leave the main party. Here they found two old people who took them into a cellar, as there was gunfire going off. They stayed here until the evening, three men from the underground came to see them, with him an English soldiers whose lorry was nearby. One underground member tried to get a message through to British lines but failed and took them into a field for the night with blankets and food from the lorry, keeping watch in turn as Germans were about. In the morning they were taken to a haystack in the village where nuns came to attend them, later that day the village was cleared and the Guards Armoured Division came through from Nijmegen to Veghel. They gave them a lift but on finding they were going into battle at Veghel they left them again and got a lift on a jeep to Uden hospital. An underground car took them to Eindhoven where they stayed the night at an RAF Hotel. Next day they went to 126 Wing at Le Coulot near Louvaine where the intelligence officer did not know where to send them, he told them to go to the town major in Brussels. Driver Albert Norton, also in the same crew, was with another man, the last to leave the aircraft, the other man was hit as he came down by a high explosive, he landed near Graves and was met by a Dutch girl. She took his chute and led him to the body an RAF man, Albert covered him with his parachute, a few minutes later a despatch rider arrived from the Duke of Cornwall's Regiment who had seen them bail out and the aircraft crash. He was taken to their HQ and then to Brigade HQ where he spent the night as his neck was giving him trouble. He was sent back through medical channels to a Casualty Clearing Station where he remained until the 24th and then on to HQ where he met a Sergeant Simpson and two airborne personnel. They arrived back in the UK on the 27th, it was though Flight Sergeant Peter Bode was killed in the fighter attack, he was 21 and came from Birmingham.

Flight Sergeant George Douglas Greenwell was recommended and awarded the Distinguished Flying Medal. He had flown thirty operations as a navigator with 196 Squadron and on the 2 August he had navigated his aircraft on two engines and the third failing, back from the Brest Peninsula to Colerne, his aircraft had been hit on the final run into the DZ.

On the 21st Flight Officer Warwick of 48 Squadron brought back from Brussels four American Glider pilots, 1st Lieutenant A. West, Flight Officer W.W. Avera, Flight Officer T.C. Campbell, and Lieutenant R.R. Neville of the 9th AAF, 442 Transport Carrier Group. West and Neville went over on D plus one and the other two D plus two day, three of them landed on the LZ. The fourth, Flight Officer Avera, was forced to cut loose some 12 miles to the north west of the LZ owing to circumstances beyond his control, and landed in a clear patch surrounded by trees. The actual LZ was to the north of the Wilhemina, 16 miles east of Tilburg. They were pulled out on D plus four Day and taken to Brussels.

Flight Officer Brian Bebarfald, RNAF, of 190 Squadron, took off from Fairford Stirling LJ-881 on the 21st to drop supplies, after successfully dropping the supplies he was hit by flak and then attacked by an enemy fighter. Flight Lieutenant Leslie Munto the wireless operator, from Vancouver, Canada, bailed out and landed 2 miles east of Zetten. On landing he sprained his ankle and was soon surrounded by Dutch people who gave him civilian clothes and took him to Zetten and hid him in a house until dark. From there he was moved to the village of Hemen. While he was there Wing Officer Morris, the rear gunner, turned up, they stayed until the 24 September when a member of the underground movement picked them up in a car and took them to advanced British unit. All the other members of the crew including Bebarfald who came from Wanganui, Wellington, New Zealand, were killed.

Flight Officer F.E. Pascoe, also of 190 Squadron, arrived at the DZ and found about twenty enemy fighters attacking each aircraft as they came in to drop their supplies, also the flak was heavy. After being hit by flak they crash- landed south of Grave, according to Pascoe and Sergeant M. Hughes, the flight engineer, they were just inside allied lines. One of the despatchers, driver Fitzhugh, was wounded and when Pascoe went to get an ambulance for him the Dutch stripped the aircraft. Driver Fitzhugh was taken away to an advance field hospital nearby and the remainder made their way back along with Flight Sergeant Armstrong the rear gunner.

They had seen Dakotas being shot up and the Germans shooting at the crews as they came down by parachute and he later saw some of their riddled remains.

Flight Officer Gerald Hagerman of 437 Squadron, was hit on the first run over the DZ, and one of the despatchers, Lieutenant Corporal Adamson, was wounded, with the outcome, not all the panniers were dropped but a second run was made successfully. As they climbed away above the cloud, six or seven FW 190's in line astern came in from the port beam. Hagerman made for the clouds but the first enemy fighter was able to get an attack in, breaking off at 100 yards. The wireless operator, Flight Sergeant John Hackett age 36, and navigator Flight Officer Mahon, RCAF, age 28, were attending to the wounded despatcher at the time and the navigator and despatcher were killed by the fighter's cannon fire. The port engine caught fire and the windscreen was smashed and the intercom rendered u/s. The second pilot warned the remainder of the crew to put on the chutes, when minutes later a fire broke out in the fuselage and the second pilot went back to order them to abandon the aircraft. The pilot left through the emergency escape hatch, the wing operator who had a slight leg wound and the despatchers, some of whom were wounded, landed 4 miles south-east of Veghel. The Dutch people provided a horse and trap to Veghel where the injured despatchers were admitted to hospital. United States Airborne troops were contacted and the uninjured helped to Brussels.

On the 16 October, Gerald Puruis Hagerman, RCAF, with twenty-one operations in his log book, was recommended for the Distinguished Flying Cross, this was approved on the 18 December.

Flight Lieutenant Beddow, after being hit in the starboard engine and fuselage, crash landed. He had tried to feather the starboard engine but then it seized and so he was flying on one engine at a height of 1,500 feet. Between Schundel and Veghel he was again hit by medium flak and the fuselage damaged, despite this he made a safe landing at Brussels Evere known as B56 and they travelled back to base on the 22nd.

Pilot Officer John Carey of 620 Squadron, crash landed near Benneken, he was on the 21st flying LJ 946.

On the 21st he was taken from a boat where he was hiding at Wolfswaard, Wageninggen.

Here he stayed for two days and received food and clothing, there were many people in the house which he thought was the local Resistance HQ. On the 22nd he was joined by three other RAF personnel –Flight Officer King, Flight Officer Newton and a Sergeant Haig. They were hidden in a tent in the undergrowth until the 23rd, they were about to cross the river in a boat when a German recce patrol arrived and they had to dash for cover. After an hour their friends produced bicycles and they split into two parties and rode into Wageningen. Later, the coast was reported clear and they crossed the river without incident and contacted the 43rd Recce Regiment. At their HQ they spent the night and after reporting to Division HQ and 39 Corps HQ on the 24 September, were taken to Brussels.

Driver W.T. Evans of 779 Coy, RASC, was flying with Pilot Officer Kenny in FZ 656 of 437 Squadron. Evans and Kenny had been trained at Blakehill airfield having volunteered for airborne duties as he always fancied flying, he did a number of varied duties such as unloading wounded from the Normandy beaches and then on to loading Dakotas at Oadby, Leicester, now a housing estate. He was issued with a .38 revolver, runner overshoes to stop them slipping in the aircraft, a flak suit, plus helmet. After getting their panniers out they were hit by flak and told to bail out, they had personal parachutes on their chest so out he went and landed in woods, he got to a hamlet and met Dutch resistance fighters who took them to their houses, they got to Antwerp and from there to England.

Flight Officer Cyril Siegert, RNAF, was recommended for the Distinguished Flying Cross on the 24 September which was later approved.

On the 21st flying with 190 Squadron he was able to drop his supplies but as he turned away he was attacked by two FW 190's, one of which damaged the aircraft but the other one was shot down by his rear gunner Flight Sergeant Jack Welton. Four further attacks followed and the aircraft was still being engaged by ground defences, despite this he was able to get his aircraft back to base.

Flight Sergeant Welton was recommended and awarded the Distinguished Flying Medal. His running commentary to the pilot of the fighter attacks had enabled him to take evasive action, and one fighter from his fire was seen to dive steeply towards the ground with smoke pouring from it, he was on his twentieth operation.

Of the force of supply aircraft sent, twenty-three were unaccounted for, seven were damaged by fighters and thirty-one by flak, making fifty-two per cent of the force sent being lost or damaged.

Aircraft Despatched	64
Gliders	Nil
Successful	87
Aircraft Lost	14

Chapter 11

Saturday 22 September 1944

The Sixth Lift

On the 22nd the weather was still poor, but although 123 aircraft were made available for another re-supply flight, no request was made, giving the ground crews time to repair aircraft and crews to rest.

The eighteen Dakotas that had taken off from Broadwell were diverted to Brussels and operated from there, and three 233 Squadron aircraft took fifty-four Spitfire drop tanks to B56 from Manston.

There was a cloud base of less than 1,000 feet over bases until 14.00 and the same conditions prevailed over the DZ's all day. Despite these conditions ten German FW 190's attacked the 1st British Airborne Division during the day.

One hundred and nineteen Typhoons supporting the 2nd Army north east of Eindhoven destroyed sixty-four (MET'S) Mechanical Enemy Transport's and three tanks. Two Typhoons were lost to flak near Eindhoven having flown in from Melsbrock, Belgium, to their new base at B78 Eindhoven, which was much more suitable for operations in this area. The units were No's 124, 137, 181, 182, and 247 Wings.

On the 22nd Flight Sergeant Semon Lievense, RCAF, from Manitoba, Canada, serving in 6080 Light Warning Unit under Wing Commander Brown, was hit in the back and killed by an 88mm shell which had landed near him in the grounds of the Hartenstein Hotel, now the Arnhem Museum. Leading Aircraftsman Eric Samwells of 6341 Light Warning Unit, also under Wing Commander Brown, was killed when he went on a patrol at Hooge Oosprong. The former a radar mechanic and the latter a radar operator, both are now buried at Oosterbeek.

On the 22nd the remainder of the Polish Parachute Brigade were dropped by Dakotas of the 9th US TCC on a site just to the west of DZ 'K', three days later than planned. The commanding general of the 9th Troop Carrier Command USAF via No 38 Group sent a message;

The personnel of Troop Carrier Command join wholeheartedly with me in a salute to the splendid officers and men of 38 and 46 Group, who have so courageously and unstintingly given their every effort under adverse weather conditions and in the face of strong enemy ground and air opposition to bring much needed support to our fellow fighting men of the airborne forces. It is General Brereton's and my wish that this message be brought to the attention of the personnel of your command.

From the first three days of re-supply operations two outstanding conclusions had been reached; the lack of communications had led to an inability to obtain up-to-date tactical information of the ground situation at Arnhem. The second was the fact that the transport aircraft and their fighter escorts had not operated from within the same UK weather zone and this had led to a high casualty rate among the transports on the 21st.

With these problems in mind, Air Commodore Darvall, the air officer commanding No 46 Group, who had witnessed at first hand the German fighter attacks on his transport aircraft during a visit to HQ 1 Airborne Corps at Nijmegen on the 21st, conferred with the air officer commanding No 38 Group and then returned to the continent. After consulting the various RAF commanders, and Generals Browning and Horrocks, an agreement was made that one of airfields in Brussels would be used by Dakotas. Having been agreed, Grave airfield was opened for Dakota operations and a plan to deal with the flak, and counter attack against known flak batteries was compiled.

Leading Aircraftsman Fitter, Frank Corbett was a member of the Royal Navy's Fleet Air Arm seconded to the RAF. He had spent his youth building Hurricanes and Stirlings at the Austin Motor Works Factory at Longbridge, Birmingham and he had joined the Royal Navy when he was 17. He went on the supply mission on the 22nd in a Stirling flown by Warrant Officer Parker, RCAF, of 570 Squadron, to aid the despatchers in the rear fuselage of the Stirling. He described the Stirling as being built like a 'Brick Outhouse' with a slow rate of climb, slow speed and a low ceiling (12,000ft) but it could take a huge hammering and was ideal for the job in hand at Arnhem. When nearing the area of the drop he sat in co-pilot's seat, as the despatcher knowing his job was capable of doing it on his own.

This was the fifth day and he described the 88mm guns on the ground being as thick as fleas on a dog's back, the aircraft took a beating on the way in and out but without getting a direct hit. One large piece of shrapnel came in through the nose shaving the bomb aimer's helmet, and ending up between the captain and Frank, himself crashing into the armour plating at the end of the navigator's table. Under such conditions a large low flying aircraft was a sitting duck and it was not easy to constantly locate a shifting drop zone on the ground, everyone in the crew who could look was looking. The drop was made successfully, to have had to go around a second time would have been suicide, this Stirling, although scarred, the skill of the pilot, got back safely. Frank, after Arnhem, went back to serving on an aircraft carrier in the Far East.

Flying Officer Norton of 620 Squadron was hit by flak which resulted in his port propeller coming off, despite this he was able to make Manston.

Also on the 22nd, 38 Group were visited by General Koenig, the commander of the Free French, who held an investiture at Netheravon where he decorated aircraft with the Croix de Guerre for aiding the expulsion of the 'Hun' from France.

On the 22nd 570 Squadron lost four aircraft and two forced landed away from base.

Congratulations to Pilot Officer Breterton, Warrant Officer Oliver, and Pilot Officer Shapley of 644 Squadron and Squadron Leader Imber, Flight Lieutenant Northmore and Warrant Officer Smith of 298 Squadrons.

Flying Officer Ashwell and crew of 644 Squadron will be pleased to hear that: "Received yesterday sixteen containers and two panniers."

The loses to 38 Group were high, with 159 aircrew missing.

The aircraft record of losses and successes was as follow's:

Aircraft Employed:	64
Gliders :	Nil
Successful:	64
Aircraft Lost:	7

Chapter 12

Saturday 23 September 1944

The Seventh Lift

Bad weather in the Arnhem area had cut down air support for forty-eight hours. On the morning of the 23rd the weather improved over the UK and in the afternoon, over the continent, a cold front cleared by 14.00 and gave good conditions. Behind it, visibility was over 8 miles with cloud five tenths to eight tenths at 3 to 3,000 feet.

The time over the drop and landing zones was fixed for late afternoon to take full advantage of the good weather, again the southern route was to be used via Bourg Leopold and Eindhoven. The Polish troops, who had returned to base on the 20th, were to be dropped at DZ-O at 14.47 by forty-two aircraft.

From 38 Group, seventy-five aircraft and from 46 Group, fifty aircraft took off carrying a re-supply of 291 tons, consisting of 1,540 containers, 235 panniers and fifty packages of supplies for the 1st Airborne Division.

An escort was provided by 193 fighters of the Air Defence Great Britain, consisting of eighteen Spitfires, three Mustang Squadrons and 586 fighters of the 8th American Air Force. On arrival they found the flak defences were as bad as on the 21st and six Stirling's and two Dakotas were shot down, plus sixty-five damaged by flak.

As before the supply was mainly in vain, as the troops on the ground were unable to lay out strip markers due to the machine gun and mortar fire. The Eureka Beacon had finally packed up and Verey signals, including flares and smoke signals, only added to the confusion, with many of the signals being put up by the Germans in attempt to lure the transport aircraft their way. Less than half the supplies fell into allied hands and it turned out to be the last re-supply of 'Market Garden'.

The German fighters on the 21st had increased from a 100 to 125 and on the 23rd from 150 to 200, of which two thirds were used against the Allied airborne operations and the remainder on the Nancy-Metz front.

Pilot Officer Walter Pring, known as 'Ralph', of 48 Squadron flying KG 370, was hit by light flak and crashed at Rosande Polder, between the River Rhine and Benedendorpsweg, near to a railway bridge. One of the despatchers', Lance Corporal Simpson, was wounded and died later of his wounds. His grave could not be located and he is now recorded on the Groesbeek Memorial, Driver Ben Hastings was made a prisoner and sent to Stalag VIIA, at Mooseburg, as was Driver Alexander Dunford, but he was sent to Stalag VIIIA at Teschen. When he bailed out his chute caught fire and instinctively he put his hands up to protect his face receiving severe burns to both, Ben Hastings was being machine- gunned as he left the aircraft and although he got down safely he was so badly wounded he could not move. It would appear that Pring had been hit by bullets as he tried to crash land the aircraft, as had Driver Crossley who was still in the aircraft when it crashed.

They crossed their own lines at 1,500 feet and on the run into the DZ were hit several times without incurring a lot of damage but on the final run in they were hit by incendiary bullets and the whole underside of the aircraft and the cockpit were ablaze. Now at 800 feet and too low to bail out, Flight Sergeant Derek Gleave shouted to Pring that they were on fire and he replied by saying he would try and crash-land the aircraft but to do so he would have to make for the other side of the Rhine, which they would reach in thirty seconds. However, the aircraft being so hot he decided he had to put it down straight away. As they came in Ralph Pring was hit by bullets and although in great pain he made a perfect landing, and in doing so saved the lives of those aboard the aircraft. Derek Gleave jumped out at the front of the aircraft and hit the ground hard, he then heard Pilot Officer Jim Springsteele and Pilot Officer Henry Coleman shouting to him to get away from the aircraft, so he got up and ran taking cover so as not to be hit, Jim told him that Ralph had not left the aircraft. Then SS troops started sniping killing Jim instantly and badly wounding Henry. With two bullets in his stomach Henry was taken to hospital but died on the operating table. Derek was taken prisoner and spent time in several camps before getting back to the UK in 1945. The aircraft was last seen with the whole underside on fire and a despatcher still pushing out the panniers.

Warrant Officer McLaughlin was flying in KG 321 of 48 Squadron and had dropped thirteen panniers and medical supplies to DZ 'V' when hit by flak in the nacelle of the port engine. When the navigator went back to examine the damage he found oil gushing out. The oil pressure gauge registered zero so he decided to make for the nearest aerodrome, which was Eindhoven. He made a tight circuit at 500 feet and had intended a crash-landing but at the last moment, when 25 feet from touch down, he decided to lower the undercarriage and although it was not fully extended he made a safe landing. They spent the night in the officer's mess at Eindhoven and the next morning joined a convoy going to Brussels, from there they were flown to the UK, along with four air dispatchers from 253 Company by Pilot Officer Jones in FL 614, who was attached to Down Ampney from Doncaster.

Warrant Officer Felton, flying KG 391, also of 48 Squadron, was hit by flak in the tail just after dropping his panniers on the DZ, there was a blinding flash, the fuselage became full of smoke and the aircraft went out of control. He had no rudder control or elevator trim in one direction, the aircraft climbed quickly but after Felton reduced the boost he exerted considerable pressure on the stick and the aircraft assumed a more or less level flying altitude at about 110mph. The despatchers were moved forward as far as possible to help to keep the nose up. He decided to make for Brussels or B56 as it was known, despite light and heavy flak on route, the wireless operator contacted flying control at B 56 and when at 500 feet, he requested permission to crash-land, which was given. On impact with the ground the port prop sliced into the fuselage and the starboard prop cut a hole in the starboard wing.

Flying Officer David Campbell of 570 Squadron flying LK 117, was hit by flak during the run over the DZ, Corporal William Hutchins, one of his air dispatchers, was wounded in both legs and his back, despite this he carried on despatching large panniers over the DZ. This was recorded in a letter from David Campbell to the officer commanding 570 Squadron and to a Captain Noakes of the RASC dated 10 October 1944. A letter was also sent by Group Captain W.E. Surplice the station commander at RAF Harwell, in which it was stated that Hutchinson had carried on despatching despite being hit in the legs and back. This was sent on to the officer commanding No 799 Company RASC (Air Defence) Great Britain Swindon on 24 September 1944. On 25 October 1944 a recommendation for the award of the Distinguished Flying Medal was submitted by Captain Noakes for the officer commanding 799 Company and approved three days later on the 28th. The final signature on the recommendation being that of Field Marshal Bernard Montgomery.

From 437 Squadron fourteen aircraft dropped 195 panniers successfully but Flying Officer Ray flying FZ 692 aborted before take off.

Flying Officer Paget, RCAF, flying KG 305, was shot down by flak and crashed at Eerschot and there were no survivors.

Flying Officer Purkis flying FZ 669 recorded in his log book that one of the air despatchers' was not wearing his 'monkey suit' during the operation over the DZ and was pulled out of the door to his death by one of the panniers over Oosterbeek. As it was not recorded on the flight manifest his name was not known but it is thought to have been Lance Corporal Clements of 800 Company who is now buried in Ravenstein.

190 Squadron could only muster seven aircraft on the 23rd and dropped 168 containers and twenty-eight panniers. 233 Squadron were able to muster seventeen aircraft. Flight Lieutenant Alastair Mackie on the 23rd was flying KG 433, he had also taken part in the re-supply on the 21st when he flew KG 430.

On the 23rd he led a formation from 233 Squadron, he described the DZ as having a weirdly festive air, with puffs of sand coloured smoke and coloured

Verey pistol rounds everywhere, with the air thick with shells he saw aircraft being destroyed. One of his air despatchers, known as 'Paddy', was having trouble getting the panniers away, probably, because of the evasive action Alastair was taking, it took three runs before all the panniers were away.

On 5 November 1944 he was recommended by the commanding officer of 233 Squadron, Wing Commander Coles, for a bar to the Distinguished Flying Cross which he had been awarded whilst with 178 Squadron in the Middle East, where he had flown thirty-three operations. On 5/6 June 1944 he had made three runs over the DZ due to the paratroopers being delayed, on the following day he re-supplied troops on the beachhead, in all flying eighty-seven operations. The recommendation for the bar to his Distinguished Flying Cross was endorsed by the commander in chief Transport Command on 18 November, and London Gazetted on 29 December 1944.

Major Arthur Rowe, SAAF, of 196 Squadron had also taken part on the 6 June and on 17 September towed a glider to Arnhem. On the 21st and 23rd he was engaged in re-supply operations and on each occasion his aircraft was hit by flak but he was able to get back to base, he was later awarded the Distinguished Flying Cross in 1945 after the The Rhine Crossing.

Flying Officer Nicoll of 271 Squadron was flying FZ 668 which was hit by flak, and one air despatcher was hit in the leg.

271 Squadron managed to drop 122 panniers and thirty-four boxes of medical supplies.

Warrant Officer Knivett Cranfield flying FZ 681 of 233 Squadron, was hit by bullets in the knee and thigh and there was a hole in the starboard wing of his aircraft 2 feet in diameter removing part of the aileron, making the aircraft difficult to control. However, he carried on to the DZ where he experienced intense flak on the run in. It was then that he was wounded again, despite this he was able to drop his panniers before handing over to his second pilot Flight Sergeant Barry Stapleford, RNAF, who flew the aircraft back to base. Cranfield's wounds were severe with his leg being hit and bleeding badly. The cockpit being full of burning cordite he managed to stay awake, as Stapleford, who had not completed his training on Dakotas, made a splendid landing at Blakehill Farm.

On 4 October, for his skill, courage and devotion to duty, Cranfield was recommended for an immediate Distinguished Flying Cross by Wing Commander Coles. This was approved by Air Marshal Conningham, Air Officer Commanding, Second Tactical Air Forces on 18 December 1944, there was nothing for Barry Stapleford.

The 23rd was a bad day for 570 Squadron. Squadron Leader Richard Cleaver, DSO, DFC, flying LK 191, was hit approaching the DZ and the aircraft was severely damaged with one engine catching fire, but he was able to drop his supplies successfully, and then with the greatest skill and determination he was able to crash-land the aircraft south of the Rhine.

Previous to joining 570 he was with 644 Squadron when he was shot down on the 6 April 1944 by flak from a Luftwaffe airfield at Cognac, but was able to evade capture and get back to the UK.

Flying Officer William Kirkham flying LK 883 was hit by flak and crashed at Planken Wambuis, west of Arnhem, he and all his crew, apart from the rear gunner Flight Sergeant Wood, and one of the air despatchers, Driver Badham of 253 Company, were killed. Flight Sergeant Wood came from Hull and joined the RAF in 1940. His aircraft was hit by light flak and set on fire flying at 500 feet, he called up the crew on the inter-com but received no reply and the aircraft crashed at Oudreemst, the other survivor Badham, had two broken ribs. Flight Sergeant Wood survived the crash and walked around the burning aircraft but failed to see anyone or hear any cries for help. He then helped Badham, the other survivor, to the cover of the woods nearby and later approached a farmhouse where he found a man with a red cross on his arm. When he told him who they were, the man replied in English that they should make for the woods that they had just left and join up with a party of paratroopers who were also in hiding. He gave them bandages which were used to try and make Badham's injuries more bearable.

As they entered the wood they were met by the paratroopers of the 10th Battalion who took them to a hideout and fed them, here they stayed for three days keeping enemy movements under observation. On the third day they were approached by two men from the Dutch resistance who took them to Ede, from there their journey was arranged for them.

Flying Officer Beck flying LJ 991 crashed at Hetern, he and one air despatcher survived but the remainder were killed. He had joined up with Flight Sergeant Bayley and Flight Sergeant Tipping who had been shot down on the 21st.

Pilot Officer Murphy flying LJ 996 crash-landed at Ghent and then returned to base.

Flying Officer Burkby flying LJ 622-V8-A had his aircraft badly damaged by flak and crash-landed at Manston.

Flying Officer Baker flying EF 298 having been hit by flak, crashed at Panoramhoeve and all were killed.

Wing Commander Donald Lee, DFC, the commanding officer of 620 Squadron, was flying LJ 873-H on the 21st, leading eleven aircraft from his squadron when his aircraft was raked by gunfire and crash-landed, on fire, in a field at Ussen, near Oss. He and his crew, including the two air despatchers returned safely on the 25th. He was awarded an immediate Distinguished Flying Cross having flown four missions during the Arnhem operations.

Flight Lieutenant Byrom of 295 Squadron, flying LJ 986, was hit by flak and one of the inboard engines was knocked out, he made an emergency landing at

Ghent and he and his crew, including the two air despatchers' from 253 Company, were safe.

Squadron Leader Richard Bunker was a flight commander with 620 Squadron. On the 23rd and in the second stream his aircraft was hit by flak knocking out one engine. When the leading aircraft was forced to land and realising the danger of the stream splitting up, he took over the lead and led the stream into the dropping zone despite the damage to his own aircraft.

On 27 September 1944 he was recommended for the Distinguished Service Order to add to his Distinguished Flying Cross and bar. He had joined the RAF in 1938 and joined 83 Squadron at RAF Scampton in 1939 at the same time as another pilot, the late Wing Commander Guy Gibson, VC, who led the famous Dambuster raid in May 1943.

In 1940 Richard was awarded his first Distinguished Flying Cross. He later joined 9 Squadron flying Lancaster's as a flight commander, and was awarded a second Distinguished Flying Cross. In June 1944 he joined 620 Squadron and in October 1944 became the commanding officer of 190 Squadron.

In April 1945 he had gone to Brussels to take petrol for the advancing army, he brought back prisoners of war to RAF Odiham then took off to return to RAF Great Dunmow with, for some unkown reason, a flat rear tyre. When he got off the ground the tail unit caught fire and the rear turret fell away from the aircraft, it was only as a result of the bravery and skill of 'Dickie' Bunker that they did not crash on to the village of Windlesham. He turned the stricken Stirling away from the village and crashed in a field 400 yards away, all were killed and apart from Richard Bunker they are now buried in their home towns. Richard for reasons unknown, is buried in Brookwood, Surrey. A memorial has now been erected by the villagers at Windlesham to the memory of him and his crew.

Wing Commander Bill Angell, DFC, had taken command of 295 Squadron on 12 September, only five days before Operation 'Market Garden'. He flew on the 17th towing a glider and on the 18th, 19th and 20th carrying twenty-four parachute containers and four panniers on each trip, other duties prevented him flying on the 23rd.

In 1945 he was awarded the Distinguished Flying Cross, having taken part in the 'Rhine Crossing' in March 1945, and was also awarded the Belgian officer of the Order of Leopold II, with Palm, and the French Croix de Guerre 1940 with Palm. In his twentyseven operations carried out in a six month tour, he had taken part in the D-Day operations, special operations to France, Holland, Denmark and Norway, nineteen operations on SOE / SAS work, seven on airborne lifts and one with Bomber Command before joining 38 Group. Previous to joining 295 Squadron he had been a flight commander with 196 Squadron.

Flying Officer Martin Mackay of 48 Squadron had been hit on the 20th. On the first run he could not get all his supplies away so went around again; despite having an engine failure. They were down to 300 feet so he feathered the starboard propeller and set off for home, gradually gaining height and landing at base on one engine. On the 23rd, he was hit again and the fuselage was severely damaged whilst over the DZ. One despatcher was wounded and as on the 20th, he was not able get his entire load away on the first run so he went around again organising his crew to help with the despatching. He was recommended for the Distinguished Flying Cross on 1 October 1944 and London Gazetted in 1945.

A Thunderbolt was shot down by a FW 190 west of the DZ and a Mosquito of 29 Squadron was shot down and both crewmen were killed. A Mustang of 129 Squadron was also shot down and the pilot killed.

Sixteen Dakotas of 512 Squadron, carried crews, personnel and equipment of 575 Squadron to Brussels Evere. They returned to base with two 512 Squadron crews who had gone missing on the 20th.

Three Dakotas of 271 Squadron, who had stayed over night at B56, returned to base with four aircrew of No 271 Squadron, who on the 21st had been reported missing.

Two glider pilots were landed at Keevil, two at Brize Norton, two of 190 Squadron and five SAS troops at Fairford.

Two Dakotas of 233 Squadron carried petrol tanks from Manston to B56 on the 22nd and returned to Broadwell and Down Ampney with casualties. One Dakota of 233 Squadron, and one of 437 Squadron, who had stayed overnight at B56, returned to Down Ampney with casualties. Two aircrew of No. 437 were reported missing on the 21st.

Anti-flak sorties were flown by eighty-eight aircraft firing rockets and dropping eighty-five bombs. Obeying the rule of 'do not fire until fired upon', they were able to strafe many defence positions and reported eighteen gun positions destroyed, and seventeen damaged.

Of the seventy-three Stirlings and fifty Dakotas despatched, two aborted, six were shot down and sixty-three damaged. Had the 78th Fighter Group not been on hand to keep the fire toll down, the casualties would have been greater.

This was to be the last re-supply attempt from the UK, the air officer commanding deciding that enough was enough and that the casualties had been too much to sustain. Two squadron commanders and two flight commanders were lost, all men with great experience and difficult to replace. On the 21st the casualties had been twenty-one per cent and on the 23rd fifty-eight per cent, with eight aircraft failing to return and a horrendous sixty-three damaged by flak, the losses were again very heavy.

Chapter 13

Sunday 24 September 1944

The Eighth Lift

There were no further re-supply drops by 38 or 46 Groups from the UK. On the 23rd, twenty-one Dakotas of No 575 Squadron, were moved to Brussels with nine bundles and 243 panniers. One army officer and seventy-two air despatchers, of which twenty were from 799 and 800 Companies. The same evening, four of the twenty-one were assigned to drop supplies to the 1st Airborne Division, two of them did not make a drop owing to not being able to identify the DZ. All returned safely, three being damaged by flak, they were escorted by thirty-six Spitfires of the 2nd Tactical Air Force and without losses, although one Dakota only just made Brussels before both of the wounded pilots collapsed at the controls.

Flight Lieutenant Brian Legge flying KG 327, and co-pilot Flight Lieutenant Hagan, were hit by machine gun fire. Legge was badly wounded in the right leg, damaging muscles and denying him the use of the leg, but despite a great loss of blood he managed to reach base; and although the runway was soft and slippery with a cross wind, he made a safe night landing. Hagan was also hit in both legs. For his efforts Legge was, on 26 September, recommended for an immediate Distinguished Flying Cross by Wing Commander Jefferson, the commanding officer of 575 Squadron and approved by the air officer commanding the 2nd Tactical Air Force on 18 December.

On the 24th the twenty-one aircraft set out on a re-supply mission, 235 panniers were dropped with food, ammunition, and thirteen bundles of bedding, some of which fell in the river. Good fighter cover, keeping the flak down, was recorded.

The remaining seventeen Dakotas gave up at Nijmegen, with fifteen of them dropping their supplies to the 82nd US Division, and two dropping loads near Grave.

On the 24th Air Commodore Darvall, air officer commanding No 46 Group who were anxious to overcome the problems of weather and poor communications between the UK and continental fighter bases, had, after flying from England to Belgium to consult with senior officers of the 2nd Tactical Air Force, one squadron was detailed to an airfield, near Brussels.

Twenty air despatchers were also sent out to Brussels from 799 and 800 Companies.

By this time the situation on the ground was such that it was no longer possible to use Eureka Beacons, as the batteries were dry, or to lay out ground signals. The only method left was by visual signals, but the enemy became aware of this and used similar signals to confuse the issue, it was not surprising that the dropping was inaccurate and most of the supplies fell into enemy hands. All four aircraft were damaged by flak.

Flying Officer Arthur Grime and Sergeant Dowall, in a Mosquito of 613 Squadron, whose mission was to harass enemy movement in the area of Emerich, Wesel, Cologne, Roermond, Venlo and Cleve, were shot down and crashed near the home of Mr Van Deelen at Randwijk near Oosterbeek, where both are now buried.

A Dakota KG 653 of No.1 Flight Unit and flown by Flight Lieutenant Korer on route to Elmas, Sardinia was shot down at Neulingen, two crew and twenty passengers were killed. When the air officer commanding 46 Group, returned from HQ 30 Company, he sent out a message "Have just returned from a visit to Nijemegen HQ 30 Corps and Airborne Corps. I saw the re-supply operations on the evening of the 23 September. Generals Horrocks and Browning and many others, expressed their admiration for the magnificent courage and determination of all crews. No one faltered and their conduct was in the highest traditions of the Royal Air Force. Many congratulations to all concerned."

Chapter 14

Sunday 25 September 1944

The Ninth Lift

On the 25th the weather conditions improved and the cloud base over the Channel went up to about 1,000 feet, allowing the American Dakotas and Troop carriers to take off from Ramsbury, Wiltshire with tons of howitzer ammunition for the 101st Airborne Division.

In the afternoon the weather again deteriorated with showers and cloud over the Channel and in the area of Holland.

There had been a demand for ninety-six panniers of rations, one medical block and small arms ammunition, this was the final re-supply mission by the 575 aircraft based at Brussels, dropping food and medical supplies west of Arnhem. At Heveadorp, seven aircraft were despatched, of which six were successful, one failing to return and three were damaged by flak, the six dropped their supplies at Hevadorp but none got into the hands of the 1st Airborne Division. They were escorted by fifty Spitfires and thirty Mustangs which encountered and took on fifty enemy fighters near Arnhem and forty near Hengelo. Two Mustangs and a Spitfire of 416 Squadron flown by Flight Lieutenant Treleaven, RCAF, Pilot Officer Phipps and Warrant Officer Hyde were lost. One was lost in the morning during an early morning patrol and another lost in the afternoon when engaging a large force of enemy fighters near Nijmegen. One German FW 190 and a Tempest of 3 Squadron flown by Flight Officer Davies and Pilot Officer Phipps, was last seen going down through cloud and Wing Officer Hyde may well have been the aircraft seen going down in flames shortly after a dog-fight with FW 190 German fighters.

Two Mitchell's of 98 Squadron flown by Flight Sergeant Williams and Pilot Officer Harrison were also lost on the 25th attacking enemy gun positions on the western suburbs of Arnhem. Again attacked by FW 190's. 401 Squadron scrambled twelve aircraft to intercept thirty enemy fighters, destroying three and damaging several others. Nine Spitfires from 441 Squadron attacked twenty ME 109 fighters which were about to attack Nijmegen Bridge, the ME 190's were forced to jettison their bombs without attacking the bridge.

The aircraft KG-449 flown by Flight Sergeant Clark that failed to return was from 575 Squadron, it crash-landed north west of Paal, Belgium, and the crew returned safely to Brussels. One despatcher, Driver Irish of 800 Company, sustained a dislocated shoulder and was evacuated to 31 Field Dressing Station. The aircraft was hit by flak over the DZ damaging the left elevator and rudder. Near Eindhoven, it flew into heavy flak, which put out the port engine and north west of Bourg-Leopold it was again hit by flak, which it was believed came from Allied troops: as no German fighters were seen in that area. So even at Arnhem in 1944 there was friendly fire!

Attacks were made on enemy gun positions by the 2nd Tactical Air Force, utilising seven Typhoons, fifty-four Mitchell's, and twenty-four Boston bombers.

At Arnhem Squadron Leader Howard Coxon who was second in command of the RAF Radar Units and senior controller, who had flown out on day one, remained in the area until the 25th collecting all the airmen he could. They fought as infantry until the withdrawal, when he with the rest of his unit attached themselves to various army units and continued to fight without food, water, sleep, and shelter for seven days. On the 25th they got to the river to be evacuated by boat, but as there were not enough boats he swam across the river and on reaching the other bank he was sent to Brussels. On the 3 December 1944 he was recommended for the Military Cross which was endorsed by Air Marshal Roderick Hill, air officer commander in chief Fighter Command.

Of the twenty-four men from the two radar units, No 6080 and 6341 despatched to Arnhem, nine were reported to have been killed, eleven were wounded or taken prisoner and only four escaped. Besides Coxon, First Lieutenant Davis, Controller, USAC, from No 6080 Squadron, Squadron Leader Wheeler, senior controller, and Flight Lieutenant Richardson, controller of No 6341, made it back to allied lines.

On the 25th, Bomber Command was approached by 21st Army Group to deliver supplies of motor transport petrol to Brussels and Melsbroek. The Allies were now advancing so quickly that they were running out of petrol. The squadrons involved were from 4 Group and included twenty-three Halifax's from 77 Squadron, twenty-two from 102 and twenty-six from 346/347 French Squadrons. In all they delivered, 952 jerry cans and 326, 340 gallons of petrol up to the last delivery on the 2 October 1944. The petrol was delivered to the airfield in Yorkshire by the US 3rd Air Force and loaded into the modified bomb bays of the Halifax bomber.

On 9 October Air Marshal Conningham, air officer commanding, 2nd Tactical Air Force, sent a letter of approval to General Bradley commanding the 12th US Army Group. It stated that the only thing that would prevent the 3rd US Army from penetrating the Seigfried Line would be the shortage of MT fuel for his armour.

On 28 September, Flying Officer Michael Wetz of 16 Squadron was recommended for the Distinguished Flying Cross. He had flown sixty-one sorties of which three were covering the Arnhem airborne landings at Nijmegen, flying low and at a low airspeed over enemy positions; taking photographs and returning to base in the dark. During these sorties he came under considerable flak and small arms fire, the recommendation was approved on 26 October 1944.

Chapter 15

Post-Mortem

On the 26th a short signal from the War Office stated that the 1st Airborne Division had been withdrawn and there were believed to be about 800 survivors. So "Market" had failed, the agony was ended and what was, perhaps the finest division this country has ever produced, almost wiped out.

The 26 September 1944 must forever remain one of the blackest days in our history.

On the 29th a message was sent from the air officer commanding of 38 Group:

Now that Operation "Market" is over, I wish to congratulate all aircrew and maintenance personnel on their magnificent work. On all sides I hear nothing but praise for the impeccable manner in which glider operations were carried out by 38 and 46 Groups and for the cool courage and determination displayed on subsequent days. Although military aim was not wholly obtained, we can console ourselves with the fact that the verdict of history will be that the operation was well worth while. The high endeavour shown in your efforts to assist our gallant friends of the First Division in their epic struggle, make me proud to have the privilege of commanding you. A special word of praise is also due to the maintenance personnel whose sterling work enabled us always to keep looking forward. WELL DONE.

The reasons for the failure at Arnhem is simple, but in hindsight was probably worth the gamble and if it had been a success would have been one of the greatest achievements of the Second World War.

From someone who was there:

Stan Lee said there was no single reason why 'Market Garden' failed. It was, as he wrote, ambitious and an imaginative plan and deserved success but airborne troops could not survive long on what they carried with them, and when the army failed to relieve the troops which had captured the bridge, the whole project was doomed. The re-supply by air ran into bad luck as regards weather, lack of fighter cover, and lack of knowledge as to the disposition of the lads on the ground, he went on to say, Jimmy Edwards referred to it as a 'shambles' but personally Stan did not think so.

So the battle finally ended on 26 September 1944.

The Royal Air Force had to contend with bad weather, intense fire power from fighters, ground flak and all the time not knowing where the exact DZ's were for dropping supplies. The areas planned to make successful supply drops were often in enemy hands but the one striking aspect of these drops was the dedication and courage of the crews. RAF and air despatchers worked to get the supplies to the men on the ground, flying straight and level at low heights and into fire power which meant that the enemy could hardly miss.

This was seen and recorded on many occasions by the men on the ground.

As a military operation it was one of those that 'if anything could go wrong it certainly did' at Arnhem. The plan was put together too quickly and as a consequence was doomed to fail and did.

Once a German army commander saw at first hand the burning Dakotas, as they flew round and round, ever lower and lower, in an attempt to drop supplies to the British soldiers below. He wrote to the Air Ministry at the end of the war and said, "When the aircraft went down a hush came over the battle-area, and for two minutes all fighting ceased, as the men on the ground, German and British spontaneously saluted, in silence, the great courage of the men who had just died."

When Operation 'Comet' was planned, it included a coup–de-main parties to attack the three bridges, Grave, Nijmegen and Arnhem but it seems now that the reason for not putting in parties such as this nearer the bridges is one for conjecture. The defence at Deelen airfield from the RAF's prospective was the major one for their objectives to drop parachutists, or the landing of gliders within a radius of, or at Arnhem itself.

The shortage of troop-carriers and the American aircrews not being able to navigate at night by was a vital factor, if two lifts had been made on the first day, it would have meant so many more troops being available. Both Air Vice Marshal Hollinghurst and General Urquhart wanted this, but General Brereton was against it, which meant two further days of transporting troops to the battle area.

Other reasons were the plan being put together too quickly and the intelligence from the Dutch of the SS Troops presence in the area of Arnhem. The radios, issued to the men on the ground, had a short range of only 3 miles, which when troops were spread over an area of 8 miles meant that there was a serious lack of communication.

The Diary of Airborne Operations at Arnhem records the following:
"The plan for this operation was as follows;-

The night before D-Day, the 17th September, 38 Group, 46 Group and some of the Groups of IX TCC are to drop paratroopers, whose main tasks would be to protect the glider LZ's and neutralise dangerous flak. After going into this matter very carefully with ADGB (Air Defence Great Britain), enemy night fighters could be prevented just for this one night from interfering with this operation.

<u>Dawn on D-Day</u>. The remaining troop carrier aircraft would land mainly gliders.

<u>At Mid-Day on D-Day</u>. The 38 Group aircraft and the other first lift aircraft to bring further gliders and paratroops.

<u>On the Evening of D-Day</u>. The second lift aircraft to bring in the balance of glider and paratroops."

In this way three complete divisions would be put on the ground in eighteen hours, probably before the Germans could bring up strong counter forces.

The concern was whether adequate reconnaissance arrangements had been made and there seemed no "alternate plan" in the event of trouble lessons learnt at "Overlord" in their opinion the Air Plan was a bad one.

Experience and common sense pointed to landing all three Airborne Divisions in the minimum of time so they could form up and collect themselves before the Germans could react. All three could have been landed in twelve hours or so but as it was, with a second lift twenty-four hours later, with half the heavy equipment the Germans were alerted and ready. The evidence shows that this second lift was disorganised or destroyed by the enemy on arrival, the result, the 1st Division had to fight its battle without a really effective glider brigade, a hopeless task.

The plan ignored so many of the lessons learned about airborne operations, many of the people planning it had no experience of airborne troop carrier operations yet they were given this vast power over the lives of the best troops and aircrew the US and England could produce.

It ended in failure but need not have failed, as a result of putting inexperienced people in charge of a highly complicated operation it did. In civil life, such a failure would result in immediate dismissal; in Russia, it would result in a court martial; in an allied democracy, the result nothing, no one had the courage to speak openly, or to act.

The planners of the ground operation found some difficulty in selecting areas for the 1st Airborne Division landings. West of Arnhem on the northern bank of the river heath, land rose to a height of about 100 feet above sea level with dry and sandy soil covered by large stretches of thick pine woods. The wide clearings were ideal for parachute and glider troops to land but on the south bank of the river lay low-lying marshy ground extending up to the Arnhem railway bridge which was intersected by ditches and if the waters of the Rhine should rise extremely it was liable to flooding. For this reason the northern bank was chosen even though ariel reconnaissance showed that large number of troops were in the area and well protected by flak.

Although on the face of it this seemed most suitable, troops were dropped at a 5 to 8 mile distance from their objective – the Arnhem bridges and the country lying in between, although good for concentrating scattered formations, was equally ideal for the purposes of the enemy defence.

Although the south side was open to flooding it would appear there was no flooding for a few days before the landings, this was known as Polder Land and only a mile from the bridge. The ditches were the main problem jeopardising safe glider landings. It's possible with the glider undercarriage being jettisoned this would have been safer, the disadvantage was not being able to swing the tail unit open to unload the vehicles, this was too much to gamble with and the Glider Pilot Regiment decided against it.

Other areas offered possibilities but were rejected as unsuitable. One, 3 miles from the bridge, was 'Malburgsche Polder' but it was enclosed by power transmission lines and ringed by a dyke 8 feet high and a battery of six heavy and six light AA guns, so was unfit for mass glider landings. It would appear that the RAF and the army were over pessimistic about the flak, landing the troops there would have been a risk worth taking.

On 17th no more than fifty fighters were launched but on the second day this had increased to between 100 and 125, and by the 23rd between 150 and 200 fighters were flying over Holland.

Between the 17 and 26 September, thirty-four, 876 troops were dropped or landed, 568 artillery weapons, 227 tons of equipment were landed.

It would appear from the records that the Germans were taken by surprise and that a parachute drop was dismissed before the Arnhem operation took place. They thought that if the whole of the 1st Airborne Division had been landed as one rather than a division east of Arnhem, success would have been greater. They did say that the area dropped was a cunning one on behalf of the allies, as it had tree cover.

Back at Down Ampney the ground crews felt very depressed and were appalled by the state of the returning aircraft, with huge holes in the wings and fuselage, and engines on fire and smoking. They thought, and who would disagree, that this was the most courageous flying of the war; in broad daylight and with a lack of fighter escorts especially the Dakotas, who were unable to defend themselves at heights of 500 feet and speeds of 120 mph, they flew into an inferno of flak.

General Brereton died in 1967 having, in 1948, become the US Secretary General of the Air Board. He had taken over the First Allied Airborne Army in

August 1944 but from his service record had little experience or background in airborne forces.

Operation 'Market Garden' was not a complete failure with passages across the Maas and Waal having been secured; to which General Kurt Student the man who was behind airborne forces in Germany said was a spring board from which to launch the final attack upon Germany.

The communications by radio was poor and without direction from the ground. Aircraft and tug crews were forced into guesswork in dropping supplies in areas already in the hands of the Germans. The only hope was the two US Air Support parties with VHF radio transmitters mounted in jeeps and known as 'kops', they were allocated to the 1st Airborne Division for ground to air links and were under the command of US officers who were not signals experts.

Unfortunately both were destroyed by shell fire on, or before, the second drop, by which time they had not made any signal contact with any allied aircraft. This was because of having the incorrect crystal frequencies installed prior to being despatched from the UK. A Lieutenant Geddes told a US Army Air Force officer serving with the RAF, and army signallers at Arnhem, that he had received the frequencies the night before the 17th and that there was no time to install crystals and fuses to test the radios.

Known targets were requested to be attacked by the 2nd Tactical Air Force but were turned down on the grounds of there being insufficient information to mount a proper strike. Many acts of supreme bravery were carried out, many unrecorded, the following are just a sample:

On 30 September 1944 aircraft and crews missing after the battle were recorded as:

38 Group -192 aircraft;
46 Group -81 Aircraft;
172 air despatchers.

Flight Sergeant Barvise had only arrived on 247 Squadron at 14:00 on the 26th when owing to the shortage of pilots he was pressed into service and detailed to attack guns and troops in the Arnhem area. On arriving over the area he proceeded to attack, releasing rockets and blazing away with cannon. He was last seen going into a steep climb weaving all the time to avoid flak, he did not call up over the radio transmitter, nor was he seen by any aircraft to have been hit.

On 15 October 1944, Flight Lieutenant Peter Burden of 233 Squadron was recommended for the Distinguished Flying Cross, he had served with 233 Squadron for eleven months, taken a glider in on the 17th and in subsequent re-supply missions, carried out towing and two re-supply sorties, his award was approved on 21 October by Air Marshal Conningham.

On 14 December, Flight Lieutenant William Dawson of 620 Squadron was recommended for the Distinguished Flying Cross having taken part in three sorties as a rear gunner, he had also gone on the first glider lift and in two subsequent re-supply missions encountered intense enemy opposition. He had previously completed one tour with Bomber Command flying sixty-two operations to France, north west Europe, the Mediterranean, and North Africa. His award was approved on 16 December 1944.

In October 1944 a message was sent to Major General R.E. Urquhart, DSO, who commanded
the 1st Airborne Division.

"In this war there has been no single performance by any unit that has more greatly inspired me or more highly excited my admiration, than the nine days action of your division between 17 and 26 September.

There is no question that those sentiments are shared by every soldier, sailor, and airmen, of the entire Allied Expeditionary Force now battling against the western boundaries of Germany.

Before the world, the proud record that your division has established, needs no embellishments from me, I should like every survivor of that gallant band to realise, not only how deeply this whole command appreciates his example of courage, fortitude and skill, but that the division's great battle contributed effectively to the success of operations to the southward of its own battleground.

Your officers and men were magnificent. Pressed from every side, without relief, reinforcements or respite, they inflicted such losses on the Nazi that his infantry dares not close with them, in an unremitting hail of steel from German snipers, machine guns, mortars, rockets, cannon of all calibres and self propelled and, tank artillery, they never flinched, never wavered. They held steadfastly.

For nine days they checked the fury of the Hun and when, on 26 September, they were ordered to withdraw across the river, they came out a proud haughty band – paratroopers, air-landing men, glider pilots, clerks, cooks and batmen, soldiers all–two thousand strong out of seven thousand five hundred that entered the battle.

The Allied Expeditionary Forces salute them.
            Signed Dwight D.Eisenhower,Supreme Commander
                                Allied Expeditionary Force."

During the Battle of Arnhem over 900 ranks of 48 and 49 Air Despatch flew 600 sorties, many flying at least two sorties and some even three. Of this number 264 were in aircraft that crash-landed or were shot down, and seventy-nine made the supreme sacrifice.

The air despatchers in one crew were ordered to bail out and found themselves amongst Polish troops, they were taken to British HQ where they were given a drink or drinks: two bottles of champagne, a bottle of red wine and a bottle of rum.

Another air despatcher when he came to bail out, found rubber dinghies burning in the doorway so he climbed on to the roller conveyer and gaining momentum shot out head first and survived. Two non commissioned officer air despatchers, one 46 and the other 49, complained of the flak, but both agreed it wasn't a patch on the gunfire on the Somme in 1918 which showed the ages of some of these men.

One officer who had returned from Arnhem said; "It was with excited hopefulness and an almost painful admiration that those on the ground watched these aircraft day by day, and for some reason always at the same hour. Flying in to drop their loads, through a continuous curtain of fire they flew on unwaveringly and very slowly, and so low that it seemed wonderful that more of them were not destroyed. Many were hit and set on fire, but continued to despatch their panniers until they fell from view; one aircraft was already on fire when it arrived over the target, but dropped half its load, circled again, losing height all the time and dropped the remainder on the second run until it went down in flames. They stuck to their course and went on, nor did they hesitate."

The losses were high, six per cent on the 18th, eight per cent on the 19th, and twenty per cent on the 21st, despite their efforts only seven point four per cent of the total tonnage dropped was collected by the men on the ground.

The men who served in the air despatchers came from all manner of backgrounds, but in a war this matters little. It's the comradeship, and the team building towards each other particularly an RAF crew that matters and keeps you alive.

Corporal Wilbye Whittaker's background was nothing like his life in the army in the Second World War. He was born in Salford in 1908, had four brothers and one sister all of whom became professional musicians. His grandfather was a member of the famous Halle orchestra, also Professor of the Oboe and Cor Anglais at the Royal Manchester College of Music where Wilbye studied the clarinet. Wilbye also played the saxophone and pre-war played with many of the top bands in the UK, including Jack Payne, Jack Hylton, Henry Hall and many others. With the saxophone, he played many recitals on the radio with the BBC, and played for many West End musicals. When war broke out in 1939 he was playing at the Victoria Palace for the show *Me and My Girl*.

In 1940 he ran the local Air Raid Warden Post in Mitcham where he was living at the time.

When he decided to enlist into the Royal Artillery, as well as being a gunner he was also a despatch rider. In March 1944 he transferred to the RASC and became an air despatcher. When he came back from Arnhem it took him some time to recover having developed a bad stammer which would come back whenever he was under stress.

On leaving the army in 1946 he went to Blackpool and played at the Ice Rink, the Opera House, the Tower Ballroom and other variety theatres. He then took up the Oboe, spent some time in London with his eldest brother Alex, who was principal oboist with the London Philharmonic Orchestra, and went on to play the Oboe in many west end shows such as *Bless the Bride* at the Adelphi Theatre in 1947. When he developed a form of neuritis, which his father also had, he stopped playing and worked for the BBC taking charge of the technical equipment needed for outside broadcasts. He also served as a local councillor for Mitcham and Wimbledon.

Edward and his crew had taken part in the initial flight on the 17 September and also a re-supply on the 19th. On the afternoon of the 19th the brothers Eddie and John Charman and a friend Reg Comber, had seen through driving rain and mist, an aircraft approaching Leith Hill, Surrey, which is about 1,000 feet above sea level. The aircraft missed the hill but hit trees close to the summit killing all three crew, today there is still a depression in the hillside where the nose of the Dakota embedded itself.

The three young men ran to the crash site and removed the three members of the crew before it burst into flames. They were:

- Edward Gibson who came from the Halesowen, West Midlands, John Holder from Kadina, Yorke Peninsula, Australia and Robert Smith from Glasgow.
    Edward had a very interesting military background having been evacuated from Dunkirk when a driver in the RASC swam out to a small boat at sea, then rowed it out to sea where he was picked up by a destroyer which took him to Margate. He joined the RAF in June 1941 and after pilot training in the USA he joined 271 Squadron, where on one occasion in January 1944 he flew as second pilot to David Lord.
- John Holder undertook his navigation training in Canada having left Australia in October 1942. He had flown with Gibson on D-Day and at Arnhem.
- Robert Smith had flown as wireless operator to Edward on 17 and 19 September.

One message the officer commanding RAF Brize Norton received expressed admiration at the way in which the RAF dropped men and supplies near Arnhem. Part of the letter read; "I would like to express to you our admiration for the RAF who flew in the re-supply; it was an unforgettable sight to see those C.47s and

Stirlings coming in at 2,500 ft in the teeth of the most terrific flak, but still calmly unloading the supplies. No matter how badly hit a plane was, we never saw one fail to unload or deviate from its course and never did any member of the crew attempt to save himself by parachute until the whole of the load had gone."

In a report on the employment of airborne forces after Arnhem, came recommendations for the further employment of such forces.

The launching of an airborne operation is an Air Force responsibility. If, in the opinion of the air commander-in-chief, the air situation, the weather, or other considerations make it likely that the operation will be unprofitable, he will order its cancellation, unless the supreme commander or (in the absence of a supreme commander) the air and army commander-in-chief by agreement, consider that the situation justifies abnormal risks.

The operation of airborne forces should be so planned that they have a strategic or major tactical affect on the operation in support of which they are launched. If airborne forces are accorded a vital role this should be stated in the plan since postponement of airborne operations will inevitably affect the main operations.

Under conditions where there is likely to be material air opposition or strong flak defences, airborne operations must generally be carried out at night, In any event this should assist in achieving surprises, though it imposes special limitations on the timing and conduct of such operations.

Airborne troops should not be landed in an area where they are immediately faced with opposition, nor should they be routed over heavily defended areas, unless the importance of their objective justifies heavy casualties.

A portion of the total available airborne forces should be held in reserve to exploit success. They should therefore be fully briefed and prepared to undertake any alternative planned task.

Airborne forces carry very limited supplies of food and ammunition. They should not, therefore, normally be used in a role requiring their separation from the main forces except for a short period and where opposition will be slight and supply by air is prearranged.

Arnhem was the most ambitious and the largest airborne operation undertaken prior to the 'Rhine Crossing' in March 1945. It was spread over three days and the re-supply over four days. It is also for question whether the operation would not have been conducted more successfully under the 2nd Tactical Air Force rather than under the 1st Allied Airborne Army. It was believed that the 2nd Tactical Air Force could have lent a greater measure of ground strafing support if the responsibility for this operation had rested in their hands. As it was the 2nd Tactical Air Force were sufficiently briefed on all aspects of the operation.

For future employment of airborne forces came the following recommendations:

1. The launching of an airborne operation was the Air Force responsibility.
2. If in the opinion of the air commander-in-chief, the air situation, the weather etc made it unlikely the operation would be unprofitable he could order its cancellation.
3. If there was likelihood of strong flak defences, operations must be carried out at night. They should not land in an area where they are faced with opposition, nor should they be routed over heavily defended areas, unless the importance of their objective justifies the acceptance of heavy casualties.
4. Airborne forces carry very limited supplies of food and ammunition. They should not, therefore, normally be used in a role requiring their separation from the main force except for a short period and unless opposition would be slight and supply by air could be pre-arranged. Gliders were mostly essential to carrying heavy support weapons which could not be dropped by parachute. It was suggested that the number of gliders used from the UK for future operations should be limited to 400 Horsa's and thirty Hamilcar's by one division.
5. A combination of parachute and glider force was essential. A glider force was required to carry the heavy support weapons, for this purpose the Horsa glider was more suitable than the US Waco. In glider borne operations, parachute troops were required to light a beacon or a flare path and provide lights or other signals to indicate the release points and landing zones for the gliders.
6. Air crews must be trained for airborne operations with airborne forces.

On 17 October 1944, the air officer commanding 38 Group sent a message of the day.

He said he would like to put on record his appreciation of the grand way in which all of you, aircrew, glider pilots and ground personnel alike, have carried out your duties. The main role had been to take the airborne forces into battle, this you have done twice with Operation 'Neptune' and 'Market'. He went on to say how successful 38 Group were in these operations. Without the courage, determination, and hard work exhibited during these operations and during the preparatory period, the outcome could have been a different one.

In the nine days of the Battle of Arnhem 2000 British troops died, a number dying as prisoners of war after the battle. They included 1174 men of the 1st Airborne Division, 219 of the Glider Pilot Regiment, ninety-two of the Polish 1st Independent Parachute Brigade, 368 men of the Royal Air Force and seventy-nine air despatchers of the RASC.

Many men were buried where they dropped, in slit trenches, field graves or mass graves dug by the Germans. After April 1945 when Arnhem was liberated by the Canadians the Grave Registration Units of the British 2nd Army moved into the area and located the hastily dug graves. A small field was offered north of Oosterbeek by the Netherlands Government to the Imperial War Graves and in June 1945 the casualties were collected and buried there. The cemetery, as we know it today, was completed in February 1946 and the original metal crosses were replaced by headstones in 1952.

The records of the Commonwealth War Graves show that at Oosterbeek there are 1759 graves, 1432 are men from the UK, Canada, Australia, and New Zealand. Also buried here are Polish soldiers, and 253 graves of men who could not be identified.

At Groesbeek there is a memorial to 138 men who have no known graves in the area of Arnhem, this number is still being increased as bodies are still being discovered.

Three holders of the Victoria Cross are buried at Oosterbeek, Flight Lieutenent David Lord is buried in Plot 4, Row B, Grave 5, two others awarded the Victoria Cross have no known grave and are remembered on the Groesbeek Memorial.

Opposite the Airborne Cemetery is a civilian graveyard with a small Commonwealth War Graves plot containing the graves of nine airmen shot down shortly before the battle.

Three miles east the Moscowa Cemetery contains the graves of thirty-six aircrew killed before the battle. Not all killed in the Battle for Arnhem are buried at Oosterbeek. Some 300 who were killed flying into battle, trying to escape or died of their wounds are buried either in the Netherlands, Belgium, the UK or the USA. Some sixty men who died in prisoner of war camps after the battle are buried in Germany, many in Berlin where there is a special plot. The plot includes men who had been prisoners of war, or died while trying to escape captivity.

In September every year since the war there is an official ceremony at Oosterbeck when flowers are put on each grave by over 1,000 school children of Arnhem.

In 1969, on the 25th Anniversary of the Battle, the Parachute Regiment spoke to the Dutch organisers of this, the first time since 1945 and said enough time had elapsed and suggested ending the annual event. But the Dutch were vehemently and emotionally opposed to the idea and so the ceremony continues and it will, it would appear, until the last man is still alive.

Not Just today,
But Everyday,
We Should,
Remember Them.

These were the words on the bottom of one of the headstones at Oosterbeek, words which would have been chosen by his family, as was their right.

As recorded on the 30 September the losses were:

38 Group 192 aircraft missing.
46 Group 81 aircraft missing and 172 air despatchers missing.

Chapter 16

The Outcome

Much was learnt at Arnhem and taken on board for Operation 'Varsity' the Rhine crossing in March 1945, the largest airborne operation of the Second World War.

Although much of the supplies went to the enemy and not the 1st Airborne Divisions the accuracy of the drops was of a very high standard over the three days of the main lift. British aircraft transported some 4,500 men, ninety-five guns and 544 jeeps or larger vehicles across 200 miles of sea and enemy-occupied territory, and delivered them up to 60 miles behind the enemy's front line.

The main lift demanded two successive flying days, a break in the weather after the first day could have been disastrous. Except for some delays to the re-supply missions, and the grounding of the covering fighters on one day out of seven, the weather did not unduly hinder the operation.

Losses to enemy flak and fighters, although mounting seriously in the latter stages, were almost negligible during the main lift: this against all expectations. The initial force was delivered as planned, at the right time and place: and to the greater extent the Germans did little, or could do little, to stop it.

An airborne force depends on the speed at which it strikes with surprise and was the main advantage, the first wave must gain complete surprise and must assemble and carry out its initial tasks with little interference. But on the second day the enemy would have been alerted and opposition would increase. The solution was to make the lifts in as short a period as possible but having sufficient aircraft in the UK to deliver them.

The German general staff would have benefited from Operation 'Neptune' and 'Market' and for future airborne operations would be better prepared.

For its mobility in the air, a large airborne force relies on complex machinery at base. For future airborne operations it would be necessary to complete the lift within a matter of hours, landing every essential unit or load before the enemy could assess the intention, and not rely on airborne reinforcement, or re-supply.

Also any plan must have a complete communication with the forces advancing on land. Operation 'Varsity' in March 1945 took on board all these points.

Lessons from 'Market' Garden showed that for low re-supply drops to be successful against heavy opposition from flak and small arms fire from the ground, every endeavour had to be made to provide the latest information, tactical and topographical, for the crews detailed and the co-operation of the fighter escorts and fighter bomber or rocket firing aircraft established. In the future all communications had to improve between the airborne forces and the re-supply area and to enlist the closest supply of the local Tactical Air Force group also, to base the twin-engine re-supply aircraft as close to the battle area as was possible, with preference to a forward fighter airfield.

One squadron of aircraft bases of within 50-100 miles of the DZ, would do the work of four based 300-400 miles away, particularly in a difficult weather area, such as the UK or Holland.

At no time in 'Market' Garden was the time to take advantage of the night training of 38/46 Group crews, although the choice of daylight for the main landing was fully justified. It is likely that that the re-supply missions would have been more successful by night, given good visual aids such as coded flares. On suitable occasions even the main force might be dropped by night using such aids, either dropped by pathfinder aircraft or set up by a marker force on the ground.

The height of the drop should also be considered, aircraft being less vulnerable if flown near ground level whilst over defended areas, climbing to dropping height a short distance from the DZ, then returning to low level until clear of defended territory.

On the losses at Arnhem:

On the basis of the flak map and reports showing a very rapid build-up of the flak guns before the date of the operation, losses up to forty per cent were predicted. The actual losses on the two days of the main lift were three aircraft from a total of 701 sorties, or less than one and half per cent, glider losses were certainly few. Much credit must be given to the anti-flak patrols and to the Bomber Command missions, all of which incurred losses. When fighter cover was lacking, losses to flak were higher than the average, with a suggestion that if fighters were in the area the flak gunners were unlikely to open fire. Fighter cover was missing in one lift and during the latter part of another. Due in the first instance to inadequate communications with the fighter bases on the continent. In the second no warning was received to the effect that part of the fighter cover was grounded by weather. Had this been known, those responsible for the despatching of re-supply aircraft may have had second thoughts. The loss of signals equipment on the LZ's was partly due to the breakdown of communications between the airborne forces and the air command post.

The parting of gliders from tugs on route was the most common failure, either by premature release, or by rope breakage. The main causes were difficulties in cloud or in the wake of other aircraft and lastly, the next most frequent cause was tug aircraft engine failure.

The Dakota was an outstanding advantage for long periods of work as a transport aircraft, however the ideal aircraft appears to be the four engine bomber type able to carry and drop reasonably bulky loads, and to tow the Hamilcar.

The General Officer Commander of 1st Division to Air Officer Commanding 38 Group:

"We were given a very good start by the RAF, the result of the dropping of the parachutists and the glider landings was quite first class. It was easily the most successful and accurate of any previously achieved, either in operations or on exercises. All units were able to move off to their tasks practically at full strength and in a very short time after landing.

We must thank you also for the efforts made to re-supply us during our nine days battle on the ground. We are full of admiration for the way in which the aircraft faced the flak, which thickened up considerable after the initial stage. The division was by then occupying a very small area, which was thickly covered either by trees or houses, and this made the re-supply task extremely difficult and hazardous."

After the Arnhem operations the Air Despatch Group were awarded their own shoulder flash, a yellow Dakota on a blue background.

His Majesty, he king, approved a squadron badge for 271 Squadron in November 1944.

The design of the badge covered paratroopers and bombs on the outward journey and on the return journey casualties.

There were a number of awards to men who took part in the Arnhem operations.

In March 1945 Flight Lieutenant Derek Boyer of 196 Squadron had completed twenty-nine operations, including all three airborne operations and Strategic Operations Executive tasks in France and Norway, also two tactical bombing operations, and a third low level attack on electrical installations in France. During the invasion of Sicily he was selected for the delivery of special sabotage troops, where accuracy without special radar aids was essential, the mission was a success. His tow to Arnhem was his most outstanding operation, when crossing the island of Overflakkee on the inwards route, he received a direct hit on the port wing and a large calibre shell tore a gaping hole between 3 and 4 feet across.

Flying below the safety speed of the Albemarle due to the heavily loaded Horsa on tow, he was further crippled by the loss of lift from the damaged wing and singled out as a straggler for further ground fire. Despite this the pilot continued undeterred for the rest of the route and delivered his glider to the right place and brought his aircraft back without further damage.

Sadly he died in a boating accident at St Peter Port Harbour in 2003 at the age of 79 while tending his motor cruiser.

Wing Commander Richard Bangay commanding 570 Squadron was awarded the Bronze Lion of the Netherlands. He had flown seventeen operations having formed 570 Squadron in 1944. Ten of his operations were Strategic Operations Executive to France, Holland and Denmark and seven to Normandy, Holland (Arnhem) and the Rhine. It was his work at Arnhem which gained him the award of the Netherlands Bronze Lion.

Wing Commander Trenham Musgrave, OBE, was recommended for the Distinguished Flying Cross in 1945. He had commanded 296 Squadron since 10 September. On 24 August 1943 he was injured in an accident whilst gaining experience flying a Horsa glider, as a result he lost his left leg, despite which he was flying again by December.

In September 1944 he took part in the initial lifts towing a glider on each occasion. On 24 March 1945 he led his squadron on Operation 'Varsity' the largest airborne operations of the Second World War in support of the 2nd Army.

Wing Commander Ernest Archer had been awarded the Air Flying Cross in June 1943 and on 31 May 1945 was recommended for the Distinguished Service Order having flown seventy-two operations, taking part in all three major airborne operations, plus Strategic Operations Executive operations to France, Holland, Norway, Denmark and SAS operations to France.

Flight Lieutenant Donald Campbell, DFC, was flying with 196 Squadron in April 1945 when recommended for a bar to his Distinguished Flying Cross. He had been awarded the Distinguished Flying Cross in August 1944 and flying Stirlings he took part in the Arnhem operations carrying out two re-supply missions flying at low level through the fiercest enemy opposition to drop his supplies accurately.

In February 1945 on returning from a bombing operation over Germany, he was attacked by a fighter but was able to get back and make a safe landing, although his rear gunner had been killed. On the 24 March he took part in the Rhine crossing, on the outward journey and over his own base the port engine failed and showed signs of catching fire, despite which he carried out the operation towing a fully loaded Horsa glider at a greatly reduced speed for two hours and forty minutes. Despite this he was able to maintain height and deliver his glider at the correct landing zone. His recommendation was signed by Wing Commander R. Turner, now the officer commanding 196 Squadron.

Pilot Officer Jack Mutton, of 298 Squadron, had flown seventy-seven operations by April 1945 when recommended for the Distinguished Flying Cross. He had, in 1941, flown as a front gunner on a Sunderland Flying boat in the Middle East for his first tour and for his second tour as a pilot with the airborne forces.

His aircraft, a Halifax, had towed gliders to Normandy, Arnhem and the Rhine Crossing; on the latter, with complete disregard to aircraft being shot down by flak around him, he was able to release his glider in the correct position.

Harry King was born in 1907 and spent his early years in India where his father was serving with the Royal Artillery, in 1926 at the age of 18 he joined the 8th Hussars in Germany. In 1931 he left the army and joined the Lancashire Police Mounted Division. Despite being in a reserved occupation he was able to join the RAF in June 1941 at the age of 33, much older than many aircrew. His navigation training was carried out in South Africa. In June 1943 he joined 271 Squadron at Doncaster and in February, 271 Squadron who had converted to C47 Dakota's, moved to Down Ampney by which time David Lord had joined the squadron and they became good friends.

In September 1944 Lord's navigator Douglas MacDonnell had gone on leave to be married, so Lord asked King if he would be his navigator on the Arnhem operations.

Harry, after bailing out, ended up in Stalag Luft I at Barth, where he met Flight Lieutenant Chalk, DFC, of 299 Squadron, who had been shot down on the same day and had posed as a paratrooper, wearing the uniform of one, to avoid being turned over to the Gestapo and possibly being executed. Harry was liberated by the United States Army from a prisoner of war camp in 1945.

In 1946 he returned to the police and was seconded to Special Police Force Corps in Germany which was responsible to the Foreign Office, there he remained until 1952 when he returned to the police in Oxfordshire and again met up with Bob Chalk. Both had been invited to the Dutch Embassy in London to receive their Dutch awards which were presented to them by Prince Bernhard.

In 1957 he left the police and became a Queen's Messenger, again with the Foreign Office.

In this role he went all over the world until forced to retire with ill- health in 1970.

David Lord had a similar career, having joined the RAF as an airman in 1936, becoming a Sergeant in 1939 and serving with 31 Squadron in India, the North West Frontier. Then he served in the desert in Libya, during which time, having been commissioned, he was awarded a Distinguished Flying Cross and then Mentioned In Despatches before joining 271 Squadron.

On 17 November 1945, Sam Lord wrote to Flight Lieutenant Bill "Flash" Kelly, a pilot colleague of David Lord. He said they had had many letters and telegrams from Lord Portal downwards and to come to Buckingham Palace with David who was to receive his Distinguished Flying Cross. On the day instead of having his photograph taken, as did the majority of recipients, David bundled his mother and father into a taxi, which he had waiting for them all the time they were inside, so they left without a photograph of the occasion. On anonther occasion when photographers were present, he took one look and said "I'd rather have a tooth out."

David went on to say that there was an investiture for his Victoria Cross award on 11 December, they asked about his best tunic which they wanted to have fitted out with medal ribbons etc. He had been awarded a number of medals including the North West Frontier medal and the Distinguished Flying Cross.

Pre-war he had trained as a priest in Spain and often knelt before a battered wooden Madonna. In 1941 when his aircraft was hit by flak over the jungles of Burma and

his compass destroyed, things looked bleak so he asked the wooden lady if she would, on

this occasion, spare him; if she did, he said he would never ask to be spared again. It was said that on 19 September 1944 he repaid this debt with his life.

On the 19th he had gone to communion and confession and when asked by the Padre what his chances were he replied "None."

Major-General Urquhart recalled the moments on the 19th when Lord was on fire as "those terrible eight minutes" which everybody who witnessed would not want to forget. Whereas the majority of the crews, including Lord's at Down Ampney, went to the Mason's Arms at Maysey Hampton a pub which was just down the road from the airfield, David Lord would stay at the airfield. His brother Frank was also an RAF pilot in South Africa. David kept himself fit by running and gave up smoking to protect his eyesight. He had crashed twice in North Africa when attacked by three enemy fighters and both sides of his head were grazed by bullets but was able to get his aircraft down and walk 10 miles across the desert to his base.

In Wrexham's Roman Catholic cathedral there is a statue of the Virgin, not made of wood as the one in Spain, but plaster. Under it is written:

> "Of your charity pray for the soul of Flt Lt David S.A. Lord VC, DFC, RAF killed in action at Arnhem, 19 September 1944, formerly an altar server in this church."

On 10 July 1945, Derek Gleave wrote to Mr Pring about the loss of his son.

Derek, was in his crew at the time of his death. He said on the run up to LZ where an isolated bunch of paratroopers were they were hit several times but didn't incur any damage. But on the final run up they were hit by incendiary bullets and the whole of the underside of the aircraft and the cabin were fully ablaze, as they were down to 800 feet at the time there was no chance of bailing out. He said he informed Ralph that the aircraft was on fire and he shouted to prepare for a crash-landing and said he was going to make for the other side of the Rhine and in thirty seconds they would have been on the other side, but being so hot, Ralph decided to put it down straight away, but as he came into land he was hit by bullets, despite this he made a perfect landing saving the lives of his crew.

Derek jumped out of the aircraft at the front and hitting the ground, lay there for a few minutes, when he came round Jim Springsteele and Henry Colman were shouting at him to get clear of the burning aircraft, Jim said Ralph never left the aircraft. The SS were sniping and killed Jim outright, badly wounded Henry, and Derek took two bullets in his stomach. They were both taken to hospital and operated on but Henry died on the operating table, Derek survived thanks to the unfailing courage of Ralph. Derek had two further operations and a spell in several camps but in July 1945 was fighting fit.

Wing Commander Reginald Altmann, DFC, was, in July 1945, recommended for a bar to his Distinguished Flying Cross.

He had flown thirty-three operations with Bomber Command 106, 408, and 83 Squadrons, flying daylight sorties over the Pas de Calais and Brest, also some night time flying laying mines. His third tour was with Transport Command carrying out nickel (Leaflet) sorties, glider towing on D-Day and at Arnhem and supply trips to France and Belgium, also the evacuation of casualties. His last tour was with 31 Squadron. David Lord had begun his operational flying with 31 Squadron in Burma.

Flight Sergeant Frank Sedgwick flying as an bomb aimer with 299 Squadron was awarded the Dutch Bronze Cross in November 1945. At Arnhem he took part in three glider lifts, his accuracy ensured the best possible positioning of the glider before release.

On 21 September 1944, his aircraft flown by Flight Lieutenant Reg Turner, was severely damaged by flak and set on fire before reaching the DZ. Despite this he continued to direct the aircraft towards the DZ and despite heavy fire from the ground released his load, but only when he was satisfied he was in the right position. After his aircraft had crash -landed he was captured and taken prisoner. The recommendation was by his former pilot and now commanding officer of 196 Squadron Wing Commander Reg Turner.

Another member of his crew was awarded the Bronze Lion, his 100 plus sorties and 1000 flying hours, Flight Lieutenant Sutton whose recommendation was again signed by Wing Commander Turner, had his Christian name omitted. He was the rear gunner in Turner's crew and showed great skill in silencing German flak batteries.

On the 21st his aircraft was hit by enemy flak and he was wounded in both legs. The hydraulic pipe lines leading to his turret were severed causing severe fire in front of and beneath the turret. Despite this he continued to operate his turret manually and maintained an accurate and continuous fire on the enemy ground positions, the flames increased in intensity and the ammunition began to explode in the feed chutes leading to the turret. He still kept up fire power until the aircraft had delivered the supplies and turned away from the Arnhem perimeter when he finally abandoned the aircraft, it was seen that his clothing was burning. After landing and with his wounds, he tried to crawl away in an endeavour to evade capture, but in doing so he was seen by the enemy just before nightfall, and taken prisoner.

Pilot Officer Denis Peel of 295 Squadron was also awarded the Dutch Bronze Cross in 1945.

Despite being hit on the 21st, he continued to fly and drop his supplies on the DZ, shortly afterwards with his starboard inner engine and starboard wing on fire, he crash-landed his aircraft safely.

Lieutenant Colonel Pierre Simond Joubert, DSO, DFC, commanding 217 Squadron and aged 48, died on 16 August 1945, whilst celebrating VJ day. He made a firework out of Verey cartridges and stuffed them into a length of clay drain pipe, with the aim of making a Roman candle. He elected, as commanding officer, to light the fuse himself and was, as always, dressed immaculately with pilot's wings and ribbons which included those from the First World War . The firework blew up in his face, he was eleven weeks short of his forty-ninth birthday and said to be the oldest operational pilot flying in the RAF. He died in RAF Wroughton hospital on the 16th and is now buried in Bath (Haycombe) Cemetery.

A sad ending to a man who had given so much, in particular to 'The Air Battle for Arnhem '.

Chapter 17

Post-War

Affixed to the outside wall of the Memorial Hall, Bodhyfryd, off Chester Road, Wrexham, is a metal plaque affixed to a stone in the shape of a headstone. It was erected by the Burgesses of Wrexham to the memory of David S.A. Lord.

The inscription:-

IN PROUD MEMORY
OF
FLT/Lt David S.A. Lord V.C. D.F.C
271 SQUADRON
ROYAL AIR FORCE (WREXHAM)
WHO, AT ARNHEM ON 19th SEPTEMBER 1944,
WHEN CAPTAIN (PILOT) OF A DAKOTA AIRCRAFT
DROPPING SUPPLIES TO BELEAGUERED TROOPS ON THE
THE GROUND, MADE A SECOND RUN IN A BURNING
AIRCRAFT TO COMPLETE DELIVERY,
ON COMPLETION HE ORDERED HIS CREW TO BAIL OUT
REMAINING AT THE CONTROLS TO ENABLE THEM TO DO SO,
THE AIRCRAFT CRASHED TO THE GROUND AND THERE WAS
ONLY ONE SURVIVOR.
FOR HIS SUPREMER SELF-SACRIFICE
HE WAS AWARDED THE VICTORIA CROSS
"HE GAVE HIS TODAY
THAT WE MAY HAVE OUR TOMORROW"
"EI ABERTH A HEIBIO"

Every year the ATC Cadets of 2279 Squadron, pay their tribute to David Lord.

After Harry King died in October 1984 his ashes were buried beneath the memorial window at the All Saints Church, Down Ampney, which is about a quarter of a mile from the old runway at the former RAF Down Ampney, the window was dedicated in June 1974. This window incorporates the squadron badge, the Airborne Pegasus and Lord's Victoria Cross and was designed by and under the driving force of Alan Hartley, with the idea coming to him after a visit to Down Ampney in 1971. He is also the secretary of the Down Ampney Association.

When the KG 374 Dakota Memorial was formed at RAF Cosford Aerospace Museum, near Wolverhampton in 1979, Harry was contacted and gave all the help and support he could to this project.

His tribute to the four army despatchers on KG 374 is worthy of a place in this book.

"These men were not volunteers like aircrew; they received no "Flying Pay", yet were, without doubt, superb in their fulfilment of duty, even though KG 374 was burning for the whole period over the Dropping Zone."

It's fair to say that David Lord's Victoria Cross is a tribute to all crews of Transport Command, their courage in the "face of the enemy" was, and still is, without approach and should never be forgotten in the history of the Second World War .

Post war, David's parents presented the Lord Trophy to Transport Command of the RAF.

Reg Turner's crashed aircraft after the Germans had vacated the area was found by a Dutch famer who cut off the fuselage above the door and transported the fuselage part to his farm where he used it as a pigsty covered with a large tarpaulin. When the famer died the pigsty was disused and became covered in weeds, when the new owner began to work on the garden it was again found. It is now at a museum in Deelen, north of Arnhem, at this museum are also pieces of Lord's Dakota KG 374.

In 2004 a new memorial was placed on the Ringdijk, near Batenburg. When Eric Pepper paid a visit there he realised attention was being given to three aircrew and despatchers of 271 Squadron, Pilot Officer Cuer KG 340, LJ 991 Flight Officer Beck 570 Son, LK 127 Flight Officer Scanlon of 620 Squadron, and also LK 121 Pilot Officer Culling of 570 Squadron at the General Cemetery at Heteren. For over 60 years a Mrs Weis Kooyman had been tending the grave of Flight Sergeant G.F. Conry-Candler, she looked after this grave as if he was her son. His grave and headstone had been paid for the by the villagers of Batenburg and not, as is usual, by the Commonwealth War Graves. Flight Sergeant Conry-Candler's pilot, Flight Lieutenant Anderson LJ 833 of 190 Squadron, had held off his stricken Stirling and was able to miss the village, other members of the crew are buried in other cemeteries in the area and three escaped by dinghy from the river Maas after the aircraft had crashed in to the water. In June 1946 the aircraft was lifted out of the River Maas and the pilot Flight Lieutenant Anderson's body recovered.

In 1994 Denis Royston, who had been shot down on the 20 September in LJ 851, flown by Wing Officer Oliver, found, with the aid of a metal detector, a piece of his aircraft. In 1995 he again went back this time with his wife and met Farmer George, his sons and daughters, who had helped him, they in turn came over to the UK for a holiday with Denis.

In 1998, Denis was presented with the axe from his aircraft, minus its wooden handle which had burnt in the crash. So much metal had been collected from the crashed Stirling that it took fourteen cartloads to take it away.

In 2004 Peter Yates was in touch with ex-Warrant Officer David Lewis, the rear gunner of a Stirling of 'A' Flight 299 Squadron. Yates was flying just forward but close to the Double Hills glider, he said there was no explosion in the air and later wrote an article on this:

"Within half-hour our flight was marred by our witnessing a tragic accident. Gazing at another Stirling with glider in tow about 200 feet below to our starboard, we saw the tail suddenly come off the glider, which just wind milled down to earth in two parts where it exploded violently! The Stirling carried on with tow rope trailing. This had a very sobering effect on all five of us!"

He had a camera, which of course was unofficial and not allowed. He took a number of pictures on the 17th and is certain one was of the Double Hills Stirling and Horsa RJ 113. In 1979 the memorial to the men killed at Double Hills was unveiled, over 1500 people and more than eighty Royal British Legion and standards paraded, the funds for this memorial being raised by the local people.

The memorial was cast in bronze resin by Nailsea sculptor Roy Cleeves, a former Royal Engineer who spent two years crafting the two statues, each figure set on a plinth with its regiment's motto beneath for the Glider Pilot Regiment, "Nothing is impossible", and the Airborne Royal Engineers, "Everywhere where Might and Glory Lead".

Each year in September some 500 people turn up to attend the service.

On the 6 November 1982, I (author) attended the 5th Annual Dinner Dance of the Aircrew Association at The Palace Hotel, Buxton, Derbyshire. Jimmy Edwards was a guest of honour at this dinner, and the evening before at a theatre the Buxton Opera House opposite the hotel, played the trombone with the RAF Central band.

At the dinner in his speech, his opening address was "I never fired a bullet and I never dropped a bomb."

This sums up the efforts and courage, particularly the men flying in Dakotas, at least the Stirling's were armed.

And about his Arnhem experience he said "I knew they were Germans attacking me because they had bloody crosses on the sides."

Later at the dance, I (author) was introduced to Jimmy and had my photograph taken with him, it was a great year for me as I had just had my first book '*The Men Who Breached The Dams*' published. I also presented him with the report he made at Down Ampney on his return to the UK from Arnhem, normally this would have been made at Brussels to MI6 but he hitched a lift back to Down Ampney so it was made to an intelligence officer of 271 Squadron. When in 1956 he applied to become a member of the RAF Escaping Society he was turned down because the criteria of becoming a member was the report to MI6 could not be located simply because it never was made. The RAES later regretted this as being a charity, Jimmy with his contacts, such as the Water Rats, would have been a great asset.

On the 18 September 1994, 50 years after the Battle of Arnhem. A memorial was unveiled to the air despatchers.

The inscription on it:

"To the memory of the air despatchers who, together with the air crew of the RAF and the RCAF, gave their lives in valiant attempts to resupply the airborne forces during the Battle of Arnhem."

The names of the seventeen air despatchers who died, and have no known graves, are written on monument panels.

RAF Down Ampney, as with many wartime airfield, is no longer used. In 2007 the last remaining building, the gymnasium at Down Ampney, was demolished to enable a small close of houses to be built. Cirencester Council Gloucestershire, invited suggestions as to the name of the close, and Alan Hartley suggested ' Joubert Close' to honour and remember a man of 271 Squadron who should never be forgotten, but sadly they did not take up the suggestion and named it after a popular farm house. Such is life for the people of Cirencester in 2007, Joubert would mean little.

At the former RAF Blakehill Farm is a monument with the inscription:

"Dedicated to the memory of those men and women who served here with 233 Squadron RAF in 1944-45.
Whether air-crew flying missions over Europe, ground staff supporting these missions, or the dedicated air ambulance nurses who flew with the casualties from the Blakehill Farm. They came from all over the Commonwealth and the British Isles to serve in the defeat of tyranny and the liberation of Europe.
" Fortis Et Fidelis"

Every year at the time of Arnhem, the school children of the area, 1,700, stand behind every airborne grave and as one lay flowers on each of them.

In 2009 the sixty-fifth anniversary of the Battle of Arnhem at Ginkel Heath, there was an estimated 50,000 people who gathered to watch a Hercules and the beloved Dakota drop 1,000 paratroopers.

RAF Fairford in Gloucestershire was constructed in 1944, it was designed to serve as a American Troop carrier and glider base for the D-Day invasion of Normandy.

It is now manned by the Americans who left in 2010, it is today also the home of the Royal International Air Tattoo, an annual air display.

RAF Keevil is 4 miles east of Trowbridge, Wiltshire. It had been marked up to be an airfield in the 1930s but it was 1941 before land was requisitioned under the emergency powers. In 1942 the Americans began using it and on the 6 September the 62nd Troop Carrier Group moved in from Florence AAF, South Carolina. It consisted of four Squadrons. When they moved out on the 15 November and the 153rd Observation Squadron moved in, they were disbanded in March 1944 when 196 and 299 RAF Squadrons moved in along with Horsa gliders manned by the GP Regiment.

Sadly, in 1965 Keevil closed, but although it was closed officially, all its facilities are still in place including many of the hard standings.

RAF Harwell was opened in February 1937 and until March 1944 was a bomber station, then it became 30 Group Airborne Forces using tug aircraft and Horsa gliders.

The station was closed in 1945 and is now the Atomic Energy Research Establishment.

A memorial to the men killed flying from RAF Harwell exists at one edge of the old airfield and a memorial service is held there annually.

RAF Brize Norton in Oxfordshire was, as with Harwell, opened in 1937. It was from here that 296 and 297 flew to Arnhem in September 1944, today it is still an RAF Station and among other things the home of No 1 Parachute Training School.

At RAF Tarrant Rushton named because it is near the village with the same name, and near Blandford Forum, Dorset. The building began in 1942 and glider operations started in October 1943 and continued until 1945, it was from here that Jim Wallwork, flying a Horsa named 'Lady Irene', when the taking, of Pegasus Bridge on the eve of D-Day June 1944. When Jim was thrown through the windscreen the first of three gliders to land there he was the first man to land in Europe on D-Day, the station was finally closed on the 30 September 1980, again a memorial is located on the roadside next to one of the surviving hangars.

Churchill said at the end of the war: "Heavy risks were taken at Arnhem, but they were justified by the great prize so nearly in our grasp." He went on to say that Arnhem was a victory, of the seven bridges planned, six were captured but Arnhem remained in enemy hands until early 1945.

What ever went wrong at Arnhem we must never forget the efforts and courage of the men of the RAF, and in particular Transport Command. They did their utmost to initially get the troops into Arnhem and then in the subsequent days to supply the troops on the ground.

The cost was high for aircraft and it's is good to know that a memorial has been erected for their efforts and sacrifice at Arnhem. The finance for this memorial £20,000 was due to Alan Hartley, the man who asked Len Wilson for a ride to Arnhem, he did not go but Len did and didn't return, the downside of Alan' efforts are that he has every year to find 532 Euros to pay the insurance premiums for the memorial. Alan is now 85 and wonders what will happen when he is not around to pay these premiums.

In 1994 Spink and Son brought out a fiftieth Anniversary Commemorative Medal for the Battle of Arnhem, it has the Pegasus Flying Horse on the obverse, and on the reverse an RAF aircraft towing a Horsa glider over the Arnhem Bridge. The ribbon is blue depicting the sky, with maroon edges for the Parachute Regiment and a black edge with golden stripe in the centre depicting the actual bridge itself.

In years to come, if any man says to you "I fought with the Arnhem Airborne Force" take your hat off to him, for he is of the stuff which England's greatness is made.

In the History of the Second World War the few of Arnhem will rank in glory with the few of the Battle of Britain.

Awards to The Royal Air Force for the Battle of Arnhem

Victoria Cross (Postumously)
Flight Lieutenant D.S.A. Lord DFC   271 Squadron

Distinguished Service Order
Wing Commander R.H. Bunker DFC   620 Squadron
Wing Commander W.E. Coles DFC AFC 233 Squadron

Bar to the Distinguished Flying Cross
Wing Commander M. Booth DFC   271 Squadron
Squadron Leader P.D. Squires   271 Squadron
Flight Lieutenant A. Mc Campbell   196 Squadron
Flight Lieutenant A.C. Mackie DFC 233 Squadron

Distinguished Flying Cross
Squadron Leader G.H. Briggs   298 Squadron
Squadron Leader C.H. Potter RCAF 295 Squadron
Squadron Leader J. Stewart   570 Squadron
Flight Lieutenant K.O. Edwards   271 Squadron
Flight Lieutenant A. Hudson   570 Squadron
Flight Lieutenant A.C. Blythe RCAF 437 Squadron RCAF
Flight Lieutenant W.J. Dawson   620 Squadron
Flight Lieutenant D.J. Boyer   295 Squadron
Flight Lieutenant B.P. Legge   575 Squadron
Flight Lieutenant W.B. Pearson RCAF 512 Squadron
Flight Lieutenant A.E. Saunders   512 Squadron
Flight Officer V.J. Blake RCAF   644 Squadron
Flight Officer AMc.P. Campbell   512 Squadron
Flight Officer G.P. Hagerman RCAF 437 Squadron RCAF
Flight Officer D.H. Hardwick   299 Squadron
Flight Officer H.H. Hancock   299 Squadron
Flight Officer S.S. Finlay RCAF   48 Squadron
Flight Officer M.R.S. Mackay   48 Squadron

Flight Officer H.J. McKinley	575 Squadron
Flight Officer L.H. Patee	48 Squadron
Flight Officer A. Turnbull	644 Squadron
Pilot Officer H. Hoysted	196 Squadron
Pilot Officer R.S. Middleton	190 Squadron
Pilot Officer N.W. Sutherland RNAF	190 Squadron
Wing Officer A.E. Smith	575 Squadron
Wing Officer K.C. Cranfield	233 Squadron
Wing Officer B.H. Harvey	299 Squadron
Flight Officer F.E. Pascoe	190 Squadron

Distinguished Flying Medal

Flight Sergeant J.R. Masini	512 Squadron
Flight Sergeant A. McHugh RCAF	437 Squadron RCAF
Flight Sergeant J.S. Welton	190 Squadron
Flight Sergeant J.A. Thompson	196 Squadron
Lieutenant Corporal W. Whittaker RASC	Air Despatcher 48 Squadron
Corporal W. Hutchinson RASC	Air Despatcher 48 Squadron

Military Cross

Flight Lieutenant R.T. Turner DFC	299 Squadron

Military Medal

Sergeant W.T. Simpton	299 Squadron
Corporal C. Burton RASC	299 Squadron
Corporal C.B. Sproston	RASC Air Despatcher 299 Squadron

Mention in Despatches

Flight Officer J. Rechenau RCAF	437 Squadron RCAF
Flight Sergeant M. Mitchell	190 Squadron

US Distinguished Flying Cross

Wing Commander T.A. Jefferson AFC	575 Squadron
Squadron Leader C.F.A. Brown	196 Squadron
Flight Lieutenant B.J. Davidson RCAF	299 Squadron
Flight Officer A.E. Andrews RCAF	620 Squadron
Flight Officer L. Decies	570 Squadron
Flight Officer J.D. Le Bouvier	190 Squadron

US Air Medal

Flight Lieutenant H.D. Simmins	620 Squadron
Flight Lieutenant H. Lanning	296 Squadron
Flight Officer K.T. Garnett	297 Squadron
Wing Officer R. Dalton	620 Squadron
Wing Officer S.T. Wells	644 Squadron
Flight Sergeant S.H. Webster	48 Squadron

Dutch Militaire Willemsorde 4th Class

Squadron Leader R.W.F. Cleaver   570 Squadron

Dutch Bronze Lion

Air Vice Marshal Sir Leslie N. Hollinghurst
    KBE CB DFC AOC 38 Gp
Wing Commander R.J.M. Bangay DFC   570 Squadron
Wing Commander J.A. Sproule DFC RCAF   437 Squadron RCAF
Assistant Squadron Leader D.C Pascall   575 Squadron
Flight Lieutenant J.S. Sutton DFM   299 Squadron
Flight Lieutenant D.F. Liddle   570 Squadron
Flight Officer F.T. Powell   196 Squadron

Dutch Bronze Cross

Flight Lieutenant W.R. Chalk DFC   299 Squadron
Flight Lieutenant H.A. King   271 Squadron –in Flight
                                                           Lieutenant Lord's crew
Flight Lieutenant J.N. Francis   299 Squadron
Flight Lieutenant J.S. Scott DFM
Flight Officer D.M. Peel   295 Squadron
Flight Officer H.M. McLeod RCAF   620 Squadron
Flight Sergeant G.D. Gleave   48 Squadron
Flight Sergeant F. H. Sedgwick   299 Squadron
Sergeant W.J. Auld   299 Squadron

Dutch Flying Cross

Group Captain A.H. Wheeler OBE   Station Commander RAF
                                                           Fairford
Air Group Captain W.E. Surplice   295/570 Squadron
Wing Commander E.L. Archer DSO AFC   296/644 Squadron
Sergeant Leader R.D. Daniell DFC   233 Squadron
Squadron Leader F.T. Cragg   575 Squadron
Flight Lieutenant G. Whitfield DFM   48 Squadron
Flight Officer G.F. Gawith   620 Squadron
Pilot Officer J.E. Ellis   196 Squadron
Pilot Officer D.S. Sellars   190 Squadron
Wing Officer J.P. Dechamplain   437 Squadron RCAF
Wing Officer K. Prowd   196 Squadron
Wing Officer W.P. Stewart   299 Squadron
Flight Sergeant J. Howes   620 Squadron

RAF Losses at Arnhem

38 Group

Squadron	Killed	POW	Wounded	Evaded	Aircraft
190	38	11	4	24	12
196	25	1	4	32	10
295	7	7		4	3
299	4	20		10	5
570	22	16	1	31	9
620	8	4	2	12	5
644					
2 Passengers					

46 Group

48	18	4	5	14	7
233	6	4		2	3
271	8	4	2	8	5
437	12	4		8	5
512	2	6	1	6	3
575	5		1	1	1
Grand Total	157	81	29	152	68

Air Despatchers

Total	79	31	34	65	
Support Squadrons	56	34			
RAF Mobile Radar	10				

Total killed including Air Despatchers   308

Squadron	Killed	POW	Wounded	Evaded	Aircraft
Lost to Flak					25
Lost to Fighters					8
Aircraft type lost:					
Stirling					44
Dakotas					24
Support Aircraft Number Lost					39
Total					107

RAF Losses at the Battle of Arnhem:
September 1944

Squadron	Date	Crew

38 Group

190 Stirling EF–263	19 September 1944	Warrant Officer S.H.Coeshott age 23 Killed Flight Sergeant S. V. Davis age 21 Killed Flight Sergeant J. G. Jeffery age 22 Killed Flight Sergeant G. S. Breckles RCAF age 19 Killed Flight Sergeant W. C. Moss age 21 Killed Sergeant G. L. Wood age 19 Killed Driver G. C. Cadle 253 Coy age 22 Killed Driver J. Courtney 253 Coy age 33 Killed

Hit by flak and crashed on fire.
Breckles, Coeshott, Davis, Jeffery, buried at St Michielsgestel, Holland
Moss, Wood, Cadle, and Courtney buried Mierlo War Cemetery.

Stirling LJ–939	19 September	Squadron Leader J.P. Gilliard DFC age 24 Killed Flight Officer N.S. McEwen age 37 Killed Squadron Leader F.N. Royle-Bantoft –passenger Survived Flight Sergeant C.T. Byrne Inj/Hospital PoW Flight Officer R.G. Cullern PoW Pilot Officer C.H. Lane RCAF PoW Flying Officer R. Lawton PoW

Driver D. Breading 253 (Airborne) RASC age 21 Killed by flak in the aircraft
Driver F. Taylor 253 (Airborne) RASC age 21 Killed by flak in the aircraft

Hit by flak, crashed in woods at Sportpark, Bliderberg Area.
Gilliard, McEwan, Breading, and Taylor all buried in Oosterbeck.

Stirling LJ–829	20 September	Flying Officer R.J. Matherson RCAF age 26 Killed Pilot Officer R.A. Davis age 27 Killed Warrant Officer T.W. Allen RCAF age 21 Killed Sergeant S.J. Cooke age 27 Killed

Squadron	Date	Crew
		Sergeant E.F. Keen age 21 Killed
		Pilot Officer K. Willett RAAF age 29 Killed
		Driver J.F. Leech 253 Airborne RASC age 22 Killed
		Lance Corporal F. Rexstrew 253 Airborne age 30 Killed

Crashed at Doorwerth.
All are buried in Oosterbeek.

Squadron	Date	Crew
Stirling EF 260	20 September	Flying Officer J.D. Le Bouvier Evaded Awarded the US Distinguished Flying Cross
		Mr Edmund Townshend War Correspondent *Daily Telegraph* Special Correspondent Evaded
		Flying Officer T. Oliver Evaded
		Flight Sergeant S.F. Sanders Evaded
		Flight Sergeant G. Kershaw PoW Stalag L7
		Sergeant G. Ryan Evaded
		Flight Sergeant D. Martin PoW Stalag L7
		Driver R.T. Watts 253 Airborne RASC Evaded
		Driver H.S. Hill 253 Airborne RASC PoW

Hit by flak port wing on fire crew bailed out.
Crashed south of the Rhine at Lijnden, Valburg
Part of crew escaped including Le Bouvier and returned to the squadron 25 September 1944.

Squadron	Date	Crew
Stirling LJ 831	20 September	Flight Lieutenant D.R. Robertson RCAF
		Flight Sergeant G.E. Thompson Wounded awarded DFM
		Flight Lieutenant L.N.L. Rosedale RCAF
		Flight Sergeant R. Alderson
		Sergeant A.G. Hopkin
		Flying Officer L.E. Prowse RCAF
		Driver W. Dungey 253 Airborne RASC
		Driver E. Garnett 253 Airborne RASC

Elvatort tabs damaged aircraft and went into a steep dive which they pulled out with the help of Flight Lieutenant Roseblade. The bomb pilot was able to make a successful belly landing in Ghent Airfield having been hit by flak over the DZ.

Squadron	Date	Crew
Stirling LJ-982	21 September	Wing Commander G.E. Harrison DFC US Silver Star Killed age 29 commanding 190 Squadron
		Warrant Officer T.B. Brierley RNAF age 21 Killed
		Pilot Officer F.G.J. Comte De Cordoue RCAF age 29 Killed
		Flying Officer N. MacKay age 35 Killed
		Warrant Officer D.M. Mathewson RNAF age 36 Killed

Squadron	Date	Crew

Flight Sergeant R. Percy age 25 DOW 23/9/1944
Flight Lieutenant N.E. Skinner DFC age 32 Killed
Lance Corporal L.H. Caldecott 253 Airborne
RASC age 22 Killed
Driver H. Gregory 253 Airborne RASC age 28
Killed

Hit by flak.
Crashed at Zethen in the same area as Herger Stirling LJ 943.
Skinner is buried in Renkum and the remainder at Oosterbeek.
Pilot Officer de Cordoue was the son of Marquis and Marquise de Cordoue of Montreal,
Quebec, Canada.

Squadron	Date	Crew
Stirling LJ-823	21 September	Flying Officer A.C. Farren Wounded PoW

Flight Sergeant F.M.T. Stone Wounded/Hospital
PoW
Flight Sergeant F. Ross Wounded after jumping
PoW
Warrant Officer L.J. Billen age 22 Killed/Drowned
Flight Sergeant W.L.P. Cairns Killed/Jumped to
low
Flight Sergeant W.H. Skewes age 23
Killed/Jumped to low
Flight Sergeant A.J.H. Brown Wounded/Hospital
PoW
Driver E. Poole 253 Airborne RASC Evaded
Corporal Woodley 253 Airborne RASC Evaded

Shot down by three fighters after being hit by flak. Flight Officer Farren was thrown through
the windscreen and injured his back.
Crashed at Haren south west of Demen.
Skewes is buried at Wijchen, Cairns is buried at Groesbeek and Billen is buried at Horssen.
The remainder of the crew survived.

Squadron	Date	Crew
Stirling LJ-833	21 September	Flight Lieutenant A. Anderson Killed/Drowned in the Maas

Flight Sergeant G.F. Conry-Candler RNAF age 20
Killed/Drowned in the Maas a spare pilot
Flight Officer D.A. Adams age 33 Killed
Flight Sergeant A.G.O. Bellamy age 20 Killed
Flight Sergeant W.G. Tolley age 21 Killed
Flight Sergeant G.E. Orange PoW
Sergeant A.J. Smith Survived
Driver L.E. Bloomfield 253 Airborne RASC
Evaded/Wounded
Driver A.E. Abbott 253 Airborne RASC age 30
Killed/Drowned in the Maas

Squadron	Date	Crew

Ditched in the Maas River south west of Nijmegen having been shot down by fighters, Adamson's body was not recovered until 1946 when the aircraft was located. Anderson and Abbott are buried at Groesbeek, Conry-Candler at Batenbur, and Adamson and Bellamy are buried at Ravenstein. The remainder survived swimming ashore. Flight Sergeant Tolley's body was recovered from the river and is now buried in Bergen–Op-Zoom War Cemetery.

Stirling LJ-943	21 September	Pilot Officer R.B. Herger RCAF age 23 Killed
		Flying Officer O.H. Antoft RCAF age 25 Killed
		Flying Officer J.K. MacDonnell RCAF age 21 Killed
		Flying Officer H.A. Thornington age 34 Killed
		Warrant Officer II L.I. Whitlock RCAF age 20 Killed
		Sergeant L.G. Hillyard Wounded/PoW
		Warrant Officer J.C. Thomas Wounded/PoW
		Driver E. Noble 253 Airborne RASC age 24 Killed
		Driver C. Parker 253 Airborne RASC age 31 Killed

Hit by flak.
Crashed near Zetten.
Antoft, Herger, MacDonnell, Thornington, Whitlock, Noble and Parker are all buried in Oosterbeek. The remainder survived.

Stirling LK 498	21 September	Flying Officer F.E. Pascoe RAAF
		Sergeant M. Hughes
		Pilot Officer R.T. Walker
		Flight Sergeant L. Couch
		Pilot Officer M. Booth
		Flight Sergeant L.N. Armstrong
		Driver H. Richardson
		Driver T.C. Fitzhugh Wounded

Hit by flak over the DZ, port wing caught fire and made a belly landing back in allied lines with the aircraft being a right off. All crew were okay.

Stirling LJ-881	21 September	Flying Officer B.A. Bebarfald RNAF age 23 Killed
		Sergeant C.F. Branson age 30 Killed
		Flight Sergeant G.A. Phillips RAAF age 21 Killed
		Pilot Officer M.J. Yarwood RNAF age 34 Killed
		Warrant Officer G. Morris RAAF Evaded
		Flight Lieutenant L.N. Munro RCAF Evaded
		Driver Hughes 253 Airborne RASC Evaded
		Driver G.E. Jones 253 Airborne RASC age 28 Died Of Wounds

Crashed at Andelst hit by flak and fighters crew bailed out
Bebarfald, Branson, Phillips, Yarwood, Jones all buried in Jonkerbosch, Nijmegen.

Squadron	Date	Crew
Stirling LJ 916	21 September	Flying Officer J.S. Hay PoW
		Flight Sergeant C.J. Duncan
		Flying Officer E.J. Clague
		Sergeant H.J. Lane
		Flight Sergeant A.G. Weston
		Flight Sergeant Povey
		Driver A. Bailey 253 Airborne RASC PoW Stalag 12a
		Driver K. Woods 253 Airborne RASC PoW

Crash landed near Tilberg after fighter attacks.

Stirling LJ 876	21 September	Flying Officer C.L. Siegert RNAF awarded Distinguished Flying Cross
		Warrant Officer V. Whillis RAAF
		Pilot Officer J.L. Peppernell RAAF
		Warrant Officer W.J. Thompson RNAF Wounded
		Sergeant D.W. Morris
		Flight Sergeant F.J. Welton awarded Distinguished Flying Medal

Shot up by twoFW 190's over DZ, Flight Sergeant Welton seen to shoot one enemy fighter down.

Stirling No Number Given	21 September	Pilot Officer N.W. Sutherland RNAF
		Flying Officer Ibbotson
		Pilot Officer C.G. Rouse RNAF
		Flight Sergeant G.D. Bartram
		Flight Sergeant I. Nixon RNAF
		Sergeant E.G. Agar
		Pilot Officer R.E.G. Vincent RNAF

Hit by flak and machine gun fire on the run up, aircraft severely damaged but the pilot was able to fly the aircraft back to the UK and land successfully.

196 Squadron Stirling EF 248	19 September	Warrant Officer K. Prowd PoW
		Flight Officer F.D. Chalkley age 23 Killed
		Sergeant D.A. Matthews Killed
		Flying Officer G.H. Powderhill age 33 Killed
		Flying Officer R.C. Gibbs RCAF age 32 Died Of Wounds 21 September 1944
		Flight Sergeant J.A. Gordon Killed
		Pilot Officer J.J. Wherry Killed
		Driver F.G. Smith 63 (Airborne) RASC age 33 Killed
		Driver W.J. Chaplin 63 RASC age 35 Died Of Wounds 11 November 1944
		Air Mechanic 2nd Class L.A. Hooker Killed H.M.S. Daedalus age 23 (Passenger)

Squadron	Date	Crew

Hit by flak
Crashed north west of Arnhem.
Flight Officer Chalkley shot by the Germans after bailing out.
Chalkley, Matthews, Powderhill, Hooker, Gibbs, all buried at Oosterbeck.
Chaplin buried at the Rheinberg War Cemetery.
Smith has no known grave name on the Groesbeek memorial

Stirling LJ 988   20 September   Warrant Officer 1 W.R. Tait RCAF age 23 Killed
Pilot Officer D.G. Benning age 22 Killed
Warrant Officer 1 E.W. Bancroft RCAF Killed
Flight Sergeant T.B. Cragg age 21 Killed
Flight Sergeant C. Mabbott Killed
Flight Sergeant A.J. Murphy Killed
Driver G. Neale 63 Airborne RASC age 18 Killed
Driver L.C. Nye 63 Airborne RASC
Wounded/PoW

Crashed at Natuurbad Doorwerth.
Tait, Benning, Bancroft, Cragg, Mabbott, Murphy and Neale are all buried in Oosterbeck.
Driver Nye was taken prisoner and held in PoW Camp X1b (Fallingbostel).

Stirling LK-556   20 September   Flying Officer J.W. McOmie Evaded
Flight Sergeant S.R. Brooks Evaded
Flying Officer G.M. Cairns Evaded
Flying Officer J.L. Patterson Evaded
Flying Officer G.F. Talbot Evaded
Sergeant D. Clough age 22 Killed
Driver R.F. Pragnell 63 Airborne RASC Killed
Corporal A.W.J. Pescodd 63 Airborne RASC age 38 Killed

Crashed landed between Valsburg and Elst having been hit by flak and the supplies caught fire.
All the aircrew survived apart from Sergeant Clough and evaded capture back to the UK. He was found dead in a field.
Driver Pragnell has no known grave and is remembered on the Groesbeek Memorial.
Corporal Pescodd and Sergeant Clough are buried in Jonkerbosch War Cemetery, Nymegen.

Stirling LJ 954   20 September   Pilot Officer J.F. Ellis Wounded
Flight Lieutenant A.E.W. Laband
Flight Sergeant W.J. Smith
Sergeant P.F.J. Barnard
Sergeant D. Noble
Warrant Officer A.B. Talbot
Corporal J.R. Jones 63 Airborne RASC
Driver Rhodes 63 Airborne RASC

Crash landed north of Brussels all safe but aircraft was badly damaged.

Squadron	Date	Crew
Stirling LJ 840	20 September	Flight Sergeant J.P. Averill Flight Sergeant C.W.G. Stevens Flight Sergeant J.H. Dowesett Flight Sergeant A.E. Yell Sergeant A.N. Haywood Lieutenant Corporal Wise 63 Airborne RASC Driver Parkham 63 Airborne RASC

Crashed whilst on fire in Betuwe south of the Rhine, having been hit by flak. All bailed out and returned.

Stirling LJ 851	20 September	Warrant Officer G.R. Oliver Evaded Flight Sergeant S.J. Oates Evaded Flight Officer C.H. Henderson RCAF Evaded Warrant Officer F.L. Steele Evaded Flight Sergeant D.E. Royston Evaded Warrant Officer L.G. Gelinas Evaded Lance Corporal Shadbolt 63 Airborne RASC PoW Driver Jones 63 Airborne RASC PoW

Crash landed at Vessum having been shot down by fighter before reaching the DZ.

Stirling EF 318	20 September	Pilot Officer C.W. King Flight Sergeant A. Tebay Flight Sergeant B.W. Curran Flight Sergeant D.G. Hunt Sergeant J.R. McGhee Sergeant J. Heslop Driver Thomas 63 Airborne RASC Wounded Driver Reed 63 Airborne RASC Wounded Force landed at Woodbridge with flak damage. Both were taken to East Suffolk and Ipswich Hospital.
Stirling LJ 947	20 September	Pilot Officer W.L. Marshall Wounded Flight Sergeant L.A. Beeson Pilot Officer G.H. Tole Wounded Warrant Officer J.F. McCarthy Sergeant W. Pyatt Flight Sergeant L.C. Harhett

Crash landed in Aslst, west of Brussels having been hit by flak.

Squadron	Date	Crew
Stirling LJ-810	21 September 1944	Flying Officer M Azouz DFC age 22 Killed Flight Sergeant P.H. Bode age 21 Killed Flight Sergeant G.D. Greenwell Evaded having bailed out awarded Distinguished Flying Medal/Wounded Flight Sergeant L. Hartman Evaded/Wounded Flight Sergeant J. McCuiggan Evaded Sergeant H.A. Turner Evaded Lance Corporal Day 63 Airborne RASC Evaded awarded Military Medal Driver A.E. Norton 63 Airborne RASC age 43 Evaded

Shot down by fighters after being hit by flak.
Crashed near Niftrick
Azouz is buried at Oosterbeek and Bode at Wijchen. Wing Officer Azouz was killed coming down in his chute.

Squadron	Date	Crew
Stirling LJ-843	21 September 1944	Flight Sergeant C.R.J. Green age 23 Killed Flight Sergeant D.J. Allway age 20 Killed Flight Sergeant R. Cowan age 21 Killed Flight Sergeant D.H. Grant age 24 Killed Flight Sergeant L. Marsh age 20 Killed Flight Sergeant R.G. Phillips age 26 Killed Driver S.V. Armand 63 Airborne RASC age 20 Killed Driver J.R. Harris 63 Airborne RASC age 27 Killed

Shot down by flak
Crashed at Wageningen.
All are buried in the Oosterbeek.

Squadron	Date	Crew
Stirling LJ-928	21 September	Flight Sergeant R.E.G. Waltrich age 23 Killed Flight Sergeant R.W. Forrest age 23 Killed Flight Sergeant S.J. Poole age 24 Killed Flight Sergeant S.A.L. Townsend age 23 Killed Lance Corporal S. Law 63 Airborne RASC age 28 Killed Driver W.H. Brook 63 Airborne RASC PoW Stalag 4B

Shot down by enemy fighter. Crashed north of Hereadorp at Johanniterweg in Doorwerth, west of Oosterbeek.
All were killed apart from Driver Brook who survived and was a PoW at Stalag 4b Muhlberg, those that were killed are buried in Oosterbeek.

Squadron	Date	Crew
295 Squadron Stirling LK-170	19 September	Flight Sergeant R.A. Hall age 22 Killed Sergeant B. Fanthorpe age 20 Killed Sergeant E.S. John age 20 Killed Flight Sergeant E.P. McDonald age 28 Killed Flight Sergeant A. Marston age 22 Killed Driver N. Enderby 253 Airborne RASC age 21 Killed Driver F.C. Holdsworth 253 Airborne RASC age 33 Killed

Hit by flak.
Crashed at Aardenburg.
The RAF aircrew have no known grave and are remembered on the Runneymede Memorial,
the two army despatchers are remembered on the Groesbeek Memorial.

Stirling LJ 652	19 September	Squadron Leader C.H. Potter DFC Flying Officer C.K. Smith Flying Officer H. Courns Flight Lieutenant W.V. Guenigualt Flying Officer G.R. Venables Sergeant A.J.T. Hill Flight Lieutenant W.W. Flynn RCAF

Force landed on one engine at Woodbridge.
Badly damaged.

Stirling LJ–618	20 September	Pilot Officer B.N. Couper RNAF age 21 Killed Sergeant D. Bowers Evaded Flight Sergeant F.T. Corcoran Evaded Flight Officer E.T.W. Harris PoW Sergeant K.H. Johnson Evaded Flight Sergeant K. Nolan Evaded

Two despatchers of 253 Airborne PoWs one possibly a Corporal J. Rose
Hit by flak
Crashed in Pfuiflijk, Druten west of Nijmegen.
Couper is buried in Puifijk. Harris a PoW remaind evaded.

Stirling LJ 115	21 September	Pilot Officer D.M. Peel PoW Stalag L1 Pilot Officer A. Barrington PoW Flight Sergeant A. Thornton PoW Flight Sergeant F.H. Jones PoW Pilot Officer R.R. Newton PoW Sergeant J. Conray PoW Driver W.G. Thompson 253 Airborne RASC Killed Driver J.F. Johnston 253 Airborne RASC Killed

Squadron	Date	Crew

Crash landed near Planken Wambuis. Hit by flak
Driver Thompson has no known grave and Johnston is buried at Jonkerbos, both having bailed out at a too low altitude, no parachute was found attached to him.

Stirling LJ 986	23 September	Flight Lieutenant E.P. Byrom
		Flying Officer P. Holroyd
		Flight Lieutenant E.R. Jordan
		Sergeant W.C. Slade
		Pilot Officer B.P. Haggort
		Sergeant R.J. Jones

Hit by flak inner-engine u/s
Emergency landing at Ghent all safe. Two despatchers from 253 Airborne RASC

| **299 Squadron** | 17 September | Flight Lieutenant R.T. Turner DFC |

Stirling LJ 971
Returned with engine trouble, glider released over base.

Stirling EF-319	19 September	Wing Commander P.B.N. Davis DSO age 28 Killed
		Flight Lieutenant F. Mason age 25 Killed
		Squadron Leader C. Wingfield age 31Killed
		Flight Lieutenant W.J. Auld PoW
		Flight Lieutenant W.R. Chalk PoW
		Flight Lieutenant J. Francis PoW
		Flight Lieutenant Y.R.W. Lovegrove Evaded
		Driver R.E. Ashton 63 Airborne RASC age 29 Killed
		Driver E.H. Shovell 63 Airborne RASC Wounded/ PoW Stalag XIIA

Shot down by flak in flames over DZ and tried to crash land.
Davis, Mason, Wingfield, and Ashton are buried in Oosterbeek. Wing Commander Davis's brother, Pilot Officer Henry Davis, was killed with 59 Squadron in 1940. His name is on the Runneymede Memorial.

Stirling EF 267	19 September	Pilot Officer C.A.R. Bayne RAAF PoW
		Flying Officer F.W. Clifford PoW
		Sergeant E.W. Dixon PoW
		Flight Sergeant W. Tee RAAF PoW
		Sergeant L.W. Robbins PoW
		Sergeant W. Hume PoW
		Driver A. Hicks 63 Airborne RASC PoW Stalag 4B
		Driver Nicolson 63 Airborne RASC PoW

Crash landed at Leur, near Wijchen.

Squadron	Date	Crew
Stirling LK 868	19 September	Flight Lieutenant G.C. Liggins Sergeant D.G. Gaskin Sergeant W.T. Simpson Flight Sergeant K. Crowther Flight Sergeant F.H. Humprey Sergeant K.W. Scott

Hit by flak and crash landed in Driel. All crew survived, four were wounded. Both air despatchers from 253 Airborne RASC survived. Simpson was awarded the Military Medal.

| Stirling LK 118 | 20 September | Flying Officer D.H. Hardwick
Pilot Officer K.B. Ketcheson RCAF Killed
Flight Sergeant White Wounded. |

Pilot Officer Ketcheson killed by machine gun fire and is buried in Brookwood Cemetery, Surrey.

| Stirling LK 645 | 21 September | Flight Lieutenant R.F.T. Turner DFC Evaded and was awarded the Military Cross
Warrant Officer B.H. Harvey Evaded
Flight Sergeant J.E. Price PoW
Flight Sergeant Sedgwick PoW
Sergeant W. Moss Evaded
Flying Officer Sutton DFM PoW Bailed out near Ewijk/Wounded
Driver Brackman 253 Airborne RASC Evaded
Corporal Sproston 253 Airborne RASC Evaded and was awarded the Military Medal |

Hit by flak crash landed near Nordelyke

| **570 Squadron**
Stirling LK 555 | 17 September | Squadron Leader J. Stewart
Flying Officer F.G.O. Wilkinson
Flying Officer J.A. Weston
Pilot Officer P.F. Clarke
Flight Sergeant A.G. Grice
Sergeant G.P. Weam |

Hit by flak returned to base.

| Stirling LK 121 | 18 September | Pilot Officer C.W. Culling age 29 Killed
Pilot Officer G.S.C. Bell RAAF age 23 Killed
Pilot Officer J.D. Baker RCAF age 21 Killed
Flight Sergeant H.E. Browne age 26 Killed
Flight Sergeant P. Pope age 21 Killed
Sergeant V. Williams age 19 Killed
Corporal J.R. Coleman RCAF age 26 Passenger Killed |

Squadron	Date	Crew

No despatchers in the crew
Hit by flak at Tiel and crashed into flames at Herteren.
All killed and are buried in Heteren General Cemetery.

Stirling LJ 913	18 September	Flight Lieutenant D F Liddle PoW
		Flying Officer H W J Leach PoW
		Flying Officer J E Brough PoW
		Flight Sergeant T Hainey PoW
		Flight Sergeant D T Stevens PoW
		Two Despatchers 253 PoWS

Hit by flak crashed landed Schaarsbergen

Stirling LK 560	18 September	Flight Sergeant N.J. Kirkman
		Flying Officer B. Swales
		Pilot Officer N.T. Whitehouse RAAF
		Pilot Officer W.H. Lash RAAF
		Flight Sergeant D.E. Hewlings
		Sergeant G.C. Coe

Crashed on take-off and swung to port, owing to loss of power from the port out putter engine.
Unable to correct glider and cast off just short of the runway, the undercarriage collapsed on landing.

Stirling AJ 594	18 September	Pilot Officer D.H. Balmer RCAF Evaded
		Pilot Officer E.G. Blight
		Flying Officer V.C. Keag
		Sergeant T. Ireland
		Flight Sergeant R.J. Kempton Evaded
		Flight Sergeant J.T. Archer PoW
		Flying Officer G.A. Mombrun Evaded
		Sergeant R.W. Crabb Passenger PoW
		Corporal A.E. Barker age 31 253 Airborne RASC
		age 31 Died Of Wounds 18 September
		Driver W.H. Bridgeman 253 Airborne RASC PoW

Hit by flak and crash landed at Zegge near Boosschenhoofd.
Four bailed out and were helped by Dutch civilians.
Corporal Barker who died of his wounds is buried in Roosendaal-en-Nispen.

Stirling LJ 944	19 September	Acting Squadron Leader Hudson
		Flight Sergeant G. Wood
		Flight Sergeant J. Kennedy
		Flight Sergeant N.G. Linton
		Sergeant P.A. Thomson
		Sergeant H. McLeland
		Lance Corporal L.G. Grantham
		Driver G. Gamage

Squadron	Date	Crew

Hurt by flak badly hit in the port engine.
Crash landed at Ghent. All returned the next day.

Stirling LJ 647	19 September	Pilot Officer E.D. Hincks
		Flight Sergeant R.L. Huckfield
		Flight Sergeant H. Fletcher
		Flight Sergeant J.P. Smith
		Sergeant K.E. Johnson
		Sergeant C. Baker

Emergency landing at Megan, west of Grave. Two despatchers from 253 Airborne RASC, all safe and returned to base.

Stirling EH 897	19 September	Pilot Officer F.J. Mortimore PoW
		Sergeant C. Baker PoW
		Flying Officer J.W. Bradstock RCAF PoW
		Flight Sergeant H.W. Klatt PoW
		Flight Sergeant J. Marshall PoW Stalag 4B
		Sergeant P. Robertson PoW
		Sergeant A.T.J. Wyatt PoW
		Driver Simpson PoW

Hit by flak and crash landed at Schaarsbergen, crew included Two despatchers from 253 Airborne RASC PoWs.

Stirling EF 306	20 September	Flying Officer H.W. McDonald RCAF
		Warrant Officer M. Frierman RCAF
		Flying Officer E.F. Siegel RCAF
		Flying Officer P.A.J. Gore RCAF
		Sergeant H.H. Bailey

Emergency landing at Benson both tyres holed, all safe.

Stirling LJ 883	23 September	Flying Officer W. Kirkham age 21 Killed
		Flying Officer M. Hand age 26 Killed
		Flying Officer D.H. Atkinson age 23 Killed
		Sergeant H. Ashton age 22 Killed
		Flight Sergeant G. Wood Survived
		Flying Officer E.C. Brown age 20 Killed
		Lance Corporal G. Reardon 253 Airborne RASC age 31 Killed
		Driver S. Badham 253 Airborne RASC Survived

Hit by flak and crashed in Planken Wambuis, west of Arnhem.
All killed and are buried in Oosterbeek.

Squadron	Date	Crew
Stirling LJ 991	23 September	Flying Officer C.M. Beck Evaded Flight Sergeant Wheatley Evaded Flight Sergeant S.P. Cormier RCAF age 23 Killed Flight Sergeant J. McGarrie age 20 Killed Flight Sergeant E.M. Milks RCAF age 20 Killed Flight Sergeant H.J. Steel RCAF age 20 Killed Driver C.W. Lightwood 253 Airborne RASC age 21 Killed

One unknown despatcher also survived
Crashed at Heteren.

Squadron	Date	Crew
Stirling LJ 996	23 September	Pilot Officer F.B.S. Murphy Flight Sergeant R.J. Bagnall Pilot Officer A.N. Hilborn RCAF Flight Sergeant D.G. Spain Flight Sergeant G. John Sergeant R.W. Dixon

Hit by flak and crash landed at Ghent, all returned to base. Two despatchers from 253 Airborne RASC.

Squadron	Date	Crew
Stirling LJ 622	23 September	Flying Officer G.J.H. Burkby Flying Officer K. Browne RCAF Sergeant R.F. Bond Sergeant R.E. Green Sergeant V. Holloway Pilot Officer D.G. Harvey

Badly damaged by flak.
Force landed Manston.

Squadron	Date	Crew
Stirling LK 191	23 September	Squadron Leader R.W.F. Cleaver Flight Sergeant A.E. Welch RCAF Sergeant G.M. Stewart Flight Sergeant L.N. Sutton Pilot Officer D.G. Harvey Warrant Officer W.F.P. Smith

Hit by flak and crash landed south of the Rhine and returned to base. Two despatchers from 253 Airborne RASC hit by flak.

Squadron	Date	Crew
Stirling EF 298	23 September	Flying Officer W. Baker RCAF age 22 Killed Flight Sergeant D.J. Blencoe age 20 Killed Sergeant R.B. Bond age 24 Killed Sergeant R.C. Booth age 22 Killed Flight Lieutenant J. Dickson DFM age 24 Killed

Squadron	Date	Crew
		Pilot Officer F.G. Totterdell age 24 Killed
		Driver R. Shore 253 Coy Airborne RASC Killed
		Driver R.W. Hayton 253 Coy Airborne RASC Killed

Hit by flak and crashed at Panoramahoeve.
All are buried at Oosterbeek apart from Shore who is commemorated on the Groesbeek Memorial.

620 Squadron   20 September   Flying Officer A.R. Scanlon RAAF age 29 Killed

Warrant Officer E.J. McGilvray RAAF age 31 Killed

Stirling LK 127   Sergeant J.W. Marshall age 22 Drowned after bailing out
Flight Sergeant R.J. Lamont BA RCAF Killed
Flight Sergeant E.B. Dane PoW/Wounded
Flight Sergeant W.J. Murray PoW/Wounded
Corporal G.A. Fowler 253 Airborne RASC age 29 Killed
Driver J.T. Hadley 253 Airborne RASC age 25 Killed

Probaly hit by flak crashed Polserstraat. Scanlon bailed out to low.
Scanlon, McGilvray, and Marshall are buried in Heteren. Lamont has no known grave and is remembered on the Runneymede Memorial. Folwer was buried in Jonkerbos and Hadley has no known grave but is remembered on the Groesbeek Memorial.

Stirling LK 548   20 September   Pilot Officer M. McHugh RAAF age 21 Killed
Flight Sergeant E.A. Bradshaw age 21 Killed
Sergeant T. Vickers age 19 Killed
Flight Sergeant N. Gascoyne Survived
Flight Sergeant J.G. Hume Survived
Sergeant D.P. Ivens Survived
Driver E.V. Heckford 398 Airborne RASC age 19 Killed
Lance Corporal J. Waring 398 Airborne RASC age 35 Killed

Hit by flak crashed Vorstenbosch.
Bradshaw, McHugh, Vickers and Waring are buried in the Groesbeek Canadian War Cemetery. Heckford has no known grave but is remembered on the Groesbeek Memorial.

Stirling LJ-830   21 September   Flying Officer H.M. McLeod PoW
Flight Sergeant H. Bate PoW/Wounded
Flying Officer J.R. Thomas RCAF Killed
Flying Officer R. Newton Evaded/Wounded
Flying Officer C.C. King Evaded

Squadron	Date	Crew
		Sergeant T. Haig Evaded
		Driver S.L. Churchyard 253 Co Airborne RASC age 22 Killed
		Driver W.G. Thompson 253 Co Airborne RASC age 25 Killed

Emergency landing near Schweilzerhohe having been damaged by flak and fighters. Rear Gunner, Flight Officer Thomas, was thrown out in the attack.
Thomas is buried in Oosterbeek. There is some doubt about the two despatchers and them being in this aircraft. Both were killed. Churchyard is buried in Oosterbeek and Thompson is on the Groesbeek Memorial having no known grave.

Squadron	Date	Crew
Stirling LJ 946	21 September	Pilot Officer J.C.L. Carey Evaded
		Flight Lieutenant D.N. Cook
		Flight Sergeant C.R. Hinden
		Sergeant L.W. Buckman
		Flight Sergeant F. Andrews PoW
		Flight Sergeant H.J. Pritchard PoW

Hit by flak and crash landed near Bennekom west of Arnhem. All survived.
Two despatchers from 253 Airborne RASC.

Squadron	Date	Crew
Stirling LJ 892	21 September	Flight Sergeant W.G. Kay Crew

Landed at Woodbridge, Kay and a Flight Sergeant Cleaver, flight engineer slightly injured, Pilot Officer Gosson's Air Bomber severely injured.
Driver's Champ and Reynolds both from 253 Airborne RASC.

Squadron	Date	Crew
Stirling LJ 847	23 September	Wing Commander D. Lee
		Flight Sergeant E. Pratt
		Flight Sergeant J.P. Baker
		Flight Sergeant B.D. Naylor
		Pilot Officer A.D. Heard DFM
		Flight Sergeant M. Hennesey
		Corporal J. Vicary 253 Airborne RASC
		Private G. Whomersley 253 Airborne RASC

Crash landed at Ussen, near Oss, crew reported safe and returned 25 September.

46 Group

Squadron	Date	Crew
48 Squadron	18 September	Flying Officer A.J.A. Lavoie RCAF age 24 Killed
		Flying Officer G.J. McKenzie RCAF Killed
Dakota		Pilot Officer V.L. Pearson RCAF age 26 (From the USA) Killed
		Pilot Officer N.J. Costin RAAF age 25 Killed

All are recorded on the Runneymede Memorial.

Squadron	Date	Crew
Dakota KG 401	19 September	Flying Officer L.R. Pattee was awarded the Distinguished Flying Cross Pilot Officer A.C. Kent Warrant Officer T. Fenwick Flying Officer F.J. MacIntyre Driver H. Davis 223 Airborne RASC age 38 Died Of Wounds after bailing out. Buried Ath (Lorrette) Belgium Lieutenant Corporal W. Whittaker 223 Airborne RASC survived and awarded the Distinguished Flying Medal

Hit by flak and crash landed in Kessel.
Crew brought back by a Blakehill Farm crew.

Dakota KG 428	19 September	Pilot Officer V.B. Christie RCAF Evaded Flight Sergeant F.E. Fuller Evaded Warrant Officer Anderson RCAF PoW Warrant Officer A.R. Fulmore RCAF PoW Driver H.W. Thomson 63 Airborne Wounded/Died in the aircraft. Corporal R. Balloch 63 Airborne Survived broke an arm Stalag XI B Lance Corporal R. Bradley 63 Airborne Survived Stalag XIB Driver R. Olderton 63 Airborne Survived

Hit by flak and small arms fire.
Crash landed north of Arnhem.

Dakota KG 423	20 September	Flying Officer M.R.S. Mackay was awarded the Distinguished Flying Cross Pilot Officer W.C. Baynes Warrant Officer W.A. Lewis Flight Sergeant R. Owen

Starboard outer hit by flak and returned on one engine.

Dakota KG 346	21 September	Captain C.H. Campbell SAAF age 25 Killed Flying Officer J.C.C. Garvey age 21 Killed Flight Sergeant J.L. Anderson age 28 Killed Flying Officer J.P. Mudge age 32 Killed Corporal H.A. Austin 223 Airborne RASC Killed age 26 Driver G.P. Sleet 223 Airborne RASC age 32 Killed

Squadron	Date	Crew
		Driver O. Morgan 223 Airborne RASC age 20 Killed
		Driver J. Robinson 223 Airborne RASC Killed age 34

Crashed Dingle Flats, Norfolk, 3 miles south-east of Bradwell Bay. Five bodies were recovered from the sea.
Garvey, Anderson and Mudge are buried in Brookwood Military Cemetery, Woking, Surrey.
Campbell has no known grave but is on the Runneymede Memorial.
Sleet has no known grave but is on the Groesbeek Memorial.
Morgan is buried in Brynannan, Glamorgan.
Austin is buried in Erith, Kent.
Robinson is in Oldham, Lancashire.

Dakota KG 417	21 September	Flying Officer J.G. Wills RCAF age 21 Killed
		Flight Sergeant D.S. Black age 22 Killed
		Flying Officer J.W. Erickson RCAF age 23 Killed
		Pilot Officer D.G. Hardy age 24 Killed
		Lieutenant H.A. Edwards 223 Airborne RASC age 27 Killed
		Lance Corporal E. Roscoe 223 Airborne RASC age 36 Killed
		Driver J. Taylor 223 Airborne RASC age 27 Killed
		Driver B. Welham 223 Airborne RASC age 38 Killed

Hit by a load from another Dakota.
Wing broken off. Crashed north of Driel.
All are buried in Oosterbeek.

Dakota KG 579	21 September	Warrant Officer, later Pilot Officer D.A. Webb RCAF age 22 Killed
		Flight Sergeant D.H.R. Plear age 26 Killed
		Pilot Officer G. Birlison age 24 Shot after bailing out
		Pilot Officer F.C. Clarke PoW/Wounded
		Lance Corporal J. Pilson 223 Airborne RASC Killed
		Driver Everett 223 Airborne RASC Evaded/Wounded
		Lance Corporal Harribin 223 Airborne RASC Evaded/Wounded
		Lance Corporal Moorcroft 223 Airborne RASC Evaded/Wounded

Hit by a fighter and crashed in Volkel. Wing Officer Webb and Lieutenant Corporal Pilson were killed after bailing out and Birlison was shot as he hung in a tree.
Plear and Webb are buried at Zeeland. Birlison and Pilson are buried at Uden.

Squadron	Date	Crew
Dakota KG 350	21 September	Squadron Leader P.O.M. Duff-Mitchell AFC Pilot Officer B.S. Edmondson Flight Officer T. Crowley Wing Commander C.M. Hallam DFC

Crash landed at B 56 Brussels after oil and fuel pipes severed.

Dakota FZ 620	21 September	Flight Sergeant S.H. Webster Evaded Flight Sergeant R. Murray Sergeant Fell Wounded Sergeant C. Rushton Corporal C. Conquest 223 Airborne Evaded Driver Fiskin 223 Evaded Driver R.C. Jones 223 Evaded Lance Corporal Hammond 223 Evaded

Crashed near Renkum near the Rhine bank.

Dakota KG 370	23 September	Pilot Officer W.R. Pring age 26 Killed Pilot Officer H.E. Colman RCAF age 19 Died Of Wounds 24 September Flight Sergeant G.D. Gleave PoW/Wounded Driver B.M. Hastings 253 Airborne RASC PoW Stalag 7a /Wounded Lance Corporal F.W.R. Simpson 253 Survived/Wounded Driver W. Aparsley 253 Survived Driver A. Dunford 253 Airborne RASC Survived PoW Driver W.T. Crossley 253 Airborne RASC Killed Pilot Officer J.L.R Springsteele RCAF Killed by a sniper on the ground

Hit by light flak and crashed at Rosande Poldar, Oosterbeek.

Colman originally buried in Arnhem Hospital gardens and Springsteele is buried in Oosterbeek. Pring has no known grave but is on the Runneymede Memorial. Crossley has no known grave but is on the Groesbeek Memorial.

Dakota KG 404	23 September	Flying Officer S.S. Finlay was awarded the Distinguished Flying Cross Pilot Officer W.J. Walsh Flight Sergeant R.L.T. Gray Pilot Officer Rice Corporal Matthews 233 Co Driver Backler 233 Co

Squadron	Date	Crew

Four despatchers one Wounded*
Crash landed near Helmond. Despatchers from 223 Airborne bailed out because of the fire after a fighter attack.
*Corporal Matthews.

Dakota KG 321	23 September	Warrant Officer S. McLaughlin Crew
		Pilot Officer L.T. Bentley
		Flying Officer F.S. Clark
		Pilot Officer S. Melidones

Emergency landing at Eindhoven airport. Four despatchers from 253 Airborne RASC.

Dakota KG 391	23 September	Warrant Officer F.F. Felton Crew
		Flight Sergeant A.W. Meecham
		Flight Sergeant K. Toyne
		Warrant Officer J.A. Chanery

One Pannier dropped in wrong place. Hit by flak.
Belly landed B 56 (Brussels).

233 Squadron	21 September	Flying Officer C.D. Hamilton RAAF age 21 Killed
		Dakota KG 566
		Flight Sergeant W.B. Wheeler RAAF age 19 Killed
		Flying Officer L.J. Firth RAAF age 21 Killed
		Pilot Officer F.B. Knight RAAF age 26 Killed
		Driver R.W. Crooks 800 Airborne RASC age 32 Killed
		Lance Corporal R. Sharpe 800 Coy Airborne RASC Killed
		Corporal J. Dellanzo 800 Coy Airborne age 30 Killed
		Driver G. Vaningen 800 Coy Airborne RASC age 20 Killed

Shot down by fighters.
All are buried but Hamilton, in Woensel, Endhoven. Hamilton has no known grave but is remembered on the Runneymede Memorial.

Dakota KG 559	21 September	Wing Commander W.E. Coles DFC AFC
		Group Captain W.M.C. Kennedy
		Flight Lieutenant A. Johnstone
		Flying Officer E.J. Sharpe Wing Officer Wounded in right thigh.
		Lance Corporal R.N. Clements 800 Airborne RASC age 29
		Fell out of the aircraft without a parachute.

Squadron	Date	Crew

Crash landed in Brussels after being damaged by flak in both wings and elevator. Clements is buried at Ravenstein.

Dakota KG 586	21 September	Warrant Officer F.R. Russell PoW
		Flight Sergeant F.H. Jones
		Warrant Officer D.C. Schofield
		Warrant Officer L. Bergens RCAF
		Corporal L.R. Ennever 800 Airborne RASC PoW
		Corporal W.R. Saddleton 800 Airborne RASC PoW
		Driver W.A. Jones 800 Airborne RASC PoW
		Driver J.H. Welsh 800 Airborne RASC Survived

Crash landed in Bennekan near Bunderkamp.

Dakota KG 399	21 September	Flying Officer T.M. Ades age 20 Killed
		Flight Sergeant G.K. Dorville age 20 Killed
		Flying Officer S.W. Dyer RAAF Evaded
		Flight Sergeant J. Hickey AFM Evaded
		Lance Corporal A. North 800 Airborne RASC PoW Stalag 6B
		Lance Corporal R. Scott 800 Airborne RASC PoW Stalag 7A
		Driver J. Warner 800 Airborne RASC PoW
		Driver G. Woodcock 800 Airborne RASC Died a PoW 27 February 1945.

Crashed at Arendonk after a fighter attack.
Ades and Dorville are buried in Valkenswaard, Holland.
All the remainder survived.

Stirling FZ 681	23 September	Warrant Officer K.G. Cranfield was awarded the Distinguished Flying Cross

Wing Officer Stapleford RNAF second pilot took over control and brought the aircraft back to base after the pilot suffered bullet wounds in the knee and thigh. A hole 2 foot in diameter was blown in the starboard wing.

271 Squadron	19 September	Flight Lieutenant D.S.A. Lord VC DFC age 30 Killed
Dakota KG 374		Flight Officer R.E.H Medhurst age 19 Killed
		Flight Officer A.F. Ballantyne age 25 Killed
		Flight Lieutenant H.A. King PoW
		Driver L.S. Harper 63 Airborne RASC age 29 Killed
		Driver J. Ricketts 63 Airborne RASC age 28 Killed

Squadron	Date	Crew
		Corporal P.E. Nixon 63 Airborne RASC age 29 Killed
		Driver A. Robotham 63 Airborne RASC age 28 Killed

Hit by flak and crashed in Reijers Camp.
All killed and are buried in the Oosterbeek War Cemetery.

Squadron	Date	Crew
Dakota KG 488	19 September	Flight Lieutenant P.A.D. Hollom
		Sergeant S. Brisk
		Flight Lieutenant F.R. Riley
		Pilot Officer G.R. Harvay

Four despatchers Evaded
Crash landed Brussels.

Squadron	Date	Crew
Dakota FZ 626	19 September	Pilot Officer J.L. Wilson age 32 Killed
		Flight Sergeant H. Osborne age 23 Killed
		Flight Sergeant R.F. French age 24 Killed
		Warrant Officer L.C. Gaydon PoW
		Driver R.C. Newth 223 Airborne RASC age 35 Died Of Wounds 23 September 1944
		Lance Corporal J. Grace 223 Airborne RASC age 28 Killed
		Driver V. Dillworth 223 Airborne RASC PoW/Wounded
		Driver W. Jenkinson 223 Airborne RASC PoW

Hit by flak and crashed north of Arnhem
Wilson, Osborne, French and Newth who died on the 23 September and were originally buried in the gardens of the Arnhem hospital, are now buried in the Oosterbeek Cemetery.
Grace's body was found in 1988 so he now has a grave but is also on the Groesbeek Memorial.

Squadron	Date	Crew
Dakota KG 365	20 September	Warrant Officer King
		Hit by cannon fire port mainplane.
Dakota KG 444	21 September	Flight Lieutenant J. Edwards Evaded/Wounded and was awarded the Distinguished Flying Cross 'Pied Piper of Barnes'
		Flight Sergeant A.W. Clarke PoW
		Flight Sergeant W.F. Randall Evaded/Wounded
		Flight Sergeant H. Sorenson PoW
		Driver H.S. Abbott 223 Airborne RASC age 19 Killed
		Driver R. Abbott age 223 Airborne RASC age 22 Killed
		Lance Corporal G. Chisholme 223 Airborne RASC age 26 Killed

Squadron	Date	Crew

Corporal Deridisi 223 Airborne RASC Evaded

Shot down by FW 190 fighters and crashed near Oploo.
All the aircrew survived but the despatchers, apart from Deridisi, were killed and are buried in Overloon.

| Dakota KG 340 'The Saint' | 21 September | Pilot Officer F.W. Cuer age 23 Killed
Warrant Officer C.A. Anderson age 23 Killed
Flight Sergeant J.N. Bayley RAAF Evaded
Flight Sergeant B. Tipping Evaded
Driver Heywood 223 Airborne RASC PoW
Corporal E.A. Slade 223 Airborne RASC PoW
Driver G. High 223 Airborne RASC age 34 Killed
Driver Robinson 223 Airborne RASC Evaded/Wounded |

Hit by flak over DZ.
Crashed Heteren.
Cuer, Anderson and High are all buried in Heteren. All the others got back.

| Dakota KG 516 | 21 September | Flight Lieutenant C.W. Mott
Flying Officer R.J. Wells
Flight Lieutenant E.J. Packer
Pilot Officer T. Kennedy
Corporal Jones 223 Co
Driver Bailey 223 Co
Driver Lane 223 Co |

Hit by flak and attacked by fighters. Bailed out near Uden.
All crew safe and arrived back on the 23 September.

| **437 Squadron**

Dakota KG 387 | 21 September | Squadron Leader R.W. Alexander RCAF DFC age 24 Killed in the air
Flying Officer W.S. McLintock RCAF age 22 Killed in the air
Flight Sergeant A. McHugh Wounded bailed out and was awarded the Distinguished Flying Medal
Flying Officer J. Rechenau RCAF Survived
Lieutenant Corporal O.R. Jones 799 Airborne RASC Survived
Corporal A.E. Hall 799 Airborne RASC age 32 Killed
Driver H. Woodward 799 Airborne RASC age 30 Killed
Driver F.G.W. Yeo 799 Airborne RASC age 19 Killed |

Squadron	Date	Crew

Shot down by fighters
Alexander and McLintock have no known grave but are remembered on the Runneymede Memorial. Hall, Woodward and Yeo are buried at Bergen-Op-Zoom, Holland.

Dakota KG 489	21 September	Flying Officer J.S. Blair RCAF age 21 Killed
		Flying Officer C.H. Cressman RCAF age 21 Killed
		Flying Officer P. Steffin RCAF age 21 Killed
		Flying Officer T.J. Brennan RCAF age 30 Killed
		Corporal G.H. Rhodes 799 Airborne RASC age 33 Killed
		Lieutenant Corporal R.A. Adams 799 Airborne RASC age 29 Killed
		Driver R.J. Claxton 799 Airborne RASC age 31 Killed
		Driver D.F. Tite 799 Airborne RASC age 19 Killed

Shot down by flak, crashed at Eerschot.
Blair, Steffin and Brennan are buried at Groesbeek Canadian War Cemetery.
Cressman has no known grave but is remembered on the Runneymede Memorial.
Rhodes, Adams, Claxton and Tite are buried at Noord-Brabant, Holland.

Dakota KG 376	21 September	Pilot Officer G.P. Hagerman RCAF bailed out was awarded the Distinguished Flying Cross
		Warrant Officer J.P. DeChamplain RCAF Wounded/ Survived
		Flight Sergeant J.C.H. Hackett age 36 Killed in the air
		Flying Officer M.S.R. Mahon RCAF age 28 Killed in the air
		Driver J. Ward 800 Airborne RASC Survived bailed out
		Corporal Latham 800 Airborne RASC Survived/Wounded
		Driver Tulley 800 Airborne RASC Survived /Wounded
		Lance Corporal J. Adamson age 29 800 Airborne Coy RASC Killed

Attacked by FW 190 at 6,000 feet, 25 miles from DZ on return to base.
Hackett and Mahon have no known grave but are on the Runneymede Memorial.
James Adamson has no known grave but is on the Groesbeek Memorial.

Dakota KG 389	21 September	Flying Officer G.P. Chambers
		Sergeant J. Pope
		Flying Officer F.H. Hill
		Flight Sergeant J. Stott

Emergency landing in Brussels, all safe. Four despatchers from 799 Airborne RASC.

Squadron	Date	Crew
Dakota KG 305	23 September	Flying Officer W.R. Paget RCAF age 28 Killed Flying Officer D.L. Jack RCAF age 21 Killed Flight Sergeant D.J. O'Sullivan RCAF age 28 Killed Warrant Officer R.I. Pinner RCAF age 25 Killed Driver F.W. Beardsley 223 Airborne RASC age 29 Killed Driver P. Williams 223 Airborne RASC age 18 Killed Corporal L.J. Clark 223 Airborne RASC age 37 Killed Corporal T.H. Baxter 223 Airborne RASC age 35 Killed

Shot by possible flak.
Crashed south west of Driel.
All are buried in Oosterbeek.

Dakota FZ 656	21 September	Pilot Officer R.A. Kenny Sergeant L. Evans RAAF Warrant Officer 1 R.E. English RCAF Pilot Officer H.H. Macaloney

Crash landed Turnhout, Belgium		Driver W.T. Evans 799 Airborne RASC Survived Driver Jenssen 799 Airborne RASC Survived Driver Jordan PoW 799 Airborne RASC Survived Lance Corporal PoW 799 Airborne RASC Survived

Dakota FZ 668		Flight Officer Nicoll

Aircraft damaged and one air despatcher wounded by shrapnel in the leg.

512 Squadron Dakota KG 570	18 September	Squadron Leader T. Southgate AFC injured Flight Lieutenant A.E. Saunders badly injured Flight Lieutenant S.W. Bryant Wounded Flying Officer J.H. Parry Wounded

Hit by flak and on fire.
Crash landed at Kesteren.
All safe and evaded. Returned 24 September.

Dakota KG 324	20 September	Pilot Officer W.H. Perry DFM age 24 Killed Warrant Officer F. Barritt Survived Warrant Officer I.O.M. Gilbert age 29 Killed Warrant Officer A.B. Friend Survived Plus two despatchers bailed out and survived.

Hit by flak and crashed at Schaijk.

Squadron	Date	Crew
Dakota KG 314	20 September	Flight Officer Campbell

Emergency landing near Brussels on one engine, all safe but one despatcher of 223 Airborne RASC wounded.

Squadron	Date	Crew
Dakota KG 418	20 September	Flight Lieutenant R.S. Matthews PoW/Wounded
		Sergeant W.C. Thompson PoW
		Warrant Officer P.B. Tonner RCAF PoW
		Warrant Officer D.W. Bromige PoW

Hit by flak.
Crash landed.   Four despatchers from 223 Airborne RASC

Tonner died of TB in Canada on 17 October 1945

Squadron	Date	Crew
575 Squadron	18 September	Flying Officer H.G.E. Henry RCAF age 25 Killed in the air
Dakota KG 328		Warrant Officer A.E. Smith Wounded and was awarded the Distinguished Flying Cross
		Flying Officer H.J.L. McKinley RCAF Wounded and was awarded the Distinguished Flying Cross

Flight Officer Henry from Manitoba, Canada, is buried in Brookwood Cemetery.
The crew attached from 437 Squadron.

Squadron	Date	Crew
Dakota KG 388	19 September	Flight Lieutenant C.R. Slack age 23 Killed
		Pilot Officer J.E.W. Caouette RCAF age 21 Killed
		F/ W [Not sure of FW meaning?] S. Monger age 22 Killed
		Pilot Officer I.L. W Holloway Killed
		Driver J. Bowers 63 Airborne RASC age 41 Killed
		Driver W.D. Cross 63 Airborne RASC age 33 Killed
		Driver R. Hodgskinson 63 Airborne RASC age 33 Killed
		Driver G.L. Weston 63 Airborne RASC age 23 Killed

Hit by flak.
RAF all buried in Oosterbeek. The army despatchers have no known graves but are on the Groesbeek Memorial.
One of the despatchers was shot by a German from one of the gun batteries that he came down by parachute near.
This was driver Robert Hodgskinson who came from Preston. Cross killed after bailing out.

Squadron	Date	Crew
Dakota KG 449	25 September	Flight Sergeant Clark

Force landed north of Pael, Belgium and crew returned the next day, all with minor injuries.

Corporal H.W. Taylor 800 Airborne RASC
Corporal H.J. Wright
Driver K.R. Irish
Driver L.G. Smith

Horsa Glider RJ 113 'D' Squadron GPR Staff Sergeant L.J. Gardner Pilot GPR age 27

	17 September	Sergeant R.A. Fraser Pilot GPR
		Lieutenant Sergeant R.H. Allen RE
		Sapper J.C. Beale RE
		Lance Corporal W.H. Burrows RE
		Sapper C.W. Calvert RE
		Sapper R. Carney RE
		Corporal A.L. Clampett RE
		Sapper A. Cutherbertson RE
		Sapper F.A.S. Davis RE
		Sapper J. Evans RE
		Sapper J. Fernyhough RE
		Sapper E.J. Godfrey RE
		Sapper A. Hall RE
		Sapper D.E. Holtham RE
		Sergeant A.F. Oakey RE.
		Lance Corporal E.V. Pickburn RE
		Sapper E.E. Sheppard RE
		Sapper A.R. Street RE
		Sapper C. Turner RE
		Sapper A.G. Watt RE
		Sapper J. Westfield RE
		Sapper J.S. Williamson RE

Crashed at Double Hills, Somerset after the tail dropped off.
All were killed and are buried in Weston-Super-Mare.
The first casualties of Arnhem.

UNITS NOT DIRECTLY INVOLVED IN ARNHEM

Squadron	Date	Crew

3 Squadron   25 September   Flying Officer W. Davies age 22 Killed

Tempest JN 819
Crashed into the sea after engine failure, 35 miles west of The Hague.
No known grave but on the Runneymede Memorial.

16 Squadron   20 September   Flying Officer J.R. Brodby age 24 Killed

Spitfire PL 896
Photo reconnaissance combat with a fighter
Buried Jonkerbosch

16 Sqaudron   20 September   Flight Lieutenant G. Bastow age 21

Spitfire PL 834
Shot down near Arnhem, evaded and returned in October 1944.
On a photo reconnaissance of the bridgehead area, to confirm the supply dropping zones to troops on the ground.
Hit by anti-aircraft fire and crash landed near Arnhem in a field full of gliders.
Awarded the Distinguished Flying Cross in 1945.

19 Squadron   17 September   Flying Officer R.A.B. Slee Killed
Mustang SR 437
Combat with a fighter.
Buried at Zeddam.

21 Squadron   17 September   Flight Lieutenant R.R. Boulter RCAF age 23 Killed

Mosquito HX 592   Flying Officer E.Q. Rawlings age 26 Killed

Shot down by flak.
Both buried at Oosterbeek.

25 Squadron   24 September   Flying Officer H.S. Cook age 24 Killed
Mosquito 300   Flight Lieutenant J.S. Limbert MID age 23 Killed

Both have no known grave but are recorded on the Runneymede Memorial.

26 September   Flight Sergeant E.A. Walker age 23 Killed
Mosquito   Warrant Officer W. Watts age 32 Killed

No known grave but recorded on the Runneymede Memorial.

Squadron	Date	Crew
29 Squadron Mosquito XIII	23 September	Flying Officer R.W. Brown RNZAF age 30 Killed Flight Lieutenant T.S.F. Meadows age 26 Killed

His fourth trip that day.
Both have no known grave but are recorded on the Runneymede Memorial.

65 Squadron	17 September	Flight Lieutenant D.G. Metzler age 23 Killed

Mustang FX 896
Crashed near Wehl.
Buried at Oosterbeek.

66 Squadron	26 September	Flight Lieutenant W. Rosser

Spitfire   PV 186
Force landed after being hit by flak, seen to leave the aircraft safely.
No known grave but on the Runneymede Memorial.

80 Squadron	17 September	Warrant Officer P.L. Godfrey age 21 Killed

Tempest EJ 519
Shot down in the North Sea off the island of Schoowen.
No known grave but his name is on the Runneymede Memorial.

	18 September	Flying Officer R.H. Hanney age 19 Killed

Tempest EJ 583
Buried Strijen.

Tempest	18 September	Flying Officer P.S. Haw age 25 Killed

No known grave on the Runneymede Memorial.

90 Squadron Lancaster LM 169	16 September	Flying Officer P.W. Tooley Killed Flying Officer A.E. Brown age 23 Killed Sergeant L.M. Gill age 36 Killed Flying Officer H. Johnson age 23 Killed Sergeant E.J. Smalldon age 21 Killed Flying Officer D.S. Thomas age 19 Killed Sergeant R. Whittington age 20 Killed

Crew buried at Dordrecht.

115 Squadron Lancaster LM 693	16 September	Flight Lieutenant P.W. Bickford RCAF Killed Flight Sergeant U.B. Butters age 21 Killed Pilot Officer D. Dawson RCAF Killed

Squadron	Date	Crew
		Pilot Officer P.L. Dooley age 19 Killed
		Pilot Officer D.G. Flood RCAF Killed
		Flying Officer A.N. Johnston RCAF Killed
		Flying Officer W.G. Scanlan RCAF Killed

Crew buried at Strijen.

Squadron	Date	Crew
98 Squadron	25 September	Flight Sergeant B.L. Williams age 21 Killed
		Flight Officer T.J. Lennie age 31 Killed
Mitchell FW 194-N		Warrant Officer Bowmaster RAAF Killed
		Flight Lieutenant C.B. Carter DFC DFM age 25 Killed

Williams and Lennie are buried at Oosterbeek and Carter has no known grave but is on the Runneymede Memorial.
Wing Officer Bowmaster escaped.

Mitchell FW 211-Y		Pilot Officer S. Harrison age 25 Killed
		Flying Officer G.R. Munton Killed
		Flight Sergeant H.M. Nottle Killed
		Flight Sergeant R.C. Taylor Evaded

Munton, Nottle, and Harrison are buried in Jonkerbos.

Mitchell FW 107		Squadron Leader C.A.H. Beck
		Flying Officer G.B. Colbourne
		Warrant Officer R.A. Willis
		Flying Officer J. Carver

Squadron	Date	Crew
107 Squadron	17 September	Warrant Officer A.G. Lewis Killed
Mosquito NS 946		Flight Sergeant G.G. Griffin age 23 Killed

Both buried at Oosterbeek.

Mosquito LR 366	17 September	Warrant Officer R.A.R.M. Woodhouse Killed
		Warrant Officer J.S. McPhee Killed

Woodhouse is buried in Heiderust and McPhee Olburgen's body was found by the police on the 27 September 1944.

Squadron	Date	Crew
132 Squadron	25 September	Pilot Officer L.J. Phipps age 24 Killed

Spitfire PL 457-V
Buried at Bergen-Op-Zoom.

	25 September	Warrant Officer J.J. Hyde age 27 Killed

Squadron	Date	Crew

Spitfire PL 316–S
Buried at Jonkerbosch.

168 Squadron   26 September   Flight Lieutenant F. Bolton age 29 Killed

Mustang AM 101
No known grave but on the Runneymede Memorial.

175 Squadron   26 September   Flight Sergeant W.R.S. Hurrell Killed

Typhoon MN 852
No known grave but on the Runneymede Memorial.

181 Squadron   22 September   Pilot Officer T.I. Pervin RCAF age 30 Killed

Typhoon JP 800
Shot down by Flak.
Buried at Groesbeek

22 September   Pilot Officer D.R.O.R. Shearburn MID age 22 Killed

Typhoon MN 241
Flak near Oosteebeers.
Buried at Eindhoven.

198 Squadron   18 September   Flying Officer J.T. Boundy DFC age 21 Killed

Typhoon JP 482
No known grave but on the Runneymede Memorial.

247 Squadron   26 September   Flight Sergeant Barwise Killed

Typhoon MM973
No known grave but on the Runneymede Memorial.

303 Squadron   18 September   Flight Sergeant S. Dworski Killed

Spitfire MH 320
Hit by flak and dived out of control from 700 feet, 8 miles south-west of Rosendahl.
Buried at Bergen-Op-Zoom.

307 Squadron   18 September   Pilot Officer K. Jaworski
Pilot Officer J. Szymilewioc

Mosquito E.223
Intruder Operation Arnhem Area
Thick fog interfered with this.

Squadron	Date	Crew
315 Squadron	20 September	Warrant Officer Sierz T. Jankowski age 25 Killed

Mustang III
Mustang escort to Stirlings.
Crashed near Jutphass.
Buried in Breda.

345 (Free French) Squadron		
	18 September	Adjutant Chief R. Maurel

Came down in the English Channel, 25 miles from Beachy Headwhile escorting transport aircraft back from Arnhem.
Presumed lost.

416 Squadron	25 September	Flight Lieutenant E.H. Treleaven RCAF age 29 Killed

Spitfire MJ 412
Buried in Oud Leusden of Amersfoort.

439 Squadron	24 September	Flying Officer R.W. Vokey RCAF age 21 Killed

Typhoon PD 465
Buried in Bergen-Op-Zoom.

441 Squadron	25 September	Pilot Officer O. McMillan RCAF age 21 Killed

Spitfire NH 151
Shot down by a fighter.
Buried in Mook War Cemetery.

Spitfire ML 360	25 September	Flight Lieutenant B. Boe RCAF age 28 Killed

Shot down by a fighter.
Buried in Mook War Cemetery.

613 Squadron	24 September	Flying Officer A.W. Grime age 23 Killed
		Sergeant J.M.C. Dowall Killed

Mosquito NT 134
Both buried in Oosterbeek.

658 Air Obs Post Squadron		
	22 September	Major P. Hazell MC MID RA age 32 Killed
Auster		Captain C.M. Corry RA age 26 Killed

Both buried in Uden.

Squadron	Date	Crew
No 1 FU Dakota KG 653	24 September	Flight Lieutenant R. Korer age 23 Pilot Officer L.A. Veary age 24

Passengers:
Sergeant G. Beckoff RAAF age 20
Corporal J.E. Allen RCAF
Leading Aircraftsman J.R.M.A. Couturier RCAF
Leading Aircraftsman H.S. Watson RCAF age 19
Aircraftsman 1 J.D. McVie RCAF
Sergeant W.F. Hughes RCAF
Leading Aircraftsman F.R.L. Gates RCAF age 21
Leading Aircraftsman J.A.R. Chevrier RCAF age 29
Leading Aircraftsman W.J.S. Lundy RCAF
Corporal F.W Sargeant RCAF age 37
Leading Aircraftsman D.J. McDonald RCAF
Leading Aircraftsman R.T. Burden RCAF
Corporal H.J. Hunter RCAF age 23
Leading Aircraftsman F.L. Kristenson RCAF age 22
Leading Aircraftsman O.E.D. Bergen RCAF age 20
Corporal J. Cumming RCAF age 32
Leading Aircraftsman J.C. Sutherland RCAF age 37
Leading Aircraftsman L.I. Beach RCAF
Leading Aircraftsman M.J.F Good RCAF age 26
Corporal L.H. Moreau RCAF

On route to Elmas, Sardinia, shot down near Neulingen.
All buried in Rheinberg War Cemetery.

6080 Light Warning Unit

Commanding Officer

Wing Commander J. Brown MBE Died of Wounds	18 September 1944
Buried in Groesbeek Canadian War Cemetery.	
Flight Sergeant S. Lievense RCAF age 27 Killed	22 September 1944
Leading Aircraftsman R. Eden age 31 Killed	20 September 1944
Both buried in Oosterbeek.	

6341 Light Warning Unit

Flight Lieutenant A.J. Tisshaw age 28 Killed	18 September 1944
Leading Aircraftsman E.A. Samwells age 21 Killed	22 September 1944
Leading Aircraftsman E.H. Lascelles age 34 Killed	18 September 1944
Aircraftsman 2 H. Highton Killed	18 September 1944
Leading Aircraftsman J. Mc Anderson age 20 Killed	18 September 1944
Leading Aircraftsman J.C. Brooks age 26 Killed	18 September 1944
Aircraftsman 1 J.R. Swann age 37 Killed	18 September 1944
All buried in Oosterbeek.	

Index

A

Abbott, Driver H.S. 162–3, 181

accuracy 40, 54, 141, 143, 147

Adams, Cpl R.A. 162, 183

Adamson, James 183

Adamson, Lieutenant Corporal 111

Adegem Canadian War Cemetery 73

Adelphi Theatre 136

AEAF (Allied Expeditionary Air Force) 12, 134

ailerons 73, 86, 120

air crews 7, 92, 138, 152

air despatchers 1–2, 5–8, 18, 57, 59, 65–6, 68–71, 73–5, 78, 87–8, 92, 94, 97–102, 105, 108–9, 119–22, 124–5, 130, 133, 135–6, 138, 140, 152, 156, 158, 170, 184

Air Force 3, 10, 53, 81, 127, 137–8

Air Force Cross 63, 94

air gunner 73, 88–9

　wireless/operator 31

　wounded 109

Air Landing Brigade 7, 24, 26, 30, 43

air officer commanding 56, 62, 68–9, 75, 82, 115, 120, 123–5, 127, 129, 138, 143

airborne 1, 20, 23, 28, 35, 38, 74, 82, 85, 122, 141, 160, 164, 176, 179

airborne assaults 22, 40

Airborne Cemetery 139

Airborne Division 3–5, 7, 9, 20–1, 23–4, 28, 60, 62, 71, 78, 117, 124, 126, 129, 131–4, 138

airborne forces 6, 12, 16, 35, 42, 62, 115, 133, 137–8, 142, 145, 152

Airborne Museum 17, 19

airborne operations 3–5, 10, 21, 26, 38, 44, 56, 131, 137–8, 141, 143–4

abortive 10

　largest 51, 137, 141, 144

aircraft 1–2, 4, 7–8, 11–16, 21, 23–4, 26–7, 30–2, 34–5, 37–50, 52–61, 63–9, 71, 73–5, 78–90, 92–105, 107, 109–12, 114–23, 125–7, 130, 133, 135–6, 140–51, 154, 160, 163–5, 175–6, 179–80, 184, 188

　abandon 46

　allied 40, 133

　crashed 107, 150

　damaged 37, 82, 90, 161

　decorated 116

　flown 51, 147

　flying supplies 107

　pathfinder 30, 142

　shot 48

　supply 55, 60, 66, 78, 113

　tug 30–1, 34, 41, 43, 153

aircrew 1–2, 7–8, 12–15, 18–19, 27, 56, 87, 92, 99, 116, 123, 129, 131, 138–9, 145, 150, 165, 182

airfields 5–6, 9–10, 12, 15, 23, 27, 36–7, 44, 68, 115, 125, 127, 146, 153

Albemarle 11–12, 21, 31, 44–5, 144

Alexander, Squadron Leader Robert 102

Allied Expeditionary Air Force (AEAF) 12, 134

allied lines 27, 48, 72, 74, 111, 127, 163

Americans 10–11, 16, 22, 34, 38, 40, 102, 104, 153

ammunition 1, 5, 35, 43, 49, 56, 94, 105, 107, 109, 124, 137–8, 148

Anderson, Flight Lieutenant 103

Anderson, Wing Officer 76, 95

anti-aircraft 21, 50, 71, 187

　intense 54

batteries 22, 103
  defences 21, 23
anti-flak patrols 142
  sorties 123
Antwerp, port of 5, 9
area, defended 137–8, 142
arms 29, 42, 47–8, 50, 57, 67–9, 102, 121
  small 42, 44, 55, 73, 78–9, 128, 142, 176
army ii, 3–4, 16–17, 20, 23, 25, 38, 48, 51, 63,
  68, 78, 93, 99, 103, 122, 130, 132, 135–6,
  139, 144–5
army air despatchers 86
Army Pigeon Service 29
Arnhem
  Bridge 18, 21, 23–4, 154
  bridges 18, 132
  first days of 13, 15
  Hospital 178, 181
  operations 15, 94, 101, 121, 132, 143–5
Astro Dome 57, 85, 94, 97, 99–100, 102
attacks 10, 12, 18, 26–7, 73, 85, 94, 97,
  99–100, 104, 107, 111–12, 127, 130, 133,
  175
Auld, Sergeant 69
Australia 85, 94, 96, 136, 139
awards 59, 68–9, 75, 119, 133–4, 143–4, 146,
  155, 157

B
bail 50, 60, 68, 74, 81, 86, 88, 94, 96–8,
  102–3, 105, 109–10, 112, 118, 135, 149
barges 40, 51, 72, 89
battle 1, 17–19, 27, 33, 38, 54–5, 68, 110,
  130–1, 133–4, 138–9, 148, 157
Battle of Arnhem 1, 6, 17, 19, 78, 134, 138,
  152–5, 160–1, 163, 165, 167, 169, 171, 173,
  175, 177, 179, 181, 183, 185, 187, 189, 191
Bayne, Pilot Officer 66
Beck, Flight Officer 95, 150
Belfast 47
Belgium 5, 64, 66, 71, 75, 87, 92, 97, 114,
  125, 127, 139, 147, 176, 186
Bergen-Op-Zoom 183, 189–91
Blakehill Farm 11, 14–15, 40, 44, 120, 152, 176
Bode, Flight Sergeant Peter 109
Bofor guns 107–8
Bomber Command 5, 10, 21–2, 42, 71, 122,
  127, 134, 147
bombers 40–2
  towing gliders 79

bombing operations, tactical 143
bombs 1, 27, 61, 126, 143, 151
Brabant 101
Bradley, Lance Corporal R. 176, 179–80
Breda 51, 191
Brereton, General 5, 40, 93, 115, 130, 132
bridges 1, 4, 9–10, 18, 21, 23–4, 27–8, 33, 53,
  57, 104, 126, 130, 132, 153–4
British troops 84–5, 99, 106–7, 138
Brize Norton 13, 123
Brown, Wing Commander 114
Browning's glider 34
Brussels 15, 20, 47, 64, 68, 71, 73, 84–7, 96,
  99, 101–3, 106, 109–12, 114–15, 118–19,
  122, 124–7, 152, 165–6, 178–80, 183, 185
bullets 1, 38, 73–4, 76, 83–4, 99–100, 102–4,
  118, 120, 146–7, 151
Bunker, Squadron Leader Richard 29, 122

C
Caen 13, 94
Canada 37, 47, 50, 63, 86, 88, 96, 111, 114,
  136, 139, 162, 185
Canadian crew 51
Canal, Albert 23, 74
Cannon, Major 51
casualties 26, 29, 38–9, 64, 78, 108, 123, 139,
  147, 152
  heavy 137–8
Chalk, Flight Lieutenant 61, 69, 145
chutes 49, 60, 84, 88, 95–6, 98, 100, 102, 105,
  110–11, 118, 148, 167
civilians 68, 98, 107–8
Clarke, Pilot Officer 99–100
Cleaver, Squadron Leader Richard 120
Clements, Lieutenant Corporal Ronald 101
Clough, Sergeant 85, 165
cockpit 16, 28, 47, 74, 76, 88, 97–8, 105, 118
Coles, Wing Commander 101, 120
Comet 5, 8–10, 21, 31, 130
communications 1, 43, 54–5, 96, 115, 124,
  130, 133, 142
Conningham, Air Marshal 98, 107, 120, 133
containers 6–8, 66, 71, 78, 82–3, 87, 90–1,
  94, 101, 107, 116–17, 119
Cork 58
courage 1, 19, 27, 51, 54, 62, 73, 120, 130–1,
  134, 138, 150–1, 154
crash land 50, 58, 74–5, 96–7, 101, 103–4,
  118, 169

Crashed 161–3, 165–8, 171, 173, 178, 180, 186–8, 191
crew 7–8, 11, 16, 21, 24, 27, 30, 35–6, 39, 44–5, 47, 50–1, 54–6, 58–61, 63, 65–7, 69–70, 72–5, 77–8, 80–91, 93–5, 97, 99, 101, 103, 105, 108–11, 114–16, 121–3, 125, 127, 130, 133, 135–7, 142, 146–7, 149–50, 160–92
Crew, Flt Sgt Kay 175
Cuer, Pilot Officer 95, 150
Cunningham, Squadron Leader John 35

D
D-Day 4–6, 11, 13–14, 28, 34, 38, 40, 51, 94, 102, 131, 136, 147, 153
  operations 82, 122
Dakota aircraft 1, 7–8, 14, 23, 29, 36, 38–40, 43, 45–7, 49, 56–8, 60, 62, 64–5, 68–9, 73, 75, 78–9, 81–3, 85, 92–8, 100, 102, 104–5, 111, 114–15, 117, 120, 123–5, 132, 136, 143, 145, 149, 151, 159, 175–86, 192
  crash 62
  damaged 83
  loads 8
  Memorial 150
  operations 115
  pilot 61, 63
  squadrons 11, 16
damage 16, 43–4, 62, 69, 73, 81, 83, 88, 102, 118, 122, 144, 147
Darvall, Air Commodore Lawrence 16, 115, 124
Dawson, Plt Off 188
Day, Lieutenant Corporal 109
Deelen 10, 23, 150
despatchers 8, 29, 40, 56–7, 60, 63–5, 68–9, 76, 94, 96, 100, 103, 105–6, 111, 115, 118–19, 123, 127, 150, 168–9, 171–3, 175, 179, 181–5
despatches 8, 29, 31, 34, 59, 63–4, 74, 76, 135, 145, 156
Distinguished Flying Cross 44, 47, 59, 64, 66, 69, 72–3, 75, 82, 86, 90, 98, 107, 112, 120–4, 128, 133–4, 144–7, 155, 164, 176, 178, 180–1, 185, 187
Distinguished Flying Medal 44, 82, 103, 110, 113, 119, 156, 176
Distinguished Service Order 69, 101, 122, 144, 155
ditches 21, 53, 86, 89, 108, 132

Doorwerth 86, 161, 167
Dorville, Flight Sergeant George 101
Dowall, Sgt 191
Down Ampney 8, 11, 14, 27, 35–6, 39–40, 44, 49, 59, 61–2, 64, 71, 73, 78–80, 93, 96, 98–9, 103, 106, 118, 123, 132, 145–6, 149–50, 152
Driel 66–7, 99, 101, 170, 177
dropping point 54–5, 80–1
dropping zone 30, 60, 67, 81, 122, 150, 187
Duff-Mitchell, Squadron Leader 101
Dutch Coast 31, 36–8, 104
Dutch resistance 20, 47, 76, 84–5, 96, 99, 121
Dyer, Flight Officer Frederick 101

E
Edwards, Lieutenant Herbert 101
Eindhoven 10, 23, 25, 40, 68, 73, 80, 97, 100, 107, 110, 114, 118, 127, 190
enemy 22–3, 37, 54–5, 77–9, 83, 108, 125, 130–1, 141, 148
  anti-aircraft 21, 37
  fighters 57, 93, 96, 103, 107, 111, 126, 146, 164, 167
  flak 66, 73, 82, 141, 148
engines 30, 34–6, 43, 45, 58, 60, 62, 65–6, 71–3, 75, 79, 82–3, 86, 88–90, 93, 96–8, 101–3, 105, 109–10, 112, 122–3, 132, 168–9, 176, 185
Europe 3, 12, 31, 39, 152–3
Evans, Driver W.T. 112, 186
Evans, Sergeant David 85
evasive action 30, 94, 97, 113
explosion 32, 34, 74, 151

F
Fairford 8, 12–13, 28, 30, 79–80, 83, 85, 123
Felton Crew, Warrant Officer 179
fighters 6, 22, 25, 35, 37, 40–1, 43, 51, 81, 84, 93–4, 97, 99–101, 104–5, 107, 113, 117, 126, 130–2, 141–2, 144, 159, 162–3, 166–7, 175, 177, 179, 182–3, 187, 191
  attacks 22, 97, 110, 113, 164, 179–80
  bases 53, 142
  bombers 61, 142
  escorts 39, 43, 53, 81, 92, 103, 115, 132, 142
Finlay, Flying Officer 97, 178
flak 13, 25, 27, 31, 37–40, 43–6, 49–50, 53–5, 57–9, 62–5, 69–70, 72, 74, 76, 78–9, 81–3,

85–6, 88–90, 93–4, 96, 98–9, 101, 103–4,
    107, 109, 111–21, 123–8, 132–3, 135, 137,
    142–3, 145–7, 159–76, 179–85, 187–8, 190
  barges 85, 88
  dangerous 6, 131
  defences 4, 43, 93, 117, 137–8
  heavy 46, 66, 84, 119, 127
  intense 27, 60, 120
  gunners 58, 142
  guns 64–5, 142
  positions 26
flight 4, 11, 13, 16, 22, 30, 39, 64, 67–9, 81,
    93, 96, 114, 151
  operational 28
flight engineer 69, 86, 90, 111, 175
flooding 38, 132
flying 3, 6, 10, 20, 24, 33–6, 39, 44–5, 47–9,
    54, 56–7, 59, 68–9, 78, 80–6, 89–90, 94,
    101, 103–4, 112, 118–22, 124, 128, 130,
    132, 134–5, 144, 151, 153
  operational 147
  pilots 35
food 1, 49, 55, 59, 67, 80, 94, 106, 110, 124,
    127
  very limited supplies of 137–8
Foreign Office 145
France 4, 12, 17, 44, 64, 94, 116, 122, 134,
    143, 147
Francis, Flight Lieutenant 69
Fraser, Sergeant 32
freedom 18–19, 39, 76
French Squadrons 127
Frost, Lieutenant Colonel 18, 104
fuel 10, 43, 85–6
Fuller, Flight Sergeant Frank 75
fuselage 16, 29, 38, 46, 56–7, 66, 71, 73–4,
    79, 83, 93–4, 97, 103–4, 111–12, 119, 123,
    132, 150

G
Gaskin, Sergeant 66
Geddes, Lieutenant 133
German
  anti-aircraft defences 22
  anti-aircraft unit 64, 68
  fighter aircraft 22, 25
  fighter attacks 115
  fighter interception 93
  fighters 93, 103, 117, 126–7
  flak batteries 147
  Panzers 20, 107

  patrols 67, 95
  resistance 4, 40
  soldiers 64, 72, 76–7, 89
  troops 23, 27, 89
Germans 3, 5–6, 9, 16, 18, 20, 22, 33, 35, 38,
    40, 47, 51, 55, 57, 66–7, 69–70, 72–3, 76–7,
    81, 84, 88–9, 93, 95, 99, 104–5, 108–10,
    117, 130–3, 139, 141, 150, 165, 185
Germany 3, 17, 21, 32, 68, 89, 93, 101,
    133–4, 139, 144–5
Ghent 72–3, 82, 92, 121–2, 169, 172–3
Gibraltar 11, 14
Gilliard, Squadron Leader 30, 71, 84
gliders 4, 6, 9–10, 12–16, 21, 23–6, 28–41,
    43–5, 47, 49–50, 52–4, 57, 61, 65–6, 72, 75,
    78–9, 92, 94, 113, 116, 120, 122, 130–1,
    133, 138, 143–5, 147, 151, 153, 169, 187
  crew 30–1
  grounded 53, 61
  landings 143
  limited 21
  missions 53–4
  operations 54, 104, 129, 153
  pilots 16, 32, 36–7, 39, 45, 48–9, 76, 94,
    123, 134, 138
  safe 132
  towed 1, 13, 30, 145
  towing 12–15, 31, 38–40, 94, 147
Glider Pilot Regiment 32–3, 132, 138, 151
Goldsmith, Flight Sergeant 88–9
grave 4, 17, 23, 70, 100, 104, 106–7, 109–11,
    118, 124, 130, 139, 150, 172, 181
  known 18, 51, 70, 97, 139, 152, 165, 168–9,
    174–5, 177–9, 183, 185, 187–90
Groesbeek 23, 139, 162–3, 190
Groesbeek Memorial 70, 118, 139, 165, 168,
    174–5, 177–8, 181, 183, 185
ground crews 27, 71, 79, 82, 86, 132
ground forces 1, 5, 80
ground operation 1, 6, 131
ground staff 50, 79, 152
ground troops 25, 27, 39
Guards Armoured Division 72, 104, 109–10
gun positions 26, 37, 108, 123
guns 16, 21, 23, 27, 40, 45–7, 64–5, 68, 79,
    93, 97, 99, 105, 107, 115

H
Haddon, Lieutenant Colonel Thomas 45, 47
Halifax 8, 11–12, 36, 38, 46, 55–6, 88–9, 127,
    145

Halifax Squadron 11, 55
Hamilcars 30–1, 36, 42–4, 46, 53–5, 92, 138, 143
  giant 49
Harrow aircraft 14
Harry Broadhurst, Air Marshal 27
Hartley, Alan 14, 19, 39, 64, 150, 152, 154
Hartman, Flight Sergeant 108–9
Harvey, Wing Officer 156, 173
Harwell (airfield) 5, 8, 12–13, 23, 25, 34, 80, 153
headstones 139–40, 149–50
Hendon 15, 39–40
Hercules aircraft 12
Heteren 95, 150, 173–4, 182
High, Driver George 95
Highton, AC2 192
Holden, Flight Sergeant 83–4
Holland 10, 17–18, 26, 31–2, 42–3, 45,
  49–50, 55–6, 68, 77, 96, 122, 126, 132, 142,
  144, 180, 183
Hollinghurst, Air Vice Marshal Leslie 16, 36,
  69, 130
Horsa gliders 13, 15–16, 23, 30–5, 38, 42–4,
  46, 53–6, 59, 66, 72, 78, 104, 138, 144,
  153–4, 186
  loaded 144
  moving towing 32
  sorties towing 13
Howie, Group Captain 62
Hudson, Squadron Leader Arthur 72
Humphrey, Flight Sergeant 66
Hurrell, Flight Sergeant 190

I

Imber, Squadron Leader 91
Independent Parachute Company 26, 29
Independent Polish Parachute Brigade Group
  53
India 58–9, 145

J

Jackson, Major 60, 62
Jenkins, Flight Lieutenant 50
Jones, Lieutenant Corporal 102–3
Jonkerbosch 163, 190
Jonkerbosch War Cemetery 165
Joubert, Lieutenant Colonel 62
Jouby, Squadron Leader 81

K

Keevil 5, 8, 12, 32–3, 35, 66, 71, 80, 87, 123,
  153

Kembs, Lieutenant Colonel 51
Kenney, John 45, 171, 179, 182
Kessel 75, 176
King George V Jubilee 107
King George VI Coronation 58
King, Harry 60, 62–3, 145, 149

L

Lancashire Police Mounted Division 145
land 4, 6, 12, 21, 23–4, 33, 36, 45, 47, 53, 61,
  98, 122, 131, 138, 142, 147, 153, 164
  troops 5
landing gear 12
landing strip 62, 71
landing zone 6, 22–5, 29–30, 36–7, 39, 43–4,
  46–7, 49, 53–5, 59–60, 63, 66, 72, 80, 117,
  138
landings 11, 22, 24, 29, 32, 34, 40, 79, 81, 132
Lawton, Flight Officer Reginald 71
Leigh-Mallory, Air Chief Marshal 48, 69
Leopold II 122
lessons 131, 142
level flight 60
Liggins, Geoff 67–8
Light Anti-Aircraft Regiment 98
light artillery 32
light flak 43, 55, 72, 74–5, 93, 101, 107, 117,
  121, 178
Light Mobile Defence 35
Light Warning Unit 114, 192
Lincoln 27
LJ 502-D 40
LJ 622-V8-A 121
LJ 851 151
LJ 913 50
LJ 991 121, 150
LJ 996 121
LK 121 50, 150
LK 127 109, 150
LK 148 33
LK 883 121
LM 693 26
load 5, 8, 28, 49–50, 53–4, 58, 60, 64, 82–3,
  98, 123, 135, 137, 141, 147, 177
  5,000lb 64
  bulky 143
  dropping 124
load containers 56
London Gazette 48, 63, 68, 109, 120, 123
London Philharmonic Orchestra 136
Lord, David 1

losses 1, 6, 10, 14–15, 26, 41, 50, 52, 66, 87, 104, 116, 123–4, 134–5, 140–2, 146
Louvaine 71, 110
Lovegrove, Lieutenant 68
low cloud visibility 72
low flying aircraft, large 115
low level airdrop techniques 12
Lowestoft 30
Luftwaffe 22, 78, 93
Luftwaffe aircraft 54
Luftwaffe airfield 121
Lyneham 8
Lyons 90
LZ 24, 31, 39–40, 43, 50, 53, 65, 80, 94, 110, 142, 146
    correct 94
    marked 29

M
Maas 133, 162
Maastricht 4
machine gun 43–4, 64, 66, 71, 73, 77, 108, 117, 124, 134, 164, 170
MacIntyre 176
Mackay 155, 161, 176
Maginot Line 16
Manchester 63
Manitoba 114, 185
manned gun turrets 56
Mannheim 9
Manston 13, 32, 45, 114, 116, 121, 123
    landed 173
    main 32
Mariaheide 107–8
Marleston Heath 45
Marquis 162
Marseilles 90
Mason, Flight Lieutenant Freddie 68
mass escape 76
mass glider landings 21, 132
Matthews, Corporal 97–8, 178–9
Mc Anderson, Leading Aircraftsman 192
Mc Campbell, Flight Lieutenant 155
McCarthy, Warrant Officer 166
McCuiggan, Flight Sergeant 167
McDonald, Flight Sergeant 168, 172, 192
McGhee, Sgt 166
McHugh, Flight Sergeant 102–3, 156, 174, 182
McHugh, Pilot Officer 45, 85
McIntyre, Flight Officer 73–5

McKenzie, Flying Officer 175
McKinley, Flying Officer 48, 156, 185
McLaughlin, Warrant Officer 179
McLeland, Sergeant 171
McLeod, Flight Officer 157, 174
McLintock, Flying Officer 102–3, 182–3
McMillan, Pilot Officer 191
McPhee, Warrant Officer 189
McQuiggan, Flight Sergeant 109–10
McVie, Aircraftsman 192
meal 87, 95, 99
Mechanical Enemy Transport 114
medal ribbons 146
Medhurst, Air Marshal 39, 63
Melrose, Staff Sergeant 71
memorial 15, 32–3, 122, 139, 151–4
    excellent 18
    flowers in the wind 17
    new 150
Memorial Committee 33
Memorial Hall 149
memorial service 153
memorial window 149
memory 18, 32–3, 38, 60, 122, 149, 152
Mere Farm House 12
metal crosses 139
metal plaque 149
MI6 152
MI9 68
Middle East 7, 120, 145
Middlesex 63, 71
Middleton, Pilot Officer 156
Military Cross 16, 109, 127, 156
Military Medal 68, 109, 156, 170
Mills, Captain Joe 36
missions 8, 30, 45, 54, 56–7, 60, 62, 71–3, 104, 121, 124–6, 133–4, 141–3, 152
    air-crew flying 152
    armed reconnaissance 25
    bomber 82
    second daylight 24
    flown 4, 144
Mitcham 135–6
Mitchell, Flight Sergeant 27, 126–7, 156
mobile radar stations 25
modified bomb bays 127
Montgomery, Field Marshal 5, 10, 20, 75, 86, 109
    HQ 20
    plan 5
monument 17, 19, 152

Mook War Cemetery 191
morphine 66
Mortimore, Pilot Officer 78
Mosquito Squadrons 54
Mosquitos 26–7, 37, 93, 123, 125, 187, 189-91
motor cycles 29, 45, 51
  lightweight 29
Mudge, Flying Officer 176–7
Munro, Flight Lieutenant 163
Munton, Flying Officer 189
Murphy, Flight Sergeant 165, 173
Murray, Flight Sergeant 174, 178
Mustang squadron 43, 53, 81, 117
Mustangs 27, 43, 89, 93, 123, 126, 188, 190–1
muster 21, 92, 119

N
Naples 9
navigation
  ability 22
  aids 48
  errors 22
navigator 12, 36, 46–7, 50, 57, 59–60, 65, 76, 84, 88, 90, 92, 95–6, 99, 109–11, 118, 145
Nazi 134
Neave, Major Airey 73
Neptune 138, 141
Netherlands 69, 139, 144
neutralise 6, 131
Neville, Lieutenant 110
New South Wales 36
New Zealand 111, 139
Newcastle-Upon-Tyne 63
nightfall 108, 148
Nijmegen 4–5, 22–3, 26, 28, 32, 35, 38, 45, 47, 67, 71–2, 80, 85, 89, 94–6, 99, 104, 110, 115, 124, 126, 128, 130, 163
Nixon, Flt Sgt 164
Nolan, Flight Officer 88
Norfolk 177
Normandy 12–13, 22–3, 28, 38, 40, 144–5
  beaches 14, 112
  landings 23
North Africa 12, 25, 32–4, 134, 146
North Sea 22–3, 25, 43, 83, 188
North Wales 58
Northern Allied Army Groups 4
Northolt 85, 89, 95
Norway 44, 71, 82, 122, 143–4

Nottle, Flight Sergeant 189
Nymegen 165

O
Oates, Jimmy 88, 166
Observation Squadron 153
officers 29, 33, 73, 76, 89, 99, 114, 134–5
Oldham 63, 177
Oosterbeek 17, 36, 65–6, 70–1, 78, 82, 92, 95, 107, 114, 119, 125, 139–40, 160–3, 165, 167, 169, 172, 174–5, 177–8, 184–5, 187–9, 191–2
Operation Comet 9
Operation Market Garden 1, 5–6, 8–10, 13–14, 18, 20–5, 34, 40, 46, 80, 117, 122, 129, 133, 138, 141–2
Operation Tonga 94
Operation Varsity 141–2, 144
operations 1–6, 8–10, 13–14, 20–5, 30–1, 36–7, 39–42, 44–5, 50–1, 53, 56–7, 63–4, 69–71, 75, 78, 80, 83, 86, 93–4, 96, 110, 113–15, 119–20, 122, 125, 129–31, 133–4, 137–8, 141–5, 147
  bombing 144
  main 137
  military 130
  perfected 91
  special 122
  textbook 30
Osborne, Flight Sergeant Herbert 65

P
Packe, Lieutenant Colonel 7
Packer, Flight Lieutenant 96
Panzers 107–8
parachute 8–9, 12–13, 21, 27–9, 38, 40, 46, 56, 62, 65, 67–8, 79, 83–5, 87, 89, 100–1, 109–11, 131–2, 137–8, 169, 179, 185
Parachute Brigade 21, 24, 28–9, 40, 42–3, 104
Parachute Regiment 18, 40, 76, 139, 154
paratroopers 6, 10, 18, 29–30, 32, 38–9, 41, 61, 69–70, 77, 79, 100, 121, 130–1, 134, 138, 143, 145–6, 153
Parry, Flight Officer Joseph 46
Pascoe, Flight Officer 111, 156
Pattee, Flight Officer 75
Pegasus Bridge 23–4, 40, 153
personnel 7, 56, 114–15, 123, 129
photo reconnaissance 187
pilot 1, 8, 11–12, 15–16, 28, 31, 33, 37–40, 44, 46–7, 49, 53–5, 57–8, 60, 62, 64–6, 68,

72, 83, 86, 88, 90, 92, 99–100, 102, 111, 113, 115, 122–3, 133, 144–5, 147, 149, 164, 180
Pilson, Lieutenant Corporal James 100
planes 29, 61–6, 79, 137
Plear, Flight Sergeant Denis 100
Polish Parachute Brigade 3, 53
positions 1, 23, 28, 45, 64, 67–8, 90, 93–4, 96, 108
    attacked anti-aircraft 10
    enemy ground 69, 148
Prior, Lieutenant Corporal 66
prisoners 33, 48, 50–1, 61, 66, 68–70, 76–8, 95, 101, 105, 118, 127, 139, 145, 147–8, 165

R
RAF aircrew 94, 168
RAF Harwell 71, 119, 153
RAF Keevil 12, 30, 32, 45, 68, 70, 109, 153
RAF Losses 158–61, 163, 165, 167, 169, 171, 173, 175, 177, 179, 181, 183, 185, 187, 189, 191
Ramsgate 30
re-supplied 120
reached 108
rear gunner 30, 34, 61, 68–9, 85, 87–8, 109, 111, 134, 144, 147, 151, 175
Rechenuc, John 102–3
resistance 10, 12, 72, 76–7
Rhine 9, 48, 56, 66, 71–3, 76–7, 85, 96, 98, 107, 118, 120, 132, 141, 144, 147, 161, 166, 173
Rice, Pilot Officer 97, 178
River Maas 103, 150
Roderick Hill, Air Marshal 127
Roosendaal 50
Rowell, Pilot Officer 66
Royal Air Force 1, 3–4, 18, 30, 125, 130, 138, 149, 155, 157
Royal Army Service Corps 6, 18, 78
Royal Flying Corps 16, 93
Royal Signals 29–30
Royle-Bantoft, Squadron Leader 71
Ruhr 5, 21, 25
Runneymede Memorial 73, 103, 168–9, 174–5, 177–9, 183, 187–90

S
Saunders, Flight Lieutenant 46–7, 155, 184
Scarlet-Streatfield, Air Vice Marshal 82

Second World War 11, 14–15, 35, 40, 47, 78, 93, 129, 135, 141, 144, 150, 154
Shadbolt, Lieutenant Corporal 86
Shapley, Pilot Officer 91, 116
shot 26–7, 39, 43–4, 51, 53, 59, 61, 64, 67–70, 76–7, 79, 83–5, 93, 95–6, 100–2, 104, 106, 111–12, 117, 119, 121, 123, 125, 135, 145, 151, 162–4, 166–7, 169, 177, 179, 182–5, 187–8, 190–2
shrapnel 48, 95, 115, 184
signals 56, 60, 75, 77, 125, 138
Simond Joubert, Major Pierre 93
Slade, Corporal 94–6
Smith, Wing Officer Bert 47
Smythe, Lieutenant Colonel 61
Somerset 32–3, 186
sorties 6, 12–15, 128, 133–4, 142, 147
    glider-pulling 14–15
Spain 146, 173
squadrons 1, 11, 14, 16, 27, 31–2, 34, 39, 44, 57, 72, 80, 83–4, 92, 102, 116, 121, 125, 127, 142, 144–5, 147, 149, 153, 161
    bomber 12–13, 94
    new 11
squadrons towing 28
Stapleford, Flight Sergeant Barry 120
Sten guns 45, 61, 76–7
Stirling 8, 11–13, 28–30, 34, 36, 38, 40, 44, 47, 49, 54, 56–8, 66–9, 71, 78–81, 84, 86, 93, 103, 115, 117, 123, 137, 151, 159, 161, 164–6, 168–9, 171–3, 175
    towing gliders 73
supplies 1–3, 6–8, 12, 19–20, 24, 35, 38–9, 43, 46, 50–1, 55–61, 66, 69, 71, 73, 75–6, 78, 80–2, 84, 86, 88, 90, 92–5, 97, 99–101, 104, 109, 111–12, 117, 120, 123–7, 130, 136–8, 141–2, 144, 148, 154, 165, 187
    dropped 38, 42, 54, 61, 73, 102, 130, 133, 149
    medical 49, 56, 118, 120
    parachuted 55

T
Tactical Air Force 27, 75, 101, 124–5, 127, 133, 137
Tomson, Lieutenant 60
tow rope 30, 33, 38–9, 45, 48–9, 53, 56, 78, 92
transport aircraft 10, 22, 26, 40, 43, 53, 104, 115, 117, 143, 191

Transport Command 10, 47, 62–3, 94, 147, 150, 154
transport crews 22
troops 1–5, 12, 20, 23–4, 29, 38, 40, 44, 46, 59–60, 72, 107, 117, 130, 132–3, 154, 187

U
underground 84, 107, 109–10
Urquhart, Major-General 20-1, 62, 146
US Army Group 127
US Troop Carriers 42–3

V
Valkenswaard Cemetery 101, 180
Vancouver 36
Veghel 93, 96, 107–11
Venlo 125
Verey
  cartridges 148
  light smoke 92
  Lights 55, 72
  pistol rounds 120
  signals 117
Victoria Cross 1, 17, 37, 58, 62–3, 65, 139, 155
victories 34, 153
villagers 12, 39, 103, 122, 150
villages 12, 32, 66–7, 72, 86–8, 95, 100, 103, 105, 108, 110–11, 122, 150, 153
VIP Transport Squadron 39
visibility 27, 56–7, 71, 73, 104, 117
  bad 55
  persistent haze 55
Vorstenbosch 85, 174

W
WAAF parachute packers 27
WAAFS 39
Wacos 16, 32, 38, 43, 72
Walsh, Pilot Officer 97–8
war 1, 10–11, 15, 17–18, 25, 48, 64–5, 70, 77–8, 84, 88, 93, 105, 130, 132, 134–5, 139, 153
  prisoners of 65, 101, 122, 138–9
Waring, Lieutenant Corporal John 85
Welton, Flight Sergeant 112-3, 164
Wheatley, Flight Sergeant 95

Wheeler, Squadron Leader 127
White, Sergeant 82
Whitfield, Flight Lieutenant 71–2
Whittaker, Lieutenant Corporal 74–5
Wijchen 109, 162, 167, 169
Wilson, Pilot Officer Len 39, 49
Winchester, Major 33
Windlesham 122
Wingfield, Squadron Leader 68-9
wireless operator 39–40, 46, 57, 69, 76–7, 81, 90, 97, 100–2, 109, 111, 119, 136
Wise, Lieutenant Corporal 166
Wolhegen 60
Wolverhampton 150
women 105, 152
  evacuating 59
Wood, Flight Sergeant 72, 121
Woodbridge 45, 166, 168, 175
Woodcock, Driver G. 800 180
woods 21, 27, 47, 55, 71, 73, 76–7, 86, 89, 106, 112, 121, 146, 160, 171
wounding 73
wounds 47–8, 65, 70, 100, 106, 118, 139, 148, 163–4, 171, 176, 178, 181, 192
  flesh 105
  multiple 103
  stomach 76
  thigh 106
wreckage 33, 54, 62, 65
Wrexham 146, 149

Y
Yarwood 163
Yates, Peter 151
York 63, 70
Yorkshire 12, 65, 127

Z
Zeddam 187
Zeeland 100, 177
zone 40, 43, 53–4, 56–7, 67, 81–2, 84, 115
  correct landing 144
  landing/drop 25
  new 55
  new supply-dropping 80
Zonehove 103